ITALY IN THE
GIOLITTIAN ERA

Giolitti in 1914

ITALY IN THE GIOLITTIAN ERA

Italian Democracy in the Making, 1900-1914

By

A. WILLIAM SALOMONE

Introductory Essay by
GAETANO SALVEMINI

Philadelphia

UNIVERSITY OF PENNSYLVANIA PRESS

Library of Congress Catalog Card Number: 59-13438
Printed in the United States of America

To My Father

and to

the Memory of My Mother

PREFACE TO SECOND EDITION

THE "revolutionary" logic of totalitarian dictatorships, of which Italian Fascism assumed the guise of one prototype, drives them all sooner or later toward a recasting of the history which they claim to fulfill or to annihilate. As in the case of liberal Italy, an ambivalent rôle is reserved to the *ancien régime* which the dictatorship seeks to destroy in idea as well as in fact: the *ancien régime* was impotent to insure its own survival and yet fertile enough to create its "revolutionary" successor. Later an epos is manipulated in order to surround the antecedents and circumstances of that strange gestation with the mystic atmosphere of great human deeds. History is drained of fact and ground into myth and myth soon hardens into dogma. Historical truth is put on the defensive while gray half-truths seek mastery over men's consciences. To try to reverse this process and restore truth is difficult not only during but even after this evolution—assuming that it really runs its course. For no matter how strenuous and objective the search for the historic actualities of the *ancien régime* may now be, it has necessarily been affected by the very process it wants to ignore toward that restoration. The triumph and hegemony of the dictatorship, even if temporary, willy-nilly assume functions of watershed and mainstream in the flow of a Nation's historic time and reality. Ironically, therefore, the claim or purpose of the fallen destroyers seems in large measure achieved: the past appears "influenced" by them even as they have affected the future. The historian's task is thereafter rendered unduly difficult and yet more necessary. He must uncover the complex palimpsest, in the search for fact, ideological layer by polemical layer, before he can once again glimpse the hard core of historical truth. The history of Italy from the Risorgimento to the coming of Fascism has been enmeshed in some such palimpsest.

This book seeks to suggest an approach to the problem of Giolitti and of his era by utilizing historical reconstruction and historiographical critique. It consists, therefore, of two very different monographs on a single aspect of modern Italian history. Section One, entitled "Italian Democracy in the Making"—together with the Chronology and Bibliography—is the text of a study which appeared as a separate volume under that title late in 1945. Nothing has been changed, added or subtracted in this re-issue of that study for a number of very special reasons. The fact is that the original volume has been out of print for many years and, not unflatteringly, the interest in and demand for it, I am told, has not altogether ceased. The Italian translation of that work is unfortunately inaccessible for some of those very people who ask about the original presentation. In turn, this may or may not be related to the good fortune which, with all its limitations, that work originally encountered in many quarters and in many ways. The most surprising and, needless to say, gratifying to me was the spur which that work apparently gave to the further study of the Giolittian era both in Italy and in the United States. Above all, any revision of that original monograph might have led to my giving in to the temptation of writing another and perhaps altogether different book on modern Italy—and that, of course, may still happen. I do not suppose that it would be immodest to say that a sort of benevolent conspiracy of potential new reader, publisher, and author is responsible for the reprint here of *Italian Democracy in the Making* in its original form but not in format.

Salvemini's "Introductory Essay" was an independent reappraisal of Giolittian politics written under the immediate stimulus of his reading of my monograph on *Italian Democracy in the Making*. Salvemini's notorious antagonism to Giolitti, his stature as historian, fighter for freedom and nonconformist, as well as the substance of his Giolittian revaluation, almost immediately turned his Essay into an autobiographical and historical document *sui generis*. It is reproduced here not only for its value as such but also as one of the important terms of reference of the discussion in Section Two of this volume.

The new monograph on "Giolittian Italy Revisited" deals with the problems of Giolitti and Italian democracy within a critical-historiographical frame of reference. Salvemini's Giolittian critiques almost inescapably suggested themselves as methodological threads. This, not only because they practically always were concerned with the heart of those problems but also because they are encountered almost ubiquitously in all the newer polemical literature on Giolitti and his era. The documentation in the three chapters in Section Two will also serve, I trust, to bring up to date, from 1945 to 1960, the materials published on Giolitti and the Giolittian period. Thus the Bibliography and the foot-note references in Section Two may perhaps now constitute a useful working bibliography on a previously much neglected phase of modern Italian history. The new critical essay seeks, essentially, to suggest the newer dimensions which an historical problem may assume in such political and ideological circumstances as arose in Italy after the fall of Fascism, the return to intellectual freedom, and the explosion of contrasting desires to revaluate the practical and moral sources of Italian national life. The homage to Salvemini contained in the Epilogue will throw, I hope, into greater relief the substance and purpose of the critical study.

If the new critical essay stimulates debates among historians and students of modern Italy, it will have served one of its main purposes. For, despite appearances and the series of grave and frequently convulsive crises through which Italy has passed since 1914, the structure of the fundamental national problem has not radically changed. That problem still involves the making of Italian democracy not merely as a fact of politics but of conscience. Progress in this direction has been immense and undeniable since the fall of Fascism. In some crucial spheres of Italian national life the basic problem still stands within a frame of reference harkening back to the Giolitti-Salvemini contrast. Whether, outside the false totalitarian alternatives of fascism and communism or beyond the persistent drives toward liberal or integral confessionalism, a genuine "third force" may rise to offer other solutions to the ancient problem no historian has the possibility of knowing or the right to predict. But a real "third force" may already very well be there. Perhaps it may consist of nothing else but the multiplicity of vital resources possessed by the Italian people. Again and again, the Italians have shown a marvelous capacity to be bigger than their politics at home and abroad. The "genius of Italy" may after all be but another name for that combination of courage, sheer work, and creativeness which has seen the Italians through even their most frightful national disasters.

I am grateful to those known and unknown students of modern Italy who for many years have persisted in their request for a second printing of my first Giolittian essay. I trust they will find the new historiographical critique of some use in their pursuit of the fascinating and challenging problems in modern Italian history. Messrs. Thomas Yoseloff, Director, and Charles Dwoskin, Editor, of the University of Pennsylvania Press, have been encouragingly responsive to the suggestions that this new volume may serve some purpose and I am most appreciative of their active and consistent interest in this work. I wish to express my deepest appreciation not only for his incisive comments and suggestions on the historiographical essay but also for his continued friendship and inspiration to Dr. Kent Roberts Greenfield. I am more grateful than I can say to my wife who has been unstinting in constructive criticism but above all in patience and understanding during the apparently endless research and writing periods.

A. W. S.

New York
December, 1959

PREFACE TO FIRST EDITION

THE purpose of this book is to present an analysis of the significant problems and currents of Italian political life at the turn of the century during the time of Giovanni Giolitti. The Italian Risorgimento has been studied in practically all its phases in Italy and abroad, and the Fascist regime has already elicited a mountain of histories and monographs. But an almost universally accepted legend had it that "hardly anything of importance" happened in Liberal Italy between the Piedmontese march on Rome in 1870 and the Fascist incursion of 1922—at least until Benedetto Croce, Gioacchino Volpe, and a few others began, for different motives, to dispel it. This was believed to be especially true of the period that takes its name from Giolitti. It was therefore dismissed with a few platitudinous and inconclusive phrases.

This work is based on the conviction that much of great import happened in Italy between 1900 and 1914 and that, contrary to common belief, it must be studied carefully for an understanding and appreciation of modern Italian history and of the Italian people. It is therefore intended as a contribution toward an understanding of pre-Fascist, Liberal-democratic Italian political life. This study makes no pretensions of being a full and complete history of Italy in the Giolittian period. It focuses attention upon the field of politics, understood in its most general sense; as a result some phases of Italian national life—finance and cultural activities, to take two extreme examples—are only touched upon indirectly. But an attempt is here made to view and present the phenomena of Giolitti and *Giolittismo* as parts of a general picture in which Italian parliamentary institutions, political parties, liberalism, socialism, nationalism, and other current ideas were significant elements. If this brief study helps to bring Giolitti and the Italy he allegedly "ruled in dictatorial fashion" a little closer to the field of history, the labor expended upon it will have been richly rewarded.

I wish to acknowledge a great debt of gratitude to Professor William E. Lingelbach of the University of Pennsylvania. Only those who have been in almost daily contact with Professor Lingelbach can fully appreciate the stimulating influence of his personality and of his learning. I have discussed many of the problems arising from this work with him and he has been most generous with his time, his patience, and with helpful suggestions. His kind encouragement will be cherished by me as the most invaluable gift of a great teacher and friend. I am indebted to Professor Gaetano Salvemini, of Harvard University, for the privilege of his inspiring friendship and for his encouragement; to Professor

Giorgio Levi Della Vida, formerly of the University of Rome and now of the University of Pennsylvania, with whom I have discussed some of the more important problems of Italian liberal thought; and to Count Carlo Sforza, who did me the honor of granting me an interview before returning to the political arena in Italy.

My researches were made possible by a George Leib Harrison Fellowship awarded me by the Graduate School of the University of Pennsylvania, by a scholarship award of the Grand Lodge of Pennsylvania of the Order Sons of Italy, and especially by a Pre-Doctoral Field Fellowship award of the Social Science Research Council in 1942–43, which assistance I acknowledge most gratefully.

The staffs of the University of Pennsylvania Library, of the Widener Library at Harvard, of the Library of Congress, of the Columbia University libraries, of the New York Public Library, and of the Philadelphia Free Library were always kind and helpful, and to them I give my thanks for their many courtesies.

A. W. S.

Philadelphia
April 1943

INTRODUCTORY ESSAY

I TALIAN political literature from 1861 to 1922 is drenched with a flood of bitter criticism about everything and everybody. To the turn of the century the Clericals regarded newborn Italy as a creation of the Evil One, and everything which was done or not done was wrong to them. After 1876, the Conservatives, who had been turned out of power and were no longer able to have their own way, found that Italy, deprived of their light, was going to rack and ruin. The Republicans, the Socialists, the Anarchists criticized men who were in power owing to the fact that they were neither Republican nor Socialist nor Anarchist. The non-party men who desired honest and efficient administration and more rapid social progress complained that the men in power were not efficient enough and not progressive enough and not honest enough or were downright dishonest. Even the politicians who were in control were disheartened by the gap which divided their everyday inconspicuous job from the alluring expectations of the men who had carried out the Italian Risorgimento.

In his *Goliath* Borgese describes with a master hand the disease which gnawed at the Italian soul after 1870: the memory of, and the nostalgia for, the grandeur of the Roman Empire, coupled with a restless urge for impossible achievements and, as a consequence, disappointment and self-vilification. Italy was crushed by her past. Instead of comparing their present with their immediate past and realizing the strides the people were making, Italians contrasted present conditions with the memories of past greatness or with dreams of impossible primacies. No measurable degree of progress could satisfy them. They had words only to lament the mediocrity, incapacity, dishonesty, failures of their politicians. A certain amount of self-criticism is a useful corrective to national smugness: it is a factor of that "divine discontent" which leads to improvements. But absurd ambitions are poisonous drugs. They create persecution-mania and make for blunders.

After Mussolini came to power Fascist propaganda overturned the procedure. Everything now became a monument of wisdom, of efficiency, of moral integrity, while everything, before the Dictator began to perform his miracles, had been wrong.

One has to take into account these two floods of misrepresentation, coming from two opposite angles, if one wants to understand the history of Italy from 1870 to 1922. Only a man endowed with a sharp critical sense can avoid the risk of misreading that history completely. Nobody would write the history of the Roosevelt Administration using only the evidence furnished by Republican or isolationist sources. Most people write recent Italian history by a method that is no more sensible.

To be sure, pre-Fascist politicians were responsible for all sorts of mistakes and misdeeds, ill-advised undertakings, unused opportunities, waste, and extravagance. Not all the problems that confronted the country were solved. Not always were the solutions reached the best nor the methods employed the most efficient. But could all problems have been solved at a moment's notice? Has there ever been in history any country which solved all its problems at one stroke and without blunders and whose politicians were monsters of untainted intelligence and moral integrity? If one judges the handiwork of Italian pre-Fascist politicians by the standards of some flawless ideal—the method of the political crusader—there is no politician who would not be sent to hell. But if one adopts the method of the historian, that is if one compares, as far as Italy is concerned, the starting point in 1861 with the point of arrival, the First World War, and the poverty of national resources with the wealth of other countries, one cannot fail to conclude that no country in Europe had made such strides in so short a time.

The author of the present book knew how to avoid the pitfalls of pre-Fascist self-vilification and Fascist propaganda. At the same time he knew how to avoid the opposite pitfalls of "idealistic" historiography, according to which (with Dr. Pangloss) everything which is real is rational and everything which is rational is good. Where most people concern themselves with passing unwarranted judgment, Mr. Salomone first endeavored to understand and then passed cautious and balanced judgment. I do not know of any book which gives a better informed and more objective account of one of the most elusive periods of Italian history, the so-called "Giolittian" years. When one learns that this is the work of a young man, one realizes that there are in this book the beginnings of an exceptionally well-gifted historian.

Mr. Salomone's book is entitled *Italian Democracy in the Making*. What does he mean by these words?

If one understands by "democracy" a political regime in which all personal and political rights are granted equally to all citizens without social, religious, or racial discrimination, and those rights are granted not only by the written law but in actual daily practice, and in addition all citizens, to the last one, intelligently and honestly share in community life, one has to admit that before the First World War Italy possessed a very low form of democracy. But does perfect democracy exist anywhere? Is not democracy in the making everywhere?

The Italian Risorgimento between 1859 and 1870 was the work of an oligarchy of upper and middle classes. The right to vote was granted only to males over twenty-five who paid a minimum of eight dollars in direct taxation and knew how to read and write. In 1871, 72.96 per cent of the population was illiterate. As a consequence, no more than 530,000 citizens were enfranchised out of a population of about 27 million, i. e., 1.98 per cent. By 1880, the enfranchised citizens had risen to 620,000, i. e., 2.18 per cent of the population. All agricultural day laborers, almost all small-holders, almost all city artisans and workers and a good many of the lower middle classes had no right to vote.

This oligarchic system was not an exception in Europe eighty years ago.

Between the Reform of 1832 and that of 1867, Great Britain had no more than 700,000 citizens on the electoral list out of a population of 32 million. She remained an oligarchy after the Reform Acts of 1867 and 1884. France had a restricted franchise before 1848; and universal suffrage, enacted in 1848, brought about Napoleon III's dictatorship in 1851. In Germany universal suffrage for the Reichstag from 1867 onward acted as a façade hiding an oligarchic social and political structure. Austria got universal suffrage only in 1908.

In Italy the Reform Act of 1882 extended the franchise to males over twenty-one who could read and write, even if they did not pay any direct taxation. At the same time, 62.80 per cent of the population, that is, almost all of the peasantry and the great majority of artisans and workmen, were still illiterate. It was only in the most progressive cities of northern Italy that workmen had begun to send their children to school. Thus in 1882, no more than two million were registered. The fact, however, remains that the electorate rose from 2.18 per cent to 6.97 per cent of the population. The urban had more electors than the rural sections of the constituencies since those who could read and write were chiefly concentrated in the cities. As a consequence, the political influence of the industrial, commercial, and intellectual classes outweighed that of the landowning class. In the cities themselves the Reform gave great influence to the lower middle classes.

In 1912 a new Reform Act added, to those who had a right to vote, all men under thirty who had served in the armed forces and all others who were over thirty. In neither of these classifications was literacy required. This was almost universal suffrage. The number of enfranchised citizens rose from three to eight and one-half million. Five and one-half million workmen and peasants submerged the old privileged body of three million.

In order to understand this reform one has to take stock of the fact that by 1911 the percentage of illiteracy had dropped to 38 per cent. Illiteracy had practically disappeared among the rising generations of northern Italy and had been sharply reduced among the youth of southern Italy. Of the young people who attained their twentieth year in 1927, and therefore had gone to school before or during the war, 87 per cent knew how to read and write. Moreover, peace-time conscription had for half a century forced men from peasant stock into the army, removing them from their villages to faraway regions, bringing them in touch with communities which followed different ways, returning them to their homes with a new outlook on life. In addition, emigration—especially emigration to North America—had brought about an upheaval of immense importance among the peasantry of southern Italy. The southern Italian peasant who emigrated not only found work but was made aware of different civilizations. When he returned home he was a new man. Last but not least it was no longer possible to leave disfranchised the majority of the Italian male population who were serving in the war for the conquest of Libya and might at any moment be expected to fight in a European war and all this at a time when even Austria was endowed with universal suffrage.

When the franchise was extended to those who did not know how to read and write, it was thought in Italy—and rightly, in my opinion—that experience of life is more important than mere literacy. A peasant might be unable to read and write but, if he had been to America and returned home with not inconsiderable savings, he possessed a greater knowledge of practical affairs than, for instance, the young gentleman who read French novels and had never faced greater difficulties than that of arranging his necktie in front of his looking-glass.

In Italy, under any voting system, no more than fifty to sixty per cent of the electorate went to the polls. This, by observers readier to pass judgment than to understand, was branded as an evidence of political inertia and hopelessness. The fact is that the same percentage prevails in the United States today. To appreciate the Italian percentage, however, one has to take stock of the fact that millions of Italian workers were far away in Central Europe or along distant Mediterranean shores or in North and South America. They naturally were not in a position to go to the polls, but their numbers were generally included in the population figures. Those men also who were under the colors—Italy had peace-time compulsory military service—were not allowed to vote. Lastly, the citizen was registered as a voter in the city where he was born; therefore, those who were away on business or as government officials had no opportunity to vote. Thus analyzed the Italian percentage compares very favorably with the American.

Parliamentary Italy did not possess the two-party system. During the eighties the traditional division between Conservatives and Democrats had vanished. The transformation of parties (*trasformismo*) had brought about in Italy the splitting up of those parties into small groups, kept together, as Mr. Salomone points out, by personal rather than ideological loyalties. According to Anglo-Saxon doctrine the two-party system is indispensable to a rightful working of a parliamentary regime. Italy lacked that blessing. Was she alone? Did she follow a universal rule or was she a scandalous exception?

During the nineteenth century in England people spoke of only two political parties: the Conservative party and the Liberal party. But the Liberal party was not a party; it was the coalition of two parties, that is, the English Liberal party and the Irish party. When the Irish party refused to coöperate with the English Liberal party and was numerically sufficiently strong to hamper the working of the House of Commons, a political paralysis resulted. But that was not the end of the world. Nobody proclaimed that the English people were incapable of living under a free regime. "We must be patient, the crisis will be solved," it was said. In the present century another party came upon the scene: the Labor party. In 1921 the Irish members went home. Thus three parties remained in England: the Conservative, the Liberal, and the Labor parties. Soon a fourth party appeared: the Communist party. Lately a fifth party has asserted itself in England: the Commonwealth party. If to all of these is added the Independent Labor party, which according to circumstance aligns itself or breaks with the Labor party, we actually see six parties performing upon the political stage. The Communist party, it is true, sends one lone member to Parliament. Presently it has no weight, but it may have more in the future. The Commonwealth party as well will certainly exert a noticeable influence. But even if the political parties should be reduced to only three, the legend of the two-party system would be seen for what it is —a legend.

Moreover, the so-called English parties are not homogeneous and compact political monoliths, as is often thought when the sacred word "party" is pronounced. During the nineteenth century the English Liberal party always had a Cobdenist Right which strenuously advocated laissez-faire doctrines, and a radical Left which demanded social reforms. Scottish Liberals, Welsh Liberals, and English Liberals are not at all the brotherly associates they often appear from afar. Within the Conservative party also there is a Left and a Right. The same thing is true of the Labor party. One of the greatest difficulties faced by party leaders is that of holding together the various groups whose ideas and interests are often in bitter conflict. The English parties are in reality coalitions of local groups which often disagree on essential points, but which are nevertheless held together by the necessity of making compromises in order to gain or to remain in power as against opposite coalitions.

In Canada there are six parties.

As for the United States, the attractive fairy-tale of sharply outlined and opposed political parties is even more imaginary than that of the two English parties. It is true that in the United States one speaks only of the Republican and the Democratic parties. But the United States are really forty-eight sections spreading over a vast continent. In each of these forty-eight sections there are two local parties, one of which is called the Democratic party and the other the Republican party. But the Republican party of California does not have a single idea in common with, for example, the Republican party of Massachusetts, while at the same time the Democratic party of Texas is as much in agreement with the Democratic party of Wisconsin as the devil with holy water. In the United States there are not two parties. There are ninety-six local parties, with many differences among them, but which come together as two large national "coalitions" for the purpose of electing the President of the Republic. Once elected the President must deal, both in the House of Representatives and in the Senate, with a hodgepodge of heterogeneous and fluctuating groups in comparison to which the groups in the pre-Fascist Italian Chamber of Deputies were a heavenly chorus. A President of the United States must shrewdly bring about among the many local groups an almost infinite number of "combinations of fortune" whose life span may be only one day and for one particular purpose, after which they disband. In this parliamentary strategy he must be prepared to utilize a subtlety and often a lack of scruples in contrast to which Giolitti's maneuvers in Italy were child's play.

In short, those political entities which in Italy one calls "parties" are known as "groups" in England and America, while those which in Italy would be coalitions of "groups" are called "parties" in England and America.

During the fifteen years preceding the First World War there was in Italy a coalition of "parties," or "groups," the Giolittian coalition. It enjoyed an almost permanent stay in power. There certainly was stability then in Italy. As a matter of fact there was even too much stability, despite the fact that Italy did not enjoy the blessing of having only two parties, a blessing which, for that matter, was also unknown to Belgium, France, Switzerland, Germany, and Austria-Hungary. Whether the Giolittian coalition's long stay in power was for Italy's good or evil is an altogether different question.

A voting system would be meaningless if it were not buttressed by freedom of the press and freedom of association.

During the nineteenth century, freedom of the press was limited in Italy by the faculty given to the Attorney General in each province to confiscate any issue of a newspaper which contained illegal material. The Government also was entitled to declare illegal such associations as it could expect to cause disturbances in public peace and could indict their members before the judiciary as "associates for the purpose of crime" (associazione a delinquere). But after 1900 no associations were any longer declared illegal. Trade union rights became unrestricted. And in 1906 the Attorney General was deprived of the power to confiscate newspapers. Italian democracy was in the making.

Town councils were elected by the citizens. But they were not autonomous bodies as in Switzerland, in England, or in the United States. There was in each one of the Italian districts (provincie) a permanent agent of the central government, the Prefetto, who was sent by the Home Secretary (Ministro degli interni) to supervise local government. This agent could annul all decisions of municipal councils. He could even remove mayors and councillors and send his own agents (commissari) to run the municipality. In 1896, A. Lawrence Lowell, in his classic work on Governments and Parties in Continental Europe, remarked that Italian administration was modeled on the French and not on the Anglo-Saxon pattern. The Italian prefect, like his French prototype, used his influence more or less openly at elections. This was the gnawing cancer of Italian democracy in the making.

The prefect was always in a position to bring pressure to bear upon the mayors and town councillors. The mayors and councillors who, during an electioneering campaign, used their influence in favor of the governmental candidate remained in office even if they were the worst scoundrels. Those who supported opposition candidates, even if they were the best possible administrators, were replaced by government commissioners. Against eventual injustice there was no redress.

Under Giolitti's rule, the interference of the prefects with local government and elections reached unprecedented heights of brutality. Where the electorate was refractory to pressure and the elected mayors and town councillors refused to bow, the prefect not only dismissed them, but "managed" local and national elections. If an election had to be carried out, the police, in league with the Government supporters, enrolled the scum of the constituencies and the underworld of the neighboring districts. In the last weeks before the polls, the opponents were threatened, bludgeoned, besieged in their homes. Their leaders were debarred from addressing meetings, or even thrown into prison until election day was over. Voters suspected of upholding the opposition were refused polling cards. Those favoring governmental candidates were given not only their own polling cards, but also those of opponents, emigrants, deceased voters, and were allowed to vote three, five, ten, twenty times. The Government candidates were always the winners. Any deputy who dared Giolitti, had to confront a bad time at his next election. In Italy people used to say that Giolitti sold prefects in order to buy deputies. Giolitti was not the first Home Secretary to "manage" elections. But he "managed" one after another three national elections (1904, 1909, 1913) and he surpassed all in clarity of purpose and lack of scruples.

But Giolitti did not strangle local government or "manage" elections all over Italy. In those sections of Italy where public opinion was alive and opposition hard to quell, he let things go their own way. It was only in backward southern Italy that Giolitti strangled local government and "managed" elections. Northern Italy was left free to run its local business as best it pleased. Not a few city governments in northern Italy were models of intelligent, honest, and efficient administration. And the worst city governments in the South were no worse than many of those of the United States. Southern Italy gave Giolitti about two hundred representatives ready to obey him under any conditions.

Northern Italy sent to the Chamber of Deputies about three hundred representatives who were split into those who favored the "boss" and those who were against him. Giolitti's majority consisted of a "solid block" from the South and those among the Northerners who were interested in playing ball with him and who, on the whole, had been freely elected. The opponents coming mostly from the North were free to protest in the Chamber of Deputies or in the press as much as they wanted. They were helpless—and hopeless. And little by little hopelessness brought "wisdom." One by one, sooner or later, they came to terms with the boss, and either they joined his flock or they carried on a mock opposition which was more useful to him than open submission.

Yet before terming Giolitti a "parliamentary dictator" one should be careful to qualify those words. A dictator is a man who suppresses freedom of speech, freedom of the press, freedom of association, and sends his opponents to jail or to the next world. Giolitti never did this. He circumvented opposition by reducing the Chamber of Deputies to the position of his maid-servant. There was in the Chamber a majority which blindly obeyed him and an opposition which was sure of always remaining in the minority and was steadily invited to come to some compromise with the master of the circus. If being a dictator means being supported by a huge parliamentary majority and therefore being able to do much as one thinks fit and necessary, Roosevelt was also a dictator in America from 1933 to

1940 and Churchill was a dictator in England from 1940 to 1945. But let us say "powerful leaders" and not "dictators." As soon as his parliamentary majority wavered Giolitti used to resign in order to allow his opponents to try their luck, keeping alert to return to the foreground as soon as his followers reorganized themselves.

Giolitti was an extraordinarily able and skilful parliamentarian. He grasped with extreme shrewdness and lightning rapidity the slightest current of opinion among the five hundred men who formed the Chamber of Deputies. But he had little sensitivity for what was going on in the country at large. Here dissatisfaction with the "managing" of elections was steadily growing among non-party citizens. He thought that he could control the electorate under universal suffrage as easily as he used to when the franchise was restricted. He never realized that the peasantry of southern Italy was no longer that of the eighties. When, in 1913, he was confronted not with a mere two or three thousand voters, but with ten thousand or more voters in a constituency to be "managed," he was forced to increase the dose of violence to insure success. He won another of his overwhelming electoral victories. But the scandals of that campaign provoked bitter indignation everywhere. On the eve of the war of 1914–18, Giolitti was the most powerful man in Parliament, but the most unpopular man in the country. Italian democracy was in the making.

Italian democracy would have needed still another generation of trial and error before becoming not a "perfect democracy" but a "less imperfect democracy."

The crisis that followed the First World War, however, was fatal to that democratic process. So long as the Italian masses had remained indifferent toward public life and had been deprived of the right of suffrage, the Royal House, the professional militarists who headed the armed forces, the big industrialists and land-owners, the chief editors of the large dailies had all been satisfied that parliamentary institutions, whether they functioned well or badly, furthered their purposes. But during the first twenty years of the present century the Italian working classes came forward demanding their place in the sun and after the war of 1914–18 they became "unruly." More than half of the members in the Italian Chamber of Deputies were now the representatives of these masses and they did not lend themselves to the traditional game of the old masters. That was the reason why the coup d'état of October 1922 (the so-called "March on Rome") was contrived by politicians blinded by class interests and by personal ambitions as well as by the leaders of the armed forces. The Giolittian method of stifling local government and of curtailing the personal and political liberties of citizens in southern Italy at election time—and only in those constituencies where the victory of the governmental candidate was necessary—was now extended and practised by the Fascists all over Italy and became permanent. And worse yet, systematic assassination was added. Now, Italy truly had a dictatorship, Mussolini's dictatorship, and not "parliamentary dictatorship." The coup d'état of October 1922 would not have taken place if a greater acquaintance with, and a more extensive practice of, democracy on the part of the people had not threatened the very roots of the conservative interests.

In the course of his researches Mr. Salomone has come upon my name and he has devoted some space in his book to my activities in Italy during the years of Giolitti. It is not up to me to comment on what he has written about me. But to one point I feel duty-bound to call the reader's attention. While during those years I practised, as well as I could, my profession of historian (which has always been my true profession), I devoted my spare time to a political crusade. The reader will find in this book the crusader and not the historian.

Looking back at the work of the crusader after thirty years, I find that I have nothing to regret. I must acknowledge, however, that I would have been wiser had I been more moderate in my criticism of the Giolittian system. My knowledge of the men who came after Giolitti in Italy as well as of countries in which I have lived during the last twenty years has convinced me that if Giolitti was not better, neither was he worse than many non-Italian politicians, and he was certainly less reprehensible than the Italian politicians who followed him. For while we Italian crusaders attacked him from the Left accusing him of being—and he was—a corrupter of Italian democracy in the making, others assailed him from the Right because he was even too democratic for their taste. Our criticism thus did not help to direct the evolution of Italian public life toward less imperfect forms of democracy, but rather toward the victory of those militarist, nationalist, and reactionary groups who had found even Giolitti's democracy too perfect. It often happens that he who seeks only the best not only fails to get it but also plunges into the worst. It is said that in the next world we shall be assigned either to hell, or purgatory, or paradise. In this world, however, there is no paradise. If, in seeking an impossible paradise, we scorn purgatory, we will surely end in hell. If it were possible for me to live again in Italy between 1900 and 1914 with that modicum of experience which I have gained during these successive thirty years, I would not omit any of my censures of the Giolittian system, but I would be more indulgent and I would regard with greater suspicion those who found pleasure in my criticism because they wanted to lead Italy in the opposite direction from that which I envisaged for her.

Perhaps I may be allowed to excuse my error with the example of a man who possessed an intelligence much greater than mine: Gaetano Mosca. The reader of this book will find in it an account of the criticism of the Italian parliamentary regime made by Gaetano Mosca when he was still very young—a young man of exceptional intelligence and moral integrity, but still quite young. It might be well to remember, however, that speaking on the bill which was to institute Mussolini's dictatorship, at the sitting of December 16, 1925 of the Italian Senate, Gaetano Mosca, by then ripe of age and experience, closed his address with the following words:

I who have always sharply criticized parliamentary government must now almost lament over its downfall. In order to judge a form of government there is one possible method, that is, to compare it with both that which has preceded it and that which has followed it. It would be premature, at this time, to speak of the latter. As to the former, the forms of government immediately preceding the parliamentary regime were such that it can be frankly asserted that this system was better than they. . . . Let us consider the road traveled from 1848 to 1914, eve of the war. Let us see what Italy was in 1848 and what she had become by 1914. We must then acknowledge that the progress made by the country during this period was immense. . . . Certainly representative parliamentary government must not and can not be immutable. As the conditions of society change political organizations are changed. But should the change have been rapid and radical, or should it have been slow and wary? This is the very grave question which vexes my soul. As an old adversary of the parliamentary regime, I believe that this problem must be solved in the most moderate and prudent manner.

Mosca too discovered that, with his criticism of the parliamentary system, he had not encouraged a moderate and prudent reform but rather the total abolition of the system. As for the results of the Fascist dictatorship in contrast with those of Italian democracy in the making, they are here before our very eyes. Let us hope that the Italians will not be the only ones to learn from that frightful experience.

GAETANO SALVEMINI

Cambridge, Massachusetts
  May 1945

CONTENTS

ILLUSTRATIONS

The illustrations are reproduced from A. William Salomone, L'eta giolittiana (Turin, 1949) by permission and through the courtesy of Francesco De Silva Editore,Turin, and "La Nuova Italia" Editrice, Florence, Italy.

GIOLITTI IN 1914   *Frontispiece*

The following illustrations appear as a group after page 114:

SECTION ONE
ITALIAN DEMOCRACY IN THE MAKING

I

HERITAGE OF THE RISORGIMENTO

*La guerra per la libertà è sacra, com'è sacro l'umano
individuo: combattetela sino all'estremo.**

MAZZINI

THE final disintegration of the Roman Empire brought in its train the beginning of Italy's tragedy. Wave after wave of former subjects and enemies of the Empire once restrained by Roman legions and the law of Rome now poured across the frontiers. Italy became the classic land of invasion. Her geographic position at the crossroads of civilization, her strategic position in the Mediterranean, her historical and cultural traditions, her reputed wealth and the glory of the name, Rome, made Italy the final prize and goal of conquerors and ravaging hordes. Across Alpine passes and from Mediterranean shores, once the floodgates were opened, poured Huns and Vandals, Visigoths and Ostrogoths, Lombards and Franks, Normans, Saracens, Germans. It is remarkable that Italy did not become a complete wasteland, that in the midst of constant battles and bloodshed, clash, and devastation, Italy slowly but surely was transformed into the thriving center of a new civilization. By the twelfth century there was an Italian people ready to be fused into an Italian nation. "The Italy of the twelfth and thirteenth centuries, though infinitely divided in the material sense, constituted a profound moral unity." [1]

There was something miraculous in Italy's assimilative powers, in her sturdy spirit of resistance, in her physical strength, in the variety of her intellectual and cultural life, in the creative plasticity of her children. Italy kept alive throughout her vicissitudes the fertile seeds of civilization. The torch of freedom was raised above the feudal world of privilege and power when the citizens of Lombardy sent the German conqueror Barbarossa scurrying back to his trans-Alpine home after the battle of Legnano (1176). The Germans, pursuing their eternal mirage of the resurrected empire, returned, and with them came the French and Spaniards. Through the coming and going of these foreign invaders could be traced the rise of an opposition whose final goal was to be the national independence of Italy. But one would be straining historical truth to see in this often-recurring opposition a systematic aspiration and a methodical struggle to unite all of Italy under one government independent of foreign domination. Unity and independence were to be realized only after Italy

---

* "The war for freedom is sacred, as the human individual is sacred: wage it unto the end." Giuseppe Mazzini, "I sistemi e la democrazia," *Scritti-Filosofia*, 2 vols. (Milan, n.d.), I, 235.

[1] Luigi Salvatorelli, *A Concise History of Italy*, tr. by Bernard Miall, p. 207.

had been further brutalized by centuries of foreign rule, political disunity, and moral stagnation.

Nowhere else, save perhaps in France and England, had the promise of early political maturity becoming complete nationhood seemed more certain. Again and again, however, that promise was to fade into a lost hope, a shadow woven of unreality and despair, an ineffectual and maddening dream. Perhaps the very multiplicity of her potentialities, the diversity of her creative spirit, the efflorescence of her achievements in culture and civilization, the consciousness and keenness of political maturity, together with the individualism of her people so often extolled, the particularism of her rulers so frequently decried, as well as the foreign arms upon her soil, all contributed to keep Italy politically enslaved and disunited.

Almost from the beginning Italians were unwilling to limit their overwhelming faith in the mind's power. In all their superb literature and philosophy one might trace the grand sweep of this aberration, for as such it came to be viewed in a world that set greater value upon other and less benign forces. Italians, at least the heads of states, the leaders and rulers of men, and the molders of their spiritual and intellectual life, became through the centuries too arrogantly proud and too increasingly blind to admit that mind and reason alone could not serve for the survival and growth of a people. In a world of naked and brutal realities—unlike the fantastic dreamworld of fifteenth and sixteenth century Italy—material strength and moral character (or at least its mask) were more formidable and effective weapons. And this blindness to reality became total just at the time that the Italians were faced by one of the most acute crises in their political life. Thus it happened that while they juggled among themselves with the balance of power in their narrow peninsula the despised "ultramontanes and barbarians," as Lorenzo de' Medici liked to call them, descended once again to spill rivers of blood in this land and to fix a foreign yoke upon them for still more centuries to come.[2] During this whole period the Italians continued to feel that there was something unreal, something at once illusive and only vaguely frightful in this series of conquests as though it were a shadow-show and not the actual tragedy which it was—a tragedy in which they themselves were the protagonists for all their passivity. Thus at the very moment when they had reached the apogée of their cultural and intellectual renaissance Italians began the descent into a centuries-long inferno of political enslavement and disunity, of economic and social stagnation, and of spiritual and moral inertia. Niccolò Machiavelli (1469–1527), and perhaps he alone, saw their tragedy in all its frightful scale and tried to sweep away the shadows and to tear off the deceptive veil with which they had obstructed their vision. But his be-

---

[2] Due to the intrigues of the ruling houses of Milan and Naples, in 1494 a French army led by King Charles VIII swept across the Western Alps and through Italy as far as Naples. Until 1559 Italy was to be the main battlefield of the Hapsburg-Valois wars. The celebrated Treaty of Cateau Cambrésis (1559) determined Hapsburg predominance in northern and southern Italy.

came a voice crying in the wilderness, unheeded, misunderstood, and despised.[3]

Long before the French Revolution, however, there began in Italy the stirrings of a new life. Those who still insist on viewing the influence of French Revolutionary and Napoleonic armies as the first and sole agents of the beginning of redemption in Italy are working under a delusion which is also an historical inaccuracy. The intellectual, moral and, in part, even the economic Risorgimento was developing in Italy almost a century before its more spectacular, essentially political, manifestations came to impress the imagination of Europe. The Italian eighteenth century has for too long a time been ignored or slighted by students of Italian history.[4] In that era Italy, it is true, was still politically divided, but a change had taken place for now bourgeois reformers and aristocratic liberals, enlightened despots and farsighted statesmen, thinkers, poets, writers of all kinds were striving to inject new life into their somnolent country. Through the work of philosophers like Vico, the historians Muratori and Giannone, scientists like Malpighi, Galvani, Volta, and Spallanzani, economists such as the brothers Pietro and Alessandro Verri, criminologists like Beccaria, legal writers like Filangeri, the littérateurs Baretti and Gozzi, the poets Parini and Alfieri, such statesmen as Bernardo Tanucci, and a thousand others, Italy in the eighteenth century was again contributing to the mainstream of European culture.

The French Revolution and Napoleon merely accelerated the tempo and enlarged the scope and goals of the political Risorgimento. It is easy, in this matter, to revive and to stir up old historical quarrels. The French invasions and conquests in Italy (1796–1815) can be viewed as no more than the exchange of one domination for another, French mastery being in some cases no better than the Austrian rule that preceded it; but whereas Austrian rule had never transcended the principles of the right of conquest and dynastic necessity, the Napoleonic whirlwind had brought an Idea as well as the Sword. A step had also been taken toward greater unity, if not yet toward national independence. Instead of the old divi-

<hr>

[3] The polemical literature on Machiavelli is vast and, while differing about the sources, it is mostly agreed about the objectives, of his patriotic fervor. In the much quoted chapter xxvi of *The Prince* entitled "Exhortation to Liberate Italy From the Barbarians," Machiavelli cried: "In order that the power of an Italian genius might be recognized, it was necessary that Italy should be reduced to her present condition . . . without a head, without order, beaten, despoiled, lacerated, and overrun, and that she should have suffered ruin of every kind. . . . Now, almost lifeless, she awaits one who may heal her wounds and put a stop to the pillaging of Lombardy, to the rapacity and extortion in the Kingdom of Naples and in Tuscany, and cure her of those sores which have long been festering."

[4] Italian scholarship has for a long time been focusing attention upon pre-French Revolution developments in Italy. The latest and most enlightening Italian studies of the Risorgimento begin with the early 18th century; see especially C. Spellanzon, *Storia del Risorgimento e dell'unità d'Italia*, 4 vols. (Milan, 1933–38); A. Omodeo, *L'età del Risorgimento italiano* (Messina, 1932); A. Ghisalberti, *Gli albori del Risorgimento italiano* (Rome, 1931); and for political thought, L. Salvatorelli, *Il pensiero politico italiano dal 1700 al 1870* (Turin, 1935).

sions, Napoleonic Italy was divided into three main sections: the provinces annexed to France (Piedmont, Liguria, Parma, Reggio, Tuscany, Umbria, and Latium); the Kingdom of Italy (Lombardy, Venetia, Trentino, Modena, Romagna, and the Marches) under Napoleon's "vicar," his stepson Eugene Beauharnais; the Kingdom of Naples under Napoleon's brother-in-law, Joachim Murat. Italy was unquestionably a French dependency, but nevertheless much constructive work was being done: free trade between the divisions of the country was introduced; many of the feudalistic privileges of the nobility and clergy were abolished; the civil and criminal codes were coördinated; a new agrarian and commercial middle class began to rise; schools and universities were reformed; civil service and administrative careers were opened on the basis of merit to the new bourgeois intellectual classes; a certain amount of freedom of the press was granted; political literature, so long as it was not overtly anti-French, was encouraged, or at least not completely muzzled.[5] Undoubtedly a new breath of life was stirring in Italy.

The fall of the Napoleonic regime in 1814–15 meant for Italy the return of the old order in its most repressive and uninspired forms. Metternich's Austria was to become the quintessence of reaction in Europe and in Italy. The Congress of Vienna (1814–15), with its fetish of restoration and its apotheosis of legitimacy, was to become the bête noire of all the forces of revolution, liberalism, nationalism, and constitutionalism on the Italian peninsula. The old rulers and princes and generals might return to their citadels of power and privilege in Milan, Florence, Bologna, Rome, Naples and a thousand other cities and regions, in the short-sighted certainty that the storm having spent itself, Italy would revert quietly to her ancient somnolence and passivity.

And indeed men were tired of wars and adventures and conquering demigods who imposed new taxes and sent their sons to die in distant battlefields. Yet not all men and not all classes of society. To be sure the peasants—and they were the overwhelming majority throughout Italy—had not felt the breath of the revolutionary gospel or the leaven of the revolutionary ideals except as those ideals masked in new forms the imposition of old oppressions. There were, however, groups of individuals all over Italy and especially in the urban North who saw in the return of the old order the end of their efforts for material and moral advancement and of the hopes for a free and united Italy. The middle classes and members of the liberal aristocracy saw themselves overwhelmed by the reëstablishment of the ancient rule, saw themselves once again reduced to an inferior position in society and excluded from participation in government by the princely bureaucracies. Thus it came to be chiefly through their agitation and work that the Risorgimento proper, that epic movement of Italian liberation whose final goal was independence and national unity, began in post-Napoleonic Italy.

[5] Cf. Gaetano Salvemini, "L'Italia politica nel secolo XIX" in *L'Europa nel secolo XIX*, I, 326–28, *passim*.

The Congress of Vienna made Austria the preponderant power in Italy. Of the ten states in Italy after 1815, five were under direct or indirect Hapsburg rule: the Kingdom of Lombardy and Venetia under the Emperor, the Grand Duchy of Tuscany, the Duchy of Modena, the Duchy of Parma, and the Duchy of Massa and Carrara.[6] Austria, moreover, came to view any change in the status quo of the other Italian states—the principal states being, of course, the Kingdom of Sardinia and Piedmont under the House of Savoy, the Papal State, and the Bourbon Kingdom of the Two Sicilies (Naples and Sicily)—as related directly to her own general interests. Her espousal and leadership of the cause of the counter-Revolution was complete and unreserved and she made Italy the testing field of all her European policies. Consequently Austria became the chief obstacle in the way of Italian independence, unity, and liberal reform.

Given the methods of the absolutist reaction in Italy, only secret societies and extreme means could be utilized at first to coördinate liberal aspirations and patriotic ends. The failure of the revolutionary outbreaks of 1820, 1821, and 1831, however, also indicated the bankruptcy of the secret societies, chief among which were the *Carboneria* and freemasonry. At this point there appeared on the historical horizon of Italy and of Europe the austere figure of Giuseppe Mazzini (1805–72). He had served his revolutionary apprenticeship among the *Carbonari* and had been among the first from their numbers to ruthlessly diagnose their weaknesses and to lay bare the ineffectual character of their activities and objectives. In 1832 Mazzini founded his Young Italy movement which was soon to blossom into a Young Europe association aimed against all reactionary governments. What, in its main lines, was the Mazzinian program?[7] Its immediate goal was the national resurrection of Italy into a free, united, and democratic republic. The ultimate goal was more visionary, a world-wide association of free peoples. Where the *Carbonari* had been a secret, aristocratic, and limited society, Mazzini wanted the substitution of an open (at least as far as the program was concerned), popular, and democratic movement. The motto of Young Italy was "God and the People"— a formula which symbolized both Mazzini's greatness and his limitations. For the God he invoked was interpreted by many of his contemporaries as a deistic abstraction remote from the "progressive" nineteenth-century world of materialistic struggles and positivistic principles. And the people he called to achieve their freedom were largely inert masses of peasants and workers completely untouched by his missionary fervor and idealistic appeals. Moreover, as one of his closest students has said, Mazzini

defined with marvelous clearness the national forces that were preparing the new history of Europe, but he associated with this rich vision of reality two great illu-

[6] For a good, brief account of the Restoration in Italy see G. F.-H. Berkeley, *Italy in the Making, 1815–1846* (Cambridge, England, 1932), pp. 25–43.

[7] Only brief generalizations can be offered in this summary. By far the best biographies of Mazzini in English are G. O. Griffith, *Mazzini, Prophet of Modern Europe* (New York, 1932) and Bolton King, *The Life of Mazzini* (New York and London, Everyman's Library, 1929).

sions: the illusion that the people were everywhere ready and anxious to rise against despotic regimes, and the illusion that the people were everywhere inspired by God with sentiments of universal justice.[8]

Nevertheless, from the time of Mazzini's appearance in the Italian revolutionary movement until the failure of his program in 1848–49, he, more than anyone else, was instrumental in keeping alive the ideal of a free and united Italy. Mazzini consecrated his life to a moral and spiritual crusade whose ultimate goal was the regeneration of mankind. In this he could not but fail. But he gave his country a political myth and a creed of liberation whose realization is, according to many of his compatriots, still possible, if not inevitable.

Perhaps what finally alienated many disciples and workers of the Mazzinian cause was not so much its utopianism as its persistent failures resulting from impracticability. The so-called Moderate program came upon the scene with the dissolution of Mazzinianism, just as Mazzinianism had risen with the discrediting of the *Carbonari* movement. The Moderates had no place in their program for violent revolution and secret societies. They were chiefly reformists who would have accepted enlightened despotism and, unlike the Mazzinians who visualized a single and democratic Italian republic, would have been satisfied with a confederation of Italian states.[9] The three great spokesmen of the Moderate program were all Piedmontese: Vincenzo Gioberti (1801–51), Cesare Balbo (1789–1853), and Massimo d'Azeglio (1798–1866).

Abbé Gioberti, in his work, *The Moral and Civil Primacy of the Italians* (*Il primato morale e civile degli italiani*), published in 1843, advanced the theory that since Italy had owed her greatness to Catholicism it was only from the Church under the guidance of an enlightened pontiff that her resurgence could come. An Italian confederation of states must come into being under the leadership of the Pope. Gioberti offered no solution, however, to the persistent problem of the Austrian occupation of Lombardo-Venetia. Many who were otherwise attracted to his program came up against the question of Austria in Italy and were turned away by his lack of an answer. The moral power of the Pope, even if completely utilized, could not alone dislodge Austria from Milan.

Cesare Balbo in his *The Hopes of Italy* (*Speranze d'Italia*) sought to straddle the dilemma. Balbo agreed with his friend Gioberti on the confederative principle, but for the papal leadership he would have substituted that of the House of Savoy, the sub-Alpine Kingdom of Piedmont. Piedmont, whose traditional policy had tended toward the absorption of Lombardy and Venetia to the east, alone possessed arms, and by these as well as by the skillful playing of European diplomacy Piedmont might induce Austria to abandon Italy and perhaps seek compensation elsewhere. Balbo's criticism of Gioberti's work was further reinforced by

---

[8] Salvemini, *op. cit.*, I, 344.

[9] On the Moderate program see Berkeley, *op. cit.*, pp. 139–53 and Guido De Ruggiero, *The History of European Liberalism*, pp. 300–12.

Massimo d'Azeglio's stirring pamphlet, *Concerning Recent Affairs in Romagna* (*Degli ultimi casi di Romagna*) wherein d'Azeglio pointed out that in spite of its traditions and historical greatness the Holy See was incompetent to bring about a regeneration of Italy, since even in the small provinces which it ruled in central Italy its administration was backward and uninspired.

The revolutionary upheavals of 1848–49 saw not only the end of the Mazzinian program, but also the failure of the Moderate programs. For a brief period they had both reached the heights of popularity. King Charles Albert of Piedmont, that Hamlet-like prince whose character and policies still elude classification, did challenge Austria in 1848 and 1849, only to meet defeat on the fields of Custoza and Novara. Moreover, he had granted a constitution to his people, the famous *Statuto* of March 4, 1848, which was to prove infinitely more important than his battles. Pope Pius IX (Pio Nono), whose pontificate was to span the most turbulent days of the Risorgimento and Italian unification (1846–78), became, for a brief moment, the hope of Italian liberals by his grant of a constitution (March 14, 1848), but the hope was shortly blasted by the Allocution of April 29.[10] Even "King Bomba," Ferdinand II of the Kingdom of the Two Sicilies, promulgated a liberal constitution. Constitutions were generously granted and violently retracted all over Italy in 1848–49. Meanwhile both Mazzini's Roman republic and Daniele Manin's Venetian republic foundered in 1849, destroyed by a combination of forces, by circumstance, by weak and ineffective support, and French and Austrian cannon. The Year of Revolutions brought disaster and disillusionment to the forces of freedom throughout Italy. And yet 1848 and 1849 were not to have been in vain. The consciousness of a free and united Italy had thereby become more acute not only among the liberal governing classes, but also among greater numbers of the middle and urban working classes. The "Italian Problem" had, furthermore, achieved the dimensions of a major European question.

From the disastrous failure of the Risorgimento proper was to stem the true unification of Italy. This was to be achieved neither as a Mazzinian republic nor a Giobertian confederation of Italian states, but rather as the result of the hegemonic expansion, conquest, and absorption of Italy by the little Kingdom of Sardinia and Piedmont. Of all the Italian states, Piedmont alone after 1848 remained true to the liberal program. From the shower of constitutions only Charles Albert's *Statuto* remained unrevoked. It was only in Turin that parliamentary life continued to thrive and liberal measures continued to be enacted. The prestige of Piedmont grew by leaps and bounds in Italy and in Europe. In the little kingdom, following d'Azeglio's preparatory ministry (1850–51), Count Camillo Benso di Cavour (1810–61) appeared upon the scene—to become the spearhead of Italian independence and unity. This shrewd

[10] See the magnificent study by Antonio Monti, *Pio IX nel Risorgimento italiano* (Bari, 1928).

Piedmontese statesman who looked like the incarnation of the prosaic and acted like a sober-minded visionary, this master of politics who breathed economics was to combine Machiavellian realism with patriotic fervor in a magnificent practical synthesis that left all Europe in wonder and admiration. For it was above all on the European stage that Cavour played his cautious game for the high stakes of Italian independence and eventually of Italian unity.[11] Mazzini's pioneering missionary work was transformed and canalized by Cavour into a workable liberal movement. The confederative principle, which he at first espoused and exploited, was later, perhaps more through the force of circumstances, repudiated in favor of the principle of centralized national unity. The famous National Society of La Farina, where Mazzinian republicans and liberal monarchists met, was secretly encouraged. At the Congress of Paris (1856), following the Crimean War, Cavour made the Italian question a responsibility of the European conscience and of international diplomacy. In 1859 he was ready to strike, with the help of Louis Napoleon's French armies, against the traditional Austrian enemy in Lombardy. Giuseppe Garibaldi (1807–82), the ex-Mazzinian "Hero of Two Worlds" and "Knight of Humanity," the adventurous and tempestuous leader of the renowned Red Shirts, won the Kingdom of the Two Sicilies and generously handed it over to Victor Emmanual II in 1860. In 1861 the Kingdom of Italy, lacking Rome and Austrian Venetia, was proclaimed. The vicissitudes of international politics and the Bismarckian drive for Prussian hegemony in Germany and German dominance in Europe gained Italy Venetia in 1866 following the Seven Weeks War between Austria and Prussia; and Rome in 1870 following the outbreak of the Franco-Prussian War. The free and united Italy of patriots' dream and martyrs' vision was now a reality, but Cavour the master had died in 1861, exhausted by the passion and strain of creating a nation. United Italy was to be plunged into the work of reconstruction and into the maelstrom of European politics bereft of the genius who might have guided her speedily and knowingly into lasting safety.

By 1870 Italy was a national state, but the gravity of many of the problems of Italian life was intensified in the peace following so long a period of spiritual, political, and military strife. Massimo d'Azeglio's dictum, "We have created Italy, now we must create Italians!" sounded like the resolve of one who, having helped to give form to a dream, strives to inject a soul into his creation.[12] But the unity so eagerly pursued and

11 William R. Thayer, *The Life and Times of Cavour,* 2 vols. (Boston and New York, 1911) is still good, but Paul Matter, *Cavour et l'unité italienne,* 3 vols. (Paris, 1922–27) ought to be consulted for findings of later scholarship.

12 Some went further than d'Azeglio; Filippo Perfetti, for example, in his *Spirito della storia d'Italia* (Prato, 1868), pp. 326–27: "We have not made the Revolution [Risorgimento], we have merely acquired the faculty to make it . . . and the right to spread over our land the blessed seed of revolution." Quoted by Carlo Curcio, *L'Eredità del Risorgimento,* p. 69.

finally attained, since it had been the work of the heroic drive of a minority,[13] could not immediately and spontaneously become the common ideal of a whole people. The Italian masses had not created Italy, for the truth was "that the great majority of the Italian people—that is, the peasantry —was absent from public life: if it could have manifested an opinion it would have been one resolutely in favor of the old regime." [14] It now became a task of immense proportions to make a conscious and living reality of Italy in the hearts and minds of millions of absentees of the Revolution.[15]

Neither the proclamation of the Kingdom in 1861 nor the occupation of Rome nine years later were final stages in the Italians' struggle to rise to full political maturity. The audacious élite, by an almost miraculous exercise of will and energy, had given Italy a new basis for dignified acceptance in the system of European states. Too many sensibilities had been wounded, too many interests touched, too many hopes and illusions blasted by the turn of events and the necessities of war for the statesmen of the new Italy to rest once political unity was attained. The revolutionary character of Italy's rise to nationhood beset her with problems which perhaps only the genius of Cavour could have solved, but Cavour was gone before his own triumph was fully achieved. Confronted by Austrian and Bourbon resentfulness, by Roman wrath and Mazzinian anathemas, and by watchful suspicions on all sides, the statesmen of the new Italy were faced with the dilemma of improvising, borrowing, adapting, or being overwhelmed. Understandably most of the solutions they adopted for their problems were not perfect but they were, by and large, adequate.[16] It was only natural that, once the first flush of victory was over, disillusionment, skepticism, and indifference should once again raise their heads in a country in which that monstrous trinity had for long been regarded as the pillars of realism. For the result of unification could not but be much less than the promise when that promise came to grips with the reality of Italian economic, social, and psychological conditions. A thousand years of calamities and of bad or indifferent governments had left too profound a heritage of physical and moral misery for even the combined genius of the people to undo it in a short space.[17] Divided political loyalties could be superficially fused around a single state, but it was infinitely more difficult to remedy the economic and social malaise of a country in which the ruling classes had little or no consciousness of this illness.[18] Small wonder that an Italian could say in 1880: "If our Liberals

[13] The phrase generally encountered is stronger in its Italian original: "La prepotenza audace di una minoranza." Arturo Labriola, *Storia di dieci anni, 1899–1909*, p. 110: "L'Italia era l'opera di una minoranza audace." Cf. also Benedetto Croce, *Storia del Regno di Napoli*, p. 260.

[14] Salvemini, *op. cit.*, I, 372.

[15] See Luigi Sturzo, *Italy and Fascismo*, p. 15.

[16] Silvio Spaventa in his *La politica della Destra* (p. 20) enumerates some of the difficulties his party, the Right, had encountered.

[17] See Giustino Fortunato, *Il Mezzogiorno e lo Stato italiano*, II, 94.

[18] Cf. Spaventa, *op. cit.*, p. 33.

had known the country better perhaps they would not have found the courage to create Italy." [19]

The greatest of all problems, that of harmonizing the South [20] with the rest of the country, a task that Cavour himself had compared in magnitude to "a war against Austria or a struggle against Rome," [21] was not understood and could not therefore be intelligently attacked. D'Azeglio himself, perhaps mistaking three centuries of different socio-economic conditions in the South for haughty Southern stolidity, is reputed to have remarked that Italy had too much "good stuff" in the North to have need of "dragging in tow this big and leaky boat of southern Italy." [22] Other expressions of similar sentiments were not lacking.[23] It took decades of hard work, sacrifice, and struggle against a mass of accumulated prejudice, ignorance, and indifference to make all of Italy conscious of the real bases of the "Question of the South." [24]

Upon the attainment of unity, the lethargy of the masses had been shaken for a brief moment in the wake of patriotic outbursts, only to relapse into a mood of bitter disillusionment and regret when the unknown and methodical Piedmontese took over the citadels of former power to convert them, it seemed, into new and more systematic forms of tyranny. "We were better off when we were worse off," and "they have made Italy only to devour her," were the people's manner of expressing their discontent at the new shape of things, and they manifested this mood in different ways. There were messianic expectations of a new redemption among the followers of one Davide Lazzaretti in the Abruzzi,[25] violent revolts in Sicily,[26] and that complex phenomenon, political and economic, socio-religious and criminal—Southern brigandage.[27]

From his exile Mazzini had for long been exhorting the people of Italy to rise and assert their rights under the banner of a God-given mission. After the accomplishment of unity in a manner so repugnant to his ideals, it was only natural that the Apostle of Liberty should see "the multitudes

---

[19] Sidney Sonnino, in a letter to P. Turiello, quoted in Curcio, *op. cit.*, p. 86.

[20] "Italy ends at the Garigliano" was a common expression.

[21] See Gaetano Zingali, *Liberalismo e Fascismo nel Mezzogiorno d'Italia*, I, 174.

[22] See Aldo Romano, "Aspetti e problemi della storia del Risorgimento nell'Italia meridionale," *Rivista Storica Italiana*, III (June 30, 1938), 56.

[23] See Croce, *op. cit.*, p. 263.

[24] The pioneers in this field were an admirable group of scholars and publicists led by Pasquale Villari, Giustino Fortunato, Leopoldo Franchetti, and Sidney Sonnino. For a penetrating essay on the group, see Enzo Tagliacozzo, *Voci di realismo politico dopo il '70.*

[25] Cf. Armando Cavalli, "Correnti messianiche dopo il '70," *Nuova Antologia*, CCLXXIV (1930), 209-15.

[26] The Palermo uprising of 1866 is briefly described by Alfredo Oriani, *La lotta politica in Italia*, III, 212-14.

[27] A. C. De Meis, in his brilliant essay "Il Sovrano" (Jan., 1868), reprinted in Francesco Piccolo, ed., *I Liberali italiani dopo il 1860*, p. 45: "When the new sovereign, the Honest King, took over his place [that of the Bourbon], there immediately broke out what the interests of the superior people has led them to call brigandage, but which impartial history will call civil war."

deluded in their high hopes" and "the middle class become more and more indifferent to its political rights." [28] But those multitudes were formed by masses of peasants who even if they had heard could hardly have understood Mazzini's formula of "God and the People"; the middle classes had been too long deprived of participation in political responsibilities to sense in any serious degree the inadequacy of their new position. The various nobilities of the former provinces had too little in common to form a basis for coöperative effort in the reconstruction of Italy and, even had they desired it, there were too many regional, traditional, and historical barriers between them to make possible a fusion of energies. The clergy, high and low, with very few exceptions kept watch, entrenched behind Vatican prohibitions and *non expedits.* Thus it came about that, unlike most of the great states among whom she was preparing to take her place, Italy was forced by a conspiracy of history and geography to launch out upon her new career without a real political class tempered, as in England, France, and even Germany, in the exercise of national power.[29]

Italian Liberalism, having served its empiric function during the Risorgimento, seemed to lose the heroic efficacy which a generation of statesmen, economists, and myth-makers had given it when the climate of political opinion began to respond to new historical processes of which world politics and imperialism were only the most violent phenomena.[30] Thereafter, economic conditions and lack of social vision, political inadequacy, and psychological malaise, a religious-political crisis and vague sentiments of spiritual frustration all joined to rob Italian Liberalism of its significance as a spiritual force and as a source of political inspiration. The only remnant of Liberalism appeared to be a skill in the art of government which succeeded in tempering its oligarchical tendencies with "an impressive façade of liberalism and democracy." [31] For fifty years the heritage of the Risorgimento and of Cavourian Liberalism seemed to have become identical with mere administrative ability and the spirit of "transformism," two currents which merged into that singular phenomenon generally described by the term *Giolittismo.*[32]

But those same fifty years saw also the gradual ascendancy and self-renewal of a people, their slow release from the bondage of history and the tyranny of geography. Falteringly, the Italian people grew into a sturdy and often turbulent, new youthfulness. Parliament might seem confused beyond understanding and raise oratory to the status of an art for art's sake: Italians would smile or curse at the confusion or sordidness of official life and politics, yet all the while they were working on their

[28] Cf. the reprint of the pamphlet of Mazzini's friend Aurelio Saffi, *Il pensiero politico e sociale di Mazzini* (Forlì, 1921), p. 37.

[29] Sturzo, *op. cit.,* pp. 69–70, *passim.*

[30] Gioacchino Volpe, *L'Italia in cammino,* p. 37.

[31] De Ruggiero, *op. cit.,* pp. 340–41. Lorenzo Giusso, *Le dittature democratiche in Italia,* has rationalized successive governments in Italy from 1876 to 1922 into a series of "democratic dictatorships."

[32] Cf. Piero Gobetti, *Risorgimento senza eroi,* p. 19.

farms or in their factories, laying the foundations for a healthy personal and national economic life. Scandals and rumors of scandals in high places might reach them—Banca Romana in 1893, Nunzio Nasi in 1907, Palazzo di Giustizia in 1913: angry Italians would speak of retribution or shrug their shoulders with the traditional *"Pazienza!"* upon their lips, but finally they would forget them in the strain of making a living and increasing their children's and country's security by striving harder at home or by the savings of their honest labor in foreign lands. Disasters of wars not of their making might strike them in their homes—Dogali in 1887, Adowa in 1896; earthquakes might uproot them from their soil—Messina and Reggio di Calabria in 1908: Italians wept and bound their wounds, all the while working to rebuild their shattered homes and to heal their broken hearts. It was this unbounded capacity for work, coupled with the lively intelligence of her people, that brought Italy in the first half century of unity from the periphery to a place well within the active circle of contemporary European civilization.

II

THE ITALIAN PARLIAMENTARY REGIME
AND ITS CRITICS

E così d'anno in anno e di ministro
In ministro, io mi scarco
Del centro destro su 'l centro sinistro
*E 'l mio lunario sbarco.**

CARDUCCI

T HE history of the Italian parliamentary regime, from the fall of the
Cavourian party of the Right on March 18, 1876 to well into the
last decade of the nineteenth century, followed a familiar Continental
pattern of political groupings and coalitions under the leadership of
changing individuals rather than that of two parties alternating in power.
The Right had been formed by an energetic group of men stemming, for
the greater part, from the ranks of the various older moderate parties.
Cavour, of course, had been unique. Under his guidance the men who
were to be his successors, Ricasoli, La Marmora, Minghetti, Lanza, Spaventa, Sella, and Peruzzi had gradually abandoned the confederative
principle of Gioberti and Balbo. Once Cavour was gone they constituted
a most admirable directing group, becoming the strongest workers for,
and the staunchest defenders of, the work of unification under Piedmontese direction. They had been a truly audacious minority which,
against great odds, had created the nation and placed it on sufficiently
solid foundations. But their religious policy and the exigency of the
occupation of Rome had gained them the enmity of the Church and,
what seemed more important, their political and social conservatism had
raised against them the democratic forces of the country. Thus, between
1860 and 1876, the opposition to the Right on the part of Mazzinian
adherents, of administrative autonomists, and progressive social reformers (vaguely associated as the Left) had given Italian political life an
apparent character of sharply defined party division. In 1876, however,
the Right not only fell from office, it ceased to exist as an organized political party. The Left was overwhelmingly victorious: it became the sole
master of the Italian Parliament. Unfortunately for Italian political life
a very un-Hegelian phenomenon thereupon took place: the victory of
the former opposition did not immediately raise up another opposition.

* "And thus from year to year and from minister to minister I shift, from Right
Center to Left Center, and live from hand to mouth." Giosuè Carducci, *Canto dell'Italia
che va in Campidoglio.*

13

It was not until the last decade of the century that the new masters were to be challenged by an Extreme Left (*Estrema Sinistra*).

The historical Right, with all the faults ascribed to it by its adversaries and candidly acknowledged by its honest members,[1] had at least brought to the government of the country a high concept of the functions of the state inspired though it was by the legalitarian theory of the Staatsrecht of German jurisprudence.[2] The men of the Left who came to power in 1876, were of similar revolutionary origin as their adversaries, although differentiated from them by social derivations and ideological traditions. The old Right had gathered its strength chiefly from the large landed, commercial, and professional classes of the North, while the "democratic" party of the Left was based on the middle, lower-middle, and urban artisan classes, and was preponderant in the South.[3] The difference between the two parties, however, was more of degree than of kind, and Silvio Spaventa could with a measure of justice assert that the government of the Left was only "a government of the Right worsened." [4]

The fall of the Right and the ascendancy of the Left has been the subject of much discussion and of no less misunderstanding. The application of political terms derived from foreign experience to Italian political situations has been the source of great confusion and has given rise to the idea that the Right and the Left represented well-defined counterparts of conservative and progressive.[5] This idea does not take into account the fact that for a long time Right and Left stood merely for differences in methods and not in fundamental ideas of government,[6] and that once Agostino Depretis had inaugurated the system of *trasformismo* even those differences became blurred.[7] March 18, 1876 marked indeed a revolutionary date in Italian parliamentary life, for thereafter the usual parliamentary struggle ceased to be possible in Italy because of the lack of party divisions.[8] From this time until the rise of the so-called *Estrema Sinistra* (Socialists, Radicals, and Republicans) toward the close of the century, the Italian Parliament became a field of contention for factions and cliques, for camarillas and organized interests, whose skirmishes and squabbles seldom touched even the fringe of political reality. Neither ideas nor practical programs were any longer weapons in the fight for responsible national power; they had become mere instruments of opportunistic transactions, jobs and influence, elections and placements.[9]

---

[1] Cf. Spaventa, *La politica della Destra*, pp. 39-45, for his speech of March 21, 1879.

[2] De Ruggiero, *The History of European Liberalism*, p. 328.

[3] Salvemini, "L'Italia politica nel secolo XIX," *L'Europa nel secolo XIX*, I, 377.

[4] Spaventa, *op. cit.*, p. 46.

[5] On the Right as a Conservative party see Stefano Iacini, "Conservatori e radicali" (1879), in F. Piccolo, ed., *I Liberali italiani*, p. 121.

[6] Romualdo Bonfadini, "I partiti parlamentari e particolarmente in Italia," *Nuova Antologia*, XLIX, 628.

[7] Benedetto Croce, *A History of Italy, 1871-1915*, p. 7.

[8] Rodolfo De Mattei, *Il problema della democrazia dopo l'unità*, p. 65, *passim*.

[9] Sturzo, *Italy and Fascismo*, p. 63, *passim*.

Still in its infancy, the Italian parliamentary system gave signs of degenerating into mere parliamentarianism.[10] Men recoiled from such confusion and at length took refuge in sterile oppositions, in scandalized admonitions, and in violent invective.[11] More diversified, parliamentary activity and the political life of the country were only more confused and, in the absence of true political divisions based on principles, they underwent, in the words of the historian of liberalism, "a process of reduction to the colourless uniformity of dust." [12]

The Italian phase of the recrudescent European phenomenon of anti-parliamentarian criticism during the latter part of the nineteenth century must therefore be related to the political and psychological atmosphere created by the fall of the Right and the rise of transformism. Various attempts have been made to present the problems of Italian democracy and the sordid chronicle of antiparliamentarian criticism, which was part of it, as intellectual developments only tenuously related to the historical moment which gave rise to them.[13] As a result the thesis has gradually won ground that there is an almost direct connection between Mazzini and fascism,[14] between the censure of parliamentary institutions by such thinkers as Gaetano Mosca and Vilfredo Pareto and the destruction of those institutions by the Fascist regime. The practice of compelling history to justify after-events shows, in this matter, some of its most absurd and dangerous implications when, not finding what it seeks, it is forced to confess, as with De Mattei, that the "general, fundamental error" of the antiparliamentarian critics was the search for "a solution in the very orbit of the infirmity," thus giving evidence of a lack of "historical initiative." [15]

From Mazzini to Salvemini the problem of Italian democracy has been considered as inherently one of moral education and of the uplifting of the masses to a consciousness of their human and political dignity. The great exile, Mazzini, had thus admonished his countrymen: "The war for freedom is sacred, as the human individual is sacred: wage it unto the end." [16] But, although the taking of Rome in 1870 had given an increased impetus to the democratic ideal in Italy, not all the exponents of democracy could view the turn of events with contented spirits. Mazzini

[10] *Ibid.*, p. 73, and Volpe, *L'Italia in cammino*, p. 36.

[11] Felice Cavallotti, the Radical leader, admonished in 1883: "Tell the young to enlarge their vision beyond this place [Parliament]. There are greater horizons, more beautiful and higher ideals than those of our politics of acrobatics, of optical tricks, of petty transactions, and 'transformations.'" Quoted by Saverio Cilibrizzi, *Storia parlamentare politica e diplomatica d'Italia*, II, 273.

[12] De Ruggiero, *op. cit.*, p. 341.

[13] For this trend, see especially Rodolfo De Mattei, "La critica antiparlamentaristica in Italia dopo l'unificazione," *Educazione Fascista*, VI (1928), No. 4, 193-201.

[14] Cf. the writings of Giovanni Gentile, especially *Origini e dottrina del Fascismo* (Rome, 1934), pp. 24-25, *passim*, on Mazzini and fascism.

[15] De Mattei, *op. cit.*, p. 200.

[16] Giuseppe Mazzini, "I sistemi e la democrazia," in *Scritti-Filosofia*, 2 vols. (Milan, n.d.), I, 235.

himself saw his great and final hope shattered and, repudiated by some of his own, he became a solitary man in whom the flame still burned brightly, if ineffectually. Even before the great event of 1870, another lonely soul of different temper had perceived the contradictions of opposed sovereignties as posing the great problem of the future: "The democratic state is an historical impossibility where society is divided into two opposite peoples, and it will always be so until their opposition ceases or is at least tempered down." [17] This conciliation of the two "opposite peoples," that is, the active ruling minorities and the passive but potentially powerful masses of the people, was to become the great task of Italian democratic forces.

The obstacles placed in the way of the realization of this democratic ideal were many and of the most complex nature. The masses themselves, especially in the South, had little consciousness of any need beyond their daily necessities, and when any attempt was made to help them they suspected even the most disinterested attention as the favors of men who expect returns. This problem of democracy, moreover, was for too long a time a source of polemical rather than realistic study; such an approach to the problem wasted the energies of its students by doctrinal interest in "forms" and models—American, Swiss, British, Roman, Athenian—when those energies should have been directed to serious efforts to create a real democracy.[18] Even when efforts were made, as in the enlargement of the suffrage in 1882 and in 1912,[19] they were attributed more to a desire to increase followers than to create new citizens [20]—when they were not actually suspected of aiding the "revolt of the masses." [21] It can nevertheless be stated that by 1914, through the concurrence of innumerable forces of which perhaps the purely ideological was not the most important, Italian democracy (incomplete, partial, and precarious though it was) had become more than a mere ideal and gave promise of a robust growth at the moment when the First World War descended upon it.

Paradoxically enough, while the problem of democracy was gradually being brought within a framework of realizable empiric objectives, the problem of the decay of the parliamentary regime seemed only to increase in size and complexity. The persisting confusion on the Italian parliamentary scene, the hopeless blurring of political ideas and programs

17 A. C. De Meis, "Il Sovrano," in F. Piccolo, ed., *op. cit.*, p. 43.

18 Cf. De Mattei, *Il problema della democrazia, op. cit.*, p. 121.

19 See *Statistiche delle elezioni generali politiche alla XXIV Legislatura, 26 ottobre e 2 novembre 1913* (Rome, 1914), p. xii, for a summary of electoral laws.

20 See an interesting editorial (Salvemini), "Il metodo giolittiano," in *L'Unità*, IX (1920), No. 4, 167.

21 Cf. Raffaele De Cesare's opinion on Luzzatti's proposal for a "modest" electoral reform, in *Cinquanta anni di storia italiana.* 3 vols. (Milan, 1911), I, 54: "A new concession to the prejudice of the extreme parties who think they are raising the political and moral level of a people by inviting ignorant masses to participation in the sovereignty. . . ."

within the ample circle of transformism,[22] the undiminishing abuses in the administrative system, and the lack of distinct political personalities contributed to a flood of criticism of, diagnoses of, and attacks upon, the workings of the parliamentary regime in Italy.

Marco Minghetti, whose ministry of the Right had been the last of that party's, in a famous speech at Naples in 1880, declared himself in favor of a constitutional regime, but warned that this form of government was subject to degeneration when the deputies ceased, as now seemed the case, to be representatives of principles and become mere tools of local interests.[23] In May of the same year Silvio Spaventa made his constructive contribution to the criticism with a speech at Bergamo invoking justice in the administration.[24] Thereafter came a long period of systematic analyses of the evils and defects of the parliamentary regime by a great host of thinkers, prominent or obscure, who each made his special contribution to the rising tide of antiparliamentarianism. Giorgio Arcoleo [25] decried the tyranny of numbers which in an assembly based on undifferentiated majorities tended, in his opinion, to be often opposed to true public opinion and the needs of government; he therefore saw the necessity for the creation of an extra-parliamentary cabinet free from the passions and whims of parliamentary majorities.[26] Pasquale Turiello [27] devoted himself to psychological analysis of parliamentary groups and parties which, he claimed, worked in and not for the country, and pointed to the fatality that compelled parties to degenerate into factions to the detriment of the national interest. Had Arcoleo's dreams of an extra-parliamentary cabinet been possible of realization, Turiello would have entrusted it with the supreme task of enacting legislation to put an end to the parliamentary regime! [28] While Francesco De Sanctis,[29] the incomparable historian of Italian literature, had seen the problem in terms of the need for a moral awakening of Italy in which the struggle for liberty should be the duty more than the right of all, Stefano Jacini, the eminent author of the Agrarian Inquiry, plead for the creation of a true Conservative party which was to serve also as a point of orientation in the troubled sea of Italian parliamentary politics.[30] It was, however, Ruggiero Bonghi who in 1884 passed the severest judgment upon the parliamentary regime not only in Italy but in all countries. Bonghi wrote:

[22] Cf. Agostino Depretis' speech at Stradella (1882), quoted by Cilibrizzi, *op. cit.*, II, 264: "We are a progressive ministry. If anyone wishes to *transform* himself and become progressive by accepting my very modest program, how can I refuse him?"

[23] See Marco Minghetti, *I partiti politici*, pp. 8-9, *passim*.

[24] For his entire speech, see Spaventa, *op. cit.*, pp. 55-105.

[25] *Il governo di Gabinetto nei governi parlamentari.*

[26] Cf. G. Barone and A. Casulli, *Il pensiero di Giorgio Arcoleo* (Milan, 1927), p. 131.

[27] *Governo e governati in Italia.*

[28] Quoted by De Mattei, "La critica antiparlamentaristica," *op. cit.*, p. 197.

[29] For De Sanctis' political thought, see his *Scritti politici*, ed. G. Ferrarelli (4th ed.; Naples, 1924).

[30] *I Conservatori e l'evoluzione naturale dei partiti politici in Italia.*

The parliamentary regime, by presuming to be representative, has in fact eliminated every representation and has placed society in a violently contradictory position in respect to its governments. . . . Truly, when I think about this regime as it still exists and unfolds itself in every country, I recall that verse: "This is a thing that will die." [31]

In the very year of Bonghi's severe verdict, an obscure young Sicilian of about twenty-four years of age launched his career as a political writer with a work which for long remained the most pitiless analysis of the evils of the parliamentary regime. Gaetano Mosca's *Teorica dei governi e governo parlamentare* (1884) [32] has been studied chiefly in connection with the history of the idea of the "élite" which Vilfredo Pareto's monumental *Trattato di sociologia generale* made a common sociological term. In the early part of his *Teorica* Mosca presented the premises of his thought, which may be briefly summarized in the following six points: (1) in "all societies regularly constituted" there is a clearly defined demarcation between the "political class," an organized ruling minority, and a more numerous class that never has participated nor does at present *really* participate in government; (2) an organized, morally superior minority always triumphs over the force of mere numbers, that is, over a disorganized majority; (3) force is of no avail to gain membership into the political class; (4) the members of the political class must possess, or must be presumed to possess, a merit or quality considered of great significance by the generality of people of the society in which they rule; (5) the cohesion, power, and very life of a state depend upon the sane coördination of forces and the power of self-renewal of the political class; (6) no political or ruling class, however constituted, ever admits the fact of its rule, but rather rationalizes its power into a "political formula" consonant with the environment and the historical moment ("The rights of men"; "God and the will of the people"; "Liberty, Equality, Fraternity"; etc.).[33]

Upon the basis of such a political philosophy Mosca built the main structure of his indictment of the Italian parliamentary regime, "a pernicious system of government which, inspired by technical ideas or metaphysical abstractions, holds of no account the knowledge of history or of human society and human character." [34] In the second part of his *Teorica* he undertook a minute examination of the organization of the Italian state from the Crown to the smallest unit of provincial and communal bureaucracy. After asserting that the Crown in Italy "reigns but does not govern," Mosca passes rapidly to a study of the character of the typical parliamentary leader, especially the Prime Minister.[35]

---

[31] Ruggiero Bonghi, "Una questione grossa: La decadenza del regime parlamentare," *Nuova Antologia*, XLV (1884), 497.

[32] Citations will be to the second edition: Gaetano Mosca, *Teorica dei governi e governo parlamentare.*

[33] *Ibid.*, pp. 16–39, *passim.*

[34] *Ibid.*, p. 166.

[35] *Ibid.*, p. 192, for a criticism of British imitation by Italy, especially of cabinet system and Prime Minister.

The successful career of a Minister in Italy, Mosca said, depended upon the combination of "moral and intellectual mediocrity, wide parliamentary experience, and the qualities of a business man"; the minister, besides, must possess a great knowledge of the human heart in general and of the character of the deputies in particular; he must know how to play upon the strings of numerous human ambitions, needs, and passions, no matter how small or how noble, all at the same time; he must know the price and the wishes of every deputy, and he must seem to grant what is asked.[36] For, Mosca observed, "since the beginning of time men have rendered their services for recompense," and the minister had innumerable opportunities and facilities to reward the faithful.[37] The illegality of these sordid maneuvers, however, the Sicilian theorist imputed more to the system which tolerated them than to the moral irresponsibility of men who were thereby placed in the dilemma of choosing between their own interest and the common good.[38]

When he came to the examination of the Italian administrative system, Mosca found that the bureaucracy charged with the task of administering the affairs of the various ministries was the most irresponsible part of the Italian body politic. This he found especially anomalous in a country which prided itself on the possession of a civil law, the interpreters of which were completely restrained within a salutary circle of guarantees and official responsibility for their actions. Administrative law, on the other hand, although of no less importance to the interest of citizens, had no such restraints and guarantees.[39] Citing examples from his own turbulent and politically backward Sicily, Mosca examined the position of the provincial and local administrators under the rule of the prefects, "the electoral agents of the Minister." It was at this point of his analysis that he began to differ from his contemporaries. For whereas most of the writers who expressed an opinion on the subject were in agreement that the political and electoral functions of the prefects were among the most deleterious causes for the decay of the parliamentary regime, Mosca confessed that he was inclined to find that form of interference in local affairs useful. Since he did not believe that the "will of the people could ever express itself freely and honestly in electoral contests," he found the interference of the central government preferable to the infleunce of local bosses and Camorristi alone.[40]

It was for the deputies that Mosca reserved his most acrid criticism and his disdain. That the deputy is the representative of the will of the majority of voters, the author of the *Teorica* said, is a legal supposition in direct contradiction to the real fact. Whoever has seen an electoral contest knows that "it is not the electors [voters] who elect the deputy, but that ordinarily it is the deputy who *has had himself elected* by the electors," since—

[36] *Ibid.*, pp. 161–62, *passim.*
[37] *Ibid.*, pp. 164–65, *passim.*
[38] *Ibid.*, p. 165.
[39] *Ibid.*, p. 175.
[40] *Ibid.*, pp. 196–97, *passim.*

and here the author brings his theory directly to the aid of his argument —a candidacy is "always the work of a group of persons gathered together for a common purpose, [the work] of an organized minority which inevitably and necessarily imposes itself upon the disorganized majority." [41] In this case the organized minority would be composed chiefly of the candidates' close friends and associates, by the prefects, by big influential electors (landowners, capitalists, professional men, etc.) and by political clubs and other such associations with their subdivisions and varieties.[42] Small wonder, Mosca said, that the Chamber of Deputies was becoming more and more "a partial and fictitious representation of the country" when by that method an ever-increasing number of living forces and politically capable elements were excluded from it. In this manner the members of the Chamber of Deputies, represented only "numbers of essentially private interests, the sum of which is by no means equal to the public interest." [43]

Mosca's criticism ended upon a note of almost violent anger against the Italian parliamentary regime. This system, he believed, was one in which the best qualities of individuals and peoples degenerated, while the "moral cowardice, the lack of all sense of justice, the cunning, the intrigue, which are exactly the qualities that lead people and states to their ruin" not only thrived but were esteemed as merits.[44] But since the system threatened to go to pieces, it was best not to oppose the impending doom, Mosca declared, for society would be the gainer thereby.

The foregoing analysis of Mosca's *Teorica* has been given in some detail because it presents in a clear, if violent and passionate form, a phase of Italian political thought by no means limited to the author alone nor to his time. It will be seen too how the current of thought represented by Mosca carried through the early anti-Liberal and antiparliamentarian forces in the first fifteen years of the twentieth century. A few comments on the work and its author may not be out of place here.

Mosca's Sicilian environment and the intellectual and social atmosphere in which he grew up were less than conducive to an optimistic view of Italian political life. His intellectual roots, moreover, grew from a mixture of the Machiavellian school of Italian thought and the positivistic philosophy of his time. The result could only be a doctrinal authoritarianism reinforced by political and social conservatism,[45] as his frequent use of Machiavellian terms [46] and his openly expressed fear of the "decay of

<hr/>

[41] *Ibid.*, p. 251.

[42] *Ibid.*, p. 252.

[43] *Ibid.*, p. 257.

[44] *Ibid.*, p. 259.

[45] Cf. Arthur Livingston's Introduction to Mosca, *The Ruling Class*, pp. xxi–xxxv, *passim*.

[46] See *Teorica*, p. 260: "Whoever lived in the Middle Ages could exclaim: 'I have seen violence.' . . . Whoever lives in our times can well assert that he has seen cabal, fraud, cunning . . . ," easily recalls Machiavelli's simile of the lion and the fox: force and cunning (*Forza e Astuzia*).

the principles of order and authority" exemplify. And last, it should be remembered that Mosca's political theories and his criticism of parliamentarianism did not begin to be seriously considered and therefore to be in vogue until the turn of the century, when they gained an unexpectedly wide audience in an atmosphere more receptive to them.

The last decade of the nineteenth century saw Giolitti's first ministry (May 1892–November 1893), the height and fall of Francesco Crispi's career (1893–96), the disaster of Adowa (March 1, 1896), the "May Days" of Milan (1898), the Pelloux military dictatorship (June 1899 to June 1900) and its culmination in the assassination of King Humbert (July 29, 1900).[47] The times seemed out of joint and Italian political life was marked by scandals and violence, repressive measures and the eclipse of freedom. The antiparliamentarian criticism continued but, on the other hand, Parliament began to redeem itself as the result of the work of a handful of strong men of former extra-parliamentary parties, the so-called Extreme Left.

On January 1, 1897 the *Nuova Antologia* published an article by Sidney Sonnino, under the pseudonym of "Un Deputato." [48] Sonnino, a Conservative of the Center, of Jewish-British-Italian extraction, urged a return to the *Statuto* by the creation of extra-parliamentary cabinets chosen by the Crown and not from parliamentary majorities which, he said, were subject to all sorts of pressures and intrigues. He advocated an enhancement of the sovereign's rights by the limitation of the powers of the elective Chamber of Deputies and by a revitalization of the Senate. Fearing the destruction of the Italian Liberal state by a Clerical and Radical-Socialist coalition, Sonnino warned that, although he did not wish to advocate Caesarism or an autocratic government, he nevertheless wanted "the liberal and representative monarchy of the *Statuto* with an effective and active Prince-Monarch unshackled from the control of a *maire du palais* called the Prime Minister." [49]

The following year Provido Siliprandi (in a voluminous work which he confessed might have been called "Chapters on the Madness of Italy," but to which he gave a much more obscure title) thus characterized what he called over-all liberalism in Italy: "Repress, do not prevent; laissez faire, laissez passer. Let the revolution be made in the most Liberal manner by priests and the people, and then shoot them down before it is too late. Let the people starve liberally in Southern regions, and then . . . more hunger and lead." [50] According to Giustino Fortunato, the great Southern writer, the new century opened with the ominous cries of "Down with the deputies!" and "The country has had enough of the deputies!" [51] The

[47] For further details on these events see below in other chapters of this work.
[48] Un Deputato, "Torniamo allo Statuto," *Nuova Antologia*, LXVII, 9–28.
[49] *Ibid.*, p. 27.
[50] Provido Siliprandi, *Capitoli teorico-pratici di politica sperimentale*, III, 212.
[51] Giustino Fortunato, "Il regime parlamentare e la XX Legislatura," *Nuova Antologia*, June 16, 1900, Fascicolo 684.

first fifteen years of the twentieth century saw no abatement of the criticism of Italian parliamentary institutions, or at least of the degeneration to which allegedly they were prey. In 1911, for example, Italian parliamentarianism was subjected to a psycho-sociological dissection by the imaginative author of a *Physiology of the Parliamentary Regime in Italy,* who arrived at the conclusion that "of all forms of political regimes, parliamentary government is the one least suited to the Italian people." [52] There was, however, during most of this period a definite change of tone and direction in the censure of parliamentarianism, for now the crisis of the Italian parliamentary regime came to be viewed in terms of one man, Giolitti, and of an alleged all inclusive instrument of destruction, *Giolittismo.*

[52] Ettore D'Orazio, *Fisiologia del parlamentarismo in Italia,* p. 452.

III

POLITICAL CURRENTS AND PARTIES
IN LIBERAL ITALY

Siamo tutti liberali . . . *

PREZZOLINI

T RANSFORMISM had done its work so well as a "crushing machine" [1] that, of the old political alignments, little was left. Even old names and labels disappeared in the general confusion, and by 1885 transformism was regarded as being so much of the essence of Italian political reality that it was hardly used as a word or discussed as a fact. [2]

Stefano Jacini's proposal for the creation of a great new Conservative party to serve as a political compass in the disoriented parliamentary scene was not realized as planned for the simple reason that it already existed. Jacini had said in 1879 that the fundamental bases for the founding of such a party should be the "unity of Italy, the legitimacy of the reigning House, and the present *Statuto*." [3] With the exception of the remnants of the old Mazzinian party, none of the remaining constitutional groups and factions failed to answer to those requirements and therefore, according to Jacini's formula, they all went to form an amorphous Conservative bloc. The various cliques that called themselves after their leaders—Depretian, Crispinian, Rudinian, Zanardellian, Giolittian, and so on—did not quarrel among themselves except for the possession of power and about differing methods of attaining similar aims. The terms that came to be used later—*ministeriali* and *antiministeriali*—seemed more nearly consonant with the actual condition of affairs. For one was in or out of the Government, for or against the Ministry, without necessarily possessing different, clear-cut political programs or political ideals.

It was, strangely enough, Giovanni Giolitti, who was to dominate Italian political life for the following fifteen years, who in a famous speech at Brusca (October 29, 1899) [4] took up Jacini's theme, but with a different aim. It was a mistake, Giolitti maintained, to fuse all parties into one great constitutional bloc since it was not only not useful but also im-

---

* "We are all Liberals. . . ." Giuseppe Prezzolini, "I cenci vecchi del liberalismo," *Il Regno*, January 31, 1904.

[1] Romualdo Bonfadini, "I partiti parlamentari in Europa e particolarmente in Italia," *Nuova Antologia*, XLIX (1894), 635.

[2] Benedetto Croce, *A History of Italy, 1871–1915*, p. 20.

[3] Cf. Stefano Jacini, "Conservatori e radicali" (1879) in Piccolo, ed., *I Liberali italiani*, p. 119.

[4] Cf. Luigi Salvatorelli, ed., *Giolitti*, pp. 33–36

possible to reconcile the radical disagreements among all those groups. "We must keep in mind," Giolitti said, "that there is no party which is not destroyed by a long tenure of power, because there is no party that once in power does not commit errors and offend many interests." [5] The party, of course, to which Giolitti was referring, was really not a party at all, but rather a small group of old die-hards inspired by Sonnino's constitutional views as expressed in his article "Return to the Constitution" and now in the ascendancy with the connivance of the reactionary clique at Court.[6]

But Giolitti's attempt to point the way to a real political party was not to be realized even within the motley groups that called themselves "Liberals" or, for that matter, among the "Giolittians" themselves. The next decade was to see spasmodic attempts to give life to a new national party capable of absorbing the divided and wasted energies of groups and factions in the name of a higher discipline and of a more effective ideal.[7] There were attempts to fuse the scattered forces of Liberalism, but to no avail. In 1904 an acute observer of the Italian political scene posed the query:

Who knows whether an Italian Liberal party exists? What is the function of a Liberal party in Italy? Is it to spread the idea of liberty? But we are all liberals nowadays, and the word "liberal" is no longer the distinguishing mark of a party, but the democratic livery worn by all parties and the common uniform of the mass of men. From L'Unità Cattolica to Enrico Ferri, from the Giornale d'Italia to the Republicans, all are Liberals. If the object of a party is to spread an idea, the Liberal party has achieved it, and precisely for this reason it is dead.[8]

It will be most interesting to notice how Giuseppe Prezzolini's "we are all Liberals" corresponded to Italian political reality and how the party label "Liberal" was applied during Giolitti's period.

For a long time it has been customary among some non-Italian observers of that period to take the label "Liberal" at its face value. The translation of that term into a different climate of political life, such as the British for example, has caused endless confusion in the interpretation of Italian political facts. Sonnino, Zanardelli, Salandra, Giolitti, all called themselves "Liberal," but their different interpretations of the term were far more important than any common derivation they might have claimed from Cavourian Liberalism. In reality, it had been the brief ascendancy of the reactionary authoritarians during the period 1898–1900 that had given the illusion of a true division between Conservatives and Liberals in Italy.[9] Once, however, the violence and repression of those years were

---

[5] *Ibid.*, p. 35.

[6] Labriola, *Storia di dieci anni*, chaps. i–iii, and Luigi Lodi, *Venticinque anni di vita parlamentare*, p. 15.

[7] De Mattei, *Il problema*, p. 86.

[8] Giuseppe Prezzolini, *supra*, quoted by Croce, *op. cit.*, p. 322.

[9] Labriola, *op. cit.*, p. 44: The period of reaction (1898–1900) "demonstrated only that there are neither reactionaries nor revolutionaries, but rather the masks of these

over, the Liberal party returned to its amorphous condition colored only by individual differences among those who claimed to be its outstanding members. Italian Liberalism as such showed itself to be concerned only with defense and preservation of the modern Italian state that had resulted from the Risorgimento and was therefore viewed as a system of repressions and restraints by the opposing and newly rising radical forces, and occasionally even by the Clerical opposition.[10]

During Giolitti's long tenure of power (1903–14), with the brief interruptions of Fortis, Sonnino, and Luzzatti, it was Sonnino and Salandra who claimed to speak in the name of classic Italian Liberalism as opposed to Giolitti's Liberal-democratic policy.

Sidney Sonnino (1847–1923) had had a scholarly, diplomatic, and financial career.[11] In 1873 he had left the diplomatic service in order to engage in studies of the Sicilian and Tuscan peasantry; in 1878 he founded the famous *Rassegna Settimanale* at Florence, and in 1901 the *Giornale d'Italia*. He served as Under-Secretary of the Treasury in 1889, and was Minister of Finance in the third Crispi Cabinet (1893–94). From 1880 to 1919 he was uninterruptedly returned to the Chamber of Deputies from the electoral district of San Casciano, Tuscany. A tall, lean figure, taciturn and solitary by temperament, austere and almost inflexible in character, unpossessed of any emotional or oratorical prowess, honest to a fault, Sonnino seldom aroused great enthusiasm.[12] Sonnino did not possess the qualities necessary to a leader of a fighting party, for, lacking facility of speech, "he refused to participate in any parliamentary debate not previously announced." His austere character made him reluctant to participate in open parliamentary battles. He ended by being "neither loved nor feared." [13] The Syndicalist Arturo Labriola commented in 1910 that Sonnino, since his political character had been formed in the years immediately following the Unification, had absorbed from that atmosphere an outlook more critical toward Liberal institutions than toward liberal doctrines. Since this critical spirit, Labriola said, could easily lead to socialism, so it could also lead, in one as lacking passion and sentiment as Sonnino to a bitter hostility toward Liberal institutions.[14]

What was Sonninian Liberalism? Sonnino's constitutional theories have already been examined in another connection. His article "Torniamo allo Statuto" (1897) was for a long time a thorn in his side and a powerful arm used against him by his political enemies, for had he not advocated therein a constitutional doctrine wholly contradictory to modern parlia-

two parties. The country, stunned by the noise of their long carnival, ended by thinking that farce is the normal condition of public life." Labriola was a Syndicalist.

[10] *Ibid.*, p. 114.
[11] For a short biography, see Jules Destrée, *Figures italiènnes d'aujourd'hui* (Brussels and Paris, 1918), pp. 1–28.
[12] Cilibrizzi, *Storia parlamentare*, III, 317–19, and Labriola, *op. cit.*, p. 47.
[13] V. Saporito, *Trenta anni di vita parlamentare*, p. 89.
[14] Labriola, *op. cit.*, p. 47. For a sustained study of Sonnino's character and political beliefs, see his *Discorsi parlamentari*.

mentary practice which, moreover, had been realized if only for a short time under Pelloux? [15] With the return of the Liberal springtide [16] and the Zanardelli-Giolitti Government of 1901, Sonnino had become the leader of a strong and rather widespread faction that fought Giolitti's domestic policies.[17] Speaking in the Chamber of Deputies on March 13, 1902, Sonnino criticized the Government for its passive attitude toward social struggles, for not class struggle, he said, but class solidarity was the foundation of a civilized society.[18] He then turned to his own party in the Chamber and asked whether they thought they had done all they could "in order to solve or at least to guide toward a solution the many social questions whose enbitterment redounds today to our country's harm." [19] It was the duty of a great constitutional party, Sonnino continued, "without distinction between the Conservative-Liberals and the Progressives, faced with the great dangers that threaten the peace and prosperity of the country" to gather together their dispersed forces in order to meet the situation manfully and boldly.[20]

The situation that called for such energetic action in Sonnino's view had been created by the radical parties and especially the Socialist party, aided by the Zanardelli-Giolitti attitude of benevolent neutrality.[21] But Sonnino soon realized that it was impossible to continue to oppose the granting of elementary political liberties to a modern people, and readily admitted his change of heart. Speaking in the Chamber on June 26, 1903, he confessed that it was unwise not to follow a generously liberal policy in internal affairs as an effective means for the political education of all classes of citizens.[22] He returned to the theme of the formation of a great Liberal bloc made up of elements of the Right, of the Center, and of the Liberal Left, exclusive of moderates and Catholics on the one side and of Progressives and Socialists on the other.[23] Giolitti was referring to this strange form of a constitutional bloc when he made the jibe at Sonnino: "Therefore your [Sonnino's] theory reduces itself to this: the Constitutional party must be one body in which the fusion of Right and Left is supported by the Center!" [24] The guiding principle of the Liberal party,

---

[15] Giolitti himself told him, in 1911, that Sonnino "voted against all Governments, whether of the Right or of the Left, except that of Pelloux"; see *Atti Parlamentari*. "Discussioni della Camera dei Deputati. Tornata dell'8 aprile 1911" (Session 1909–13), XI, 13717.

[16] Cf. Giovanni Giolitti, *Memorie della mia vita*, I, 162–84.

[17] Lodi, *op. cit.*, p. 94.

[18] *Atti Parlamentari*. "Discussioni della Camera dei Deputati. Tornata del 13 marzo 1902" (Session 1902–04), I, 97.

[19] *Ibid.*

[20] *Ibid.*, p. 98.

[21] Giolitti, *op. cit.*, I, 175: "We found ourselves in the situation of being accused from one side of leaving the restraints too loose, and on the other of being considered too lukewarm friends of Liberal principles."

[22] Michele Viterbo, *Sidney Sonnino*, p. 33, and Lodi, *op. cit.*, p. 94.

[23] G. Rabizzani and F. Rubbiani, eds., *Sonnino*, pp. 18–19, *passim*.

[24] *Atti Parlamentari*. "Discussioni della Camera dei Deputati. Tornata dell'8 aprile 1911" (Session 1909–11), XI, 13717.

Sonnino said in 1911, "must be simply the general interest of the whole nation" irrespective of creed or social class; its ends to be attained through the "orderly development of Liberal institutions." [25] Two years later he said that it was not sufficient merely to propose reforms, that it was necessary for the Liberal party to realize those reforms which would bring the common people closer to the state.[26] In his electoral speech of September 27, 1913, Sonnino said: "We must grant freedom even to those who fight against freedom; we must show ourselves generous and equanimous even toward those who wish to base every social relation upon the class struggle." [27] And on the same occasion he revealed the patriotic strain in his Liberal Conservatism when he asserted: "We have the duty of reconquering for our children a more civil Italy, that is, [an Italy] more advanced, more upright, wealthier, stronger, and more respected." [28]

It was Antonio Salandra, a Southerner, who perhaps stood closest to Sonnino in his political beliefs. He had had a successful parliamentary career and had served, almost upon his entering the Chamber, as Under-Secretary of State and later as Minister of Agriculture in the second Pelloux Cabinet. A man of austerity, but of a Southern quality that often made austerity seem haughtiness, trained in law and philosophy, reserved and aloof, possessing an unmistakable capacity for the happy (or unhappy) phrase,[29] Salandra was a man of character. The coming of the First World War was to thrust upon him the heavy burden of guiding the Italian state through the period of precarious neutrality and the first year of the conflict.

Salandra claimed, politically, direct descent from the Right, and of the Right he seemed to have retained all its rigidity of doctrine with little of its flexibility of outlook. As early as 1875 he had written that the ideal of the modern state consisted in the participation of all political "competents" in the government of the state and in the entrusting of the conduct of public affairs to the aristocratic and chosen few.[30] This was the theory of rule by the optimate that he never completely abandoned. During the decade preceding his succession to Giolitti in 1914, Salandra remained inflexible in his opposition to the disruptive forces which he believed to be rising with the conscienceless aid of Giolitti to a position of influence in the country. It was by a strange twist of fate that Salandra himself should have been Prime Minister during that turbulent "Red Week" of June 1914 when it seemed that those forces he dreaded so much would assault the very citadels of power in the state.[31] During the great debate on the State monopoly of life insurance, in June 1911, however,

25 Rabizzani and Rubbiani, *op. cit.*, p. 20; Sonnino, *op. cit.*, III, 446.
26 Rabizzani and Rubbiani, *op. cit.*, pp. 25–26, *passim*.
27 *Ibid.*, p. 24.
28 Viterbo, *op. cit.*, p. 24.
29 It was Salandra who in 1914 coined the phrase *sacro egoismo* (sacred egoism).
30 Antonio Salandra, "La dottrina della rappresentanza personale," in his *Politica e Legislazione*, p. 29.
31 For "Red Week" and the Salandra Government, see chap. v, below.

Salandra made one of the most eloquent speeches against the Government proposal, in the name of freedom from the further encroachments of the state on the social and economic life of the nation.[32] As the peroration of his learned address, Salandra said:

> I ask myself: Is the task of Italian Liberalism then exhausted? Has it been only a brief tale? Has it been only a midsummer night's dream? Must we see once again the chilling specter of the state-as-patron, of the paternal state which, I repeat, is the same in its essence whether it be founded upon electoral suffrage or upon bureaucratic organs? . . . It is not capitalism you will succeed in demolishing! You will create a new capitalism, a monstrous being that will enmesh us all in its inextricable net and that will stifle the economic life of the country. (*Interruptions on the Extreme Left. Signs of warm approval on the Right and in the Center*).[33]

The following year Salandra himself answered his own query when he said that the task of the Liberal party was not yet exhausted and that, amid the insufficiency of the popular parties and the irreconcilable contradictions between those "who do not dare to call themselves Catholics" and modern thought, only the Liberals, the Conservatives and the Progressives could continue in their half-century's work of directing the destinies of the Italian State.[34] But it was in his electoral speech of Lucera (October 19, 1913) that Salandra synthesized his Liberal doctrines and beliefs.[35] He said: "I am a Liberal of the ancient and classical school. I belong to the party that was created by Camillo di Cavour; that can still govern the country along the lines set by him. . . ."[36] Such a Liberal, Salandra continued, was one who held aristocratic rule to be the foundation of the state; who maintained the fullest sovereignty of the state compatible with the widest exercise of spiritual and material activities within the law; one who believed that individual freedom was the animating spirit of social well-being; one who subordinated every desire of progress and every personal or social aspiration to the preservation, greatness, and exaltation of the fatherland: liberalism in Italy had meant, and must continue to mean, patriotism.[37] This categorical identification of liberalism and patriotism was derived in Salandra, as in Sonnino, from his anti-Socialistic and anticlerical bias, and was also closely related to the doctrine of the state as an ethical entity, strong and authoritative, possessing rights that might transcend those of individuals. It was upon premises such as these that men of the Right like Salandra were able to rationalize their belief that it was the task of the Italian Liberal-Conservative bourgeoisie not merely to resist the encroachments of socialism, but,

[32] The speech is reprinted in F. Piccolo, ed., *op. cit.*, pp. 223–43.

[33] *Ibid.*, p. 343.

[34] A. Salandra, *La politica nazionale e il partito liberale*, pp. 20–22, *passim*.

[35] *Idem*, "Il partito liberale nell'ora presente e i compiti della nuova legislatura," in *L'Eloquenza*, III (1913), Nos. 9–10, 324–33.

[36] *Ibid.*, p. 326.

[37] *Ibid.*, p. 327.

actively, to take the leadership in the fulfillment of popular aspirations away from the Socialists. The diffusion of small landed property was the most solid barrier against the spread of agrarian socialism, for, Salandra said, "our hard-working peasants are Socialists through their desire for land," that is, "in order to cease to be Socialists." [38]

The Liberal thought of Sidney Sonnino and Antonio Salandra represented in their political, social, and economic derivations and doctrines a small but powerful circle that viewed the Giolittian regime with misgivings and suspicions. Their patronizing attitude toward the lower classes, their suspicious fear of the extreme parties, their doctrine of the strong State, their identification of Liberalism, that is, conservatism, with patriotism, were to remain for a long time influential currents in the Italian political scene. They were perhaps the outstanding Italian examples of the fate of the translation of nineteenth-century approaches into different social and ideological environments. It was ironic indeed that, when, after the First World War, the Italian Liberal state had become a shadow of its former self they should have been exalted by its destroyers as prophetic critics rather than as its strongest mentors.

The Liberalism of the "Cavourian school," as Salandra had called it, was in reality one of the staunchest conservative forces in Italian political and social life. Its stronghold was in the North and in particular in Milan, where the powerful and enlightened *Corriere della Sera* was identified with the large industrial and financial interests of that great city. At the beginning of the twentieth century, attempts were made in this stronghold at more purely Liberal propaganda and education, starting with the Milanese *L'Idea Liberale* (founded in 1899), the Florentine (later Roman) *Rinnovamento,* and the *Azione,* founded at Milan by Alberto Caroncini and Paolo Arcari in 1914.[39] The old Bolognese daily, *Il Resto del Carlino,* was used for Liberal propaganda in the elections of 1913 by a group of men who called themselves Young Liberals (*Giovani Liberali*), and were led by Giovanni Borelli, Giovanni Amendola, Ettore Maroni, Caroncini, and others. These Young Liberals intended to inject new life into the old forces of Liberalism, which they regarded as incapable of gaining a hold upon the minds of the new generations of Italians. The old Liberalism and socialism were in need of being transformed and synthesized, and this could be accomplished, it was thought, only by men who could steer a middle course between the exaggerated individualism of the old school and the materialistic collectivism of the Socialists.[40] Given the condition of national affairs and the confused state of the national psychology, in the face of "the hodge-podge of this democracy of ours," wrote Giovanni Borelli in 1905, the Young Liberals, rather than repeating the "old dry

[38] *Ibid.,* p. 331.

[39] On the Italian press during the period, see Adolf Dresler, *Geschichte der italianischen Presse,* III, 1-37.

[40] For a good synthesis of the Young Liberal movement and its doctrines, see Alberto Caroncini, *Problemi di politica nazionale;* also, Mario Viana, "Giovanni Borelli poeta, artista, letterato, agitatore politico," in *La Vita italiana* (August, 1933), pp. 162 ff.

formulas of the various democracies," would go forward "in the knowledge of truth, in the light of the future, toward the fundamental renovation of life and society." [41] The truth, however, was that despite its
significance as a symptom of the times, the Young Liberal movement
remained a brave but ineffectual attempt by a group of intelligent young
Italians to set themselves against the current of radical-democratic forces.

By 1914 all attempts to reorganize the elements of the Italian Liberal-
Conservative groups into a single body had ended in failure. The fighting
Florentine periodical, *La Voce* (although some of the more outstanding
Young Liberals had contributed articles to it on art, literature, and phi-
losophy) called Italian Liberals reactionaries who had for too long a time
shown little or no interest in the fate of the lower classes:

> From 1870 to date, the bourgeoisie has offered us fifty years of political lazi-
> ness. Its consciousness—with few exceptions—has never gone beyond the bounda-
> ries of local interests. Its attitude toward the masses has been, at its best, one
> of diffidence; in the South, one of hostility. . . . Will it be able to rise again
> suddenly? That would be very fine, but for the present we must doubt its prob-
> ability.[42]

The Italian Liberal party, commented Carlo Manes, should be called the
"Great Absentee" of Italian political life, for in Italy there was no organization of local political groups bound by a community of interests and
ideas that could properly be called a Liberal party.[43] Explain the thing
as you please, Manes said, "the fact is that outside the Chamber the Liberal party is unknown among the masses." [44] The cycle seemed to have
been completed with these disturbing comments. From 1900 to 1914 the
Conservatives who called themselves Liberals had tried and had failed
to create the party they so strenuously desired. But these self-styled "Liberals" who, according to all the evidence, had little or no standing in the
country at large, were throughout the period among the most influential
groups in the Chamber of Deputies. It is a fact worthy of the greatest
emphasis that they formed the parliamentary majority without, however,
possessing the cohesion necessary to make them independent arbiters of
their own political fate or of the nation's government.

Of the political parties that had for some time been regarded as extra-
constitutional and that made up the *Estrema* the Republican party could
claim possession of the longest tradition.[45] Stemming from the scattered
remnants of the old Mazzinian parties, the Republicans had been torn

---

[41] Giovanni Borelli, "I giovani liberali e il problema della scuola," in F. Piccolo,
ed., *op. cit.*, p. 205.

[42] Editorial, "La crisi del partito liberale," *La Voce*, V (November 20, 1913), No. 47,
1199.

[43] Carlo Manes, "I partiti politici italiani nell'ora presente," *L'Eloquenza*, III (December 20, 1913), Nos. 9-10, 312.

[44] *Ibid.*, p. 313.

[45] For a history of the Republican party in Italy, see Pio Viazzi, *Il partito repubblicano*.

by self-contradictions in policies as well as in ideas and programs. They were for long divided among themselves as unitarians and federalists, antimonarchists and parliamentarians, Irredentists and antimilitarists, Catholics and anticlericals. Their only form of positive program was itself a negation: opposition.[46] In a country that seemed slowly to be reconciling itself to monarchical institutions, they had come to be regarded as an outworn anachronism.[47] One of their leaders, Salvatore Barzilai, after his expulsion from the party, remarked that it had had a tendency (which, as shall be seen, was certainly not unique in the Republican party) toward becoming a council of the elect, especially at its congresses; and yet, he added, to accentuate the contradictions within the party, he himself at the Ancona congress of 1914 succeeded in having a resolution sponsoring an increase in armaments passed in a quarter of an hour in an atmosphere which was still largely antimilitaristic! [48]

The Republicans had their strongholds in the North, in the Romagna, where their struggles with the Socialists became at times very turbulent, in the central provinces of the Marches, and in Apulia in the South. But as a party their numbers gradually dwindled, while those of the other two parties of the *Estrema*—the Socialist and the Radical—grew during the same period.[49] Of them perhaps more than of any other group it could be said that the whole was less than the sum of its parts, for while they were strong in personalities, they were weak as a party. They had had Giovanni Bovio, the philosopher,[50] and Matteo Renato Imbriani; they had Salvatore Barzilai, the great orator; they had Roberto Mirabelli, the expert on constitutional law; they had the fighting Giuseppe Gaudenzi and Innocenzo Cappa.[51] In the Chamber of Deputies the Republicans were among the most acrid critics of Giolitti, in whom some of them suspected a mere obsequious servant of the monarchy. For his part, Giolitti made the vow, in April 1903, that by his policy of "liberty for all within the limits of the law" he would show that the Republican party no longer had a reason for being, and even before the end of his regime he practically succeeded in realizing his promise.[52] The Romagnuole Alfredo Oriani said in 1906 that the Republican party since the death of Mazzini had survived only as "the echo of a name and the shadow of a ghost" and that individual Republicans were merely "positivists in philosophy, atheists in morality, and Socialists in their minimum program." [53] After the elections

[46] Ernest Lémonon, *De Cavour à Mussolini*, p. 35.

[47] *Ibid.*, pp. 33–34, *passim*.

[48] Salvatore Barzilai, *Luci ed ombre del passato*, p. 133.

[49] In 1901 the Republicans sent 29 deputies to the Chamber, but in 1913 they had only 16. Cf. Bolton King and Thomas Okey, *Italy Today*, p. 74, and the article, "La prima prova del suffragio allargato," *Nuova Antologia*, CLXVIII (November 16, 1913), 334–38.

[50] On Bovio, see Croce, *op. cit.*, pp. 212–13.

[51] For brief sketches of outstanding Republicans, see Barzilai, *op. cit.*, pp. 332–33.

[52] *Atti Parlamentari*. "Discussioni della Camera dei Deputati. Tornata del 1 aprile 1903" (Session 1902–04), VII, 6960.

[53] Alfredo Oriani, *Rivolta ideale*, 3rd ed., pp. 154–55, *passim*.

of 1913, the party had little weight in Italian political life and seemed condemned to a sterile intransigence.[54]

The Radical party, too, traced its origins to Mazzini's party of Action, but it was only in 1890 that it became differentiated from all the other groups which claimed similar derivation from the famous Pact of Rome of May 13, 1890.[55] The Pact of Rome was the work of eminent men who had gathered to give concrete form to the various political currents which went under the name of democratic. Giovanni Bovio, Felice Cavallotti, Ernesto Nathan, and others formulated a program of action long regarded as the most revolutionary outside of Socialist programs. Among the most significant points expressed in the Pact were: the right of the nation to be consulted in its supreme interests and in the use of its blood and money; the revision or extension of Articles 5, 44, and 45 of the *Statuto;* [56] protection of the free exercise of the representative mandate; full parliamentary control of the Government; a law on administrative liberty; decentralization; the greatest possible popular participation in active politics; the conversion of ecclesiastical properties; labor legislation.[57] The Radical party itself drew its strength from the middle, lower middle, and artisan classes of the North, chiefly from Lombardy, Venetia, Emilia, and Tuscany, and it had a powerful organ of public opinion in the Milanese daily *Il Secolo*. The electoral strength of the Radicals was in the ascendancy during the period. In 1900 they had thirty-four seats in the Chamber and the elections of 1913 saw that number rise to seventy.[58]

The Radicals were as a whole inspired by a democratic-bourgeois ideology founded, they believed, upon the realistic consideration of Italian political and economic conditions. They were inclined to be pacifistic and exponents of a foreign policy consonant with what they regarded as the very limited resources of the country. Francesco Saverio Nitti, one of their leaders, said in 1907, "We have no empire to conquer and the whole future to jeopardize." [59] They were therefore suspicious of increasing state control and wished, at least until 1912, to limit the action of the State to its great functions of creating order and security.[60] But despite the possession of eminent political and intellectual figures such as Nitti himself, Ettore Sacchi, Edoardo Pantano, Luigi Credaro, Giulio Alessio, and Vincenzo Giuffrida, the Radical party never succeeded in finding great support throughout the country since its programs were considered too nebulous. As a party, the Radicals lacked a solid organization and the

[54] C. Manes, *op. cit.,* p. 305.

[55] For the early history of the Radicals, see Alberto La Pegna, *Per l'idea democratica,* pp. 39–82.

[56] *Statuto,* Art. 5: "The Executive power devolves upon the King alone . . ."; Art. 44: on the election of deputies after a dispossession of mandate; Art. 45: on the arrest of, and criminal procedure against, a deputy during a session of the Chamber.

[57] Cf. pamphlet, *Il Patto di Roma del 13 maggio 1890* (Milan, 1890), *passim.*

[58] King and Okey, *op. cit.,* p. 75. See also *France-Italie, revue mensuelle,* I (December 1, 1913), No. 6, 347.

[59] F. S. Nitti, *Il Partito radicale e la nuova democrazia industriale,* p. 152.

[60] *Ibid.,* p. 153.

spirit of political initiative necessary to a really fighting group. Despite their electoral gains they became more and more estranged from the masses of the people and were finally reduced, as one of them later said, to a parliamentary expression whose sole power consisted in their weight of numbers in the Chamber.[61] The Radicals were almost completely domesticated by Giolitti who, in 1904, had one of their leaders, Giuseppe Marcora, elected to the presidency of the Chamber of Deputies,[62] and formed his Cabinet of 1911 chiefly with their support, having given Nitti the portfolio of Agriculture, Industry, and Commerce. The Radicals themselves, however, by a sort of unconscious political revenge, in March 1914 passed to the opposition and, by determining the fall of Giolitti, indirectly contributed to the close of a period of Italian history in that fateful spring.[63]

[61] La Pegna, op. cit., pp. 11–12, passim.
[62] Giolitti, op. cit., I, 217: "The election of Marcora to the presidency [of the Chamber of Deputies] answered perfectly my expectation. . . . That nomination was the first decisive step by which the Radical party began to undertake the responsibilties of government."
[63] On the fall of Giolitti in 1914, ibid., II, 510, and Lodi, op. cit., p. 164.

IV

CATHOLICS IN POLITICS

*I cattolici scendono in campo ed il rafforzamento dello
Stato ne risulta inevitabile.**

MARIO MISSIROLI

THE Radical party could claim no monopoly of Italian democratic currents for, long before it formulated its program of action with the Pact of Rome of 1890, there had been the germs of an Italian Christian Democracy attempting to break through the official irreconcilability of Catholicism and democracy. As early as 1881 Monsignor G. B. Savarese had tried to show that there was no irreconcilable contradiction between the moral teachings of the Church and the social aspirations of democracy.[1] Subsequently as a counteraction to the rising tide of socialism, the Church had, by a series of encyclicals and official acts, attempted to translate her own moral and humanitarian ideals into concrete suggestions aiming to stem the materialistic teachings of socialism by herself pointing to possible checks for the most ruthless abuses of capitalism. *Rerum novarum,* of May 15, 1891, had been only the most forceful and complete statement of a social faith.[2]

In Italy, as early as January 1895, the *Unità Cattolica* of Turin had written: "We Catholics, through the origins of our faith, through the constant tradition of the Church, through the very history of Italy, are we not intimately democratic? If radicalism ceases to be irreligious it will find us very close at hand." In June of the same year it said: "We are ready to clasp hands with the men who, representing the traditions of our ancestors, are preparing for Italy the sane future of an honest and strong democracy." [3]

Long before Italian Christian Democracy became a movement with definite political policies, local Catholic groups and organizations, especially in the north of Italy, had carried on a widespread work of gradual social improvement.[4] Bergamo became the stronghold of Catholic organization which sponsored some of the best rural coöperative movements

---

* "As Catholics enter the arena the strengthening of the state is the inevitable result," Mario Missiroli, *La Monarchia socialista—Estrema Destra,* p. 183.

[1] Cf. De Mattei, *Il problema,* p. 115.

[2] See also *Apostolici numeris* (December 28, 1878), *Libertas* (June 20, 1888), *Graves de communi* (January 18, 1901), and the *Istruzione della Sacra Congregazione degli Affari Ecclesiatici* (January 27, 1902).

[3] Quoted by De Mattei, *op. cit.,* p. 118.

[4] On the working-class Catholic organizations in Italy since 1870, see the magnificent and complete publication of the Italian Ministry of Agriculture, Industry, and Commerce, *Le organizzazioni cattoliche in Italia.*

in Italy.[5] Christian Democracy as such was an attempt to unify and canalize into a definite social and political movement, with an ideology of its own, the potentially resourceful though dispersed forces of North Italian Catholic organization.[6] But it was precisely this aim of the Christian Democrats that ran counter to the official line of conduct prescribed by the Vatican for strictly political activities of Italian Catholics. When, for example, on November 4, 1903, after the Christian Democratic congress at Bologna, the Bolognese Catholic newspaper *L'Avvenire d'Italia* remarked that now that "Christian Democracy had found its track" it should follow it "full blast," it received the official retort that, as far as tracks were concerned, there was not one alone, but two, and they ran in opposite directions: there was the track of obedience to the Church and the track "of thinking, talking, and acting as one pleased." [7]

As far as Italian Catholics were concerned, the track of obedience to the Church ran back to 1870 and 1874, to Pius IX and the thorny Roman Question.[8] As a protest against the "usurpation" of Rome by the new King of Italy, Italian Catholics had been enjoined by the *non expedit* and Don Margotti's formula of *nè eletti nè elettori* (neither voters nor candidates) from participation in Italian political life. From Pius IX to Pius X no official act of the Church had so far sanctioned any relaxation of the admonishment, but by a sort of tacit and benevolent conspiracy the newly risen Catholic forces had begun to encroach upon systematic abstention, and furthermore a new generation of Catholics had risen who had not lived through the hectic times of the Roman occupation.[9] The "sacrilegious usurper," instead of collapsing had, in fact, grown stronger with the years. Although the rural masses had remained faithful to the Church, Socialist forces were gradually weaning away the urban proletariat. Among the results of the official friction between Church and state in Italy was the inroads made by the "irreligious" Socialists.[10] A "question" of so many years' standing, involving so many phases of Italian Catholic life, could not and was hardly expected to be answered in a day.[11] There were daily opportunities to show that the antagonism between Church and state was becoming more acute, as was clearly shown in 1904, following President Loubet's and Delcassé's visit to Rome.[12]

[5] For a brief account of the Bergamo coöperative movement, see King and Okey, *Italy Today*, pp. 189–92.

[6] On Italian Christian Democracy, see especially Filippo Meda, *Il programma politico della democrazia cristiana*; Romolo Murri, *La politica clericale e la democrazia*; G. Toniolo, *L'unione popolare fra i cattolici d'Italia*; Ernesto Vercesi, *Il movimento cattolico in Italia, 1870–1922*.

[7] See De Mattei, *op. cit.*, p. 119, and the documentary *La Democrazia cristiana davanti ai Documenti Pontifici* (Venice, 1904).

[8] Cf. Luigi Sturzo, *Church and State*.

[9] Corrado Barbagallo, *L'Italia dal 1870 ad oggi*, p. 67.

[10] Cf. Gaetano Salvemini, "L'Italia nel secolo XIX," in *L'Europa nel secolo XIX*, I, 378–80.

[11] See S. William Halperin, *The Separation of Church and State in Italian Thought from Cavour to Mussolini*.

[12] The visit of the French President, Loubet, took place on April 24, 1904, and it was

There seemed to be no end to the rumors of scandal and mutual recrimina-tions, and public opinion was hotly aroused on both sides.

The excitement throughout the country produced a strong reaction in the Chamber of Deputies and it was in answer to interpellations by the Republican deputy Pilade Mazza and the Radical Cornelio Guerci that Prime Minister Giolitti was forced to proclaim his formula for the rela-tions of Church and state in Italy. On May 30, 1904, Giolitti said in the Chamber: [13]

> As far as ecclesiastical policy is concerned, we believe there are no changes to be made. . . . Our principle is this: that the state and the Church are two paral-lels which should never meet. Woe to the Church the day it should wish to in-vade the powers of the state! Freedom for all within the limits of the law: this is our program. And as we apply it to all parties outside the Constitution on the one hand, we apply it to those who are outside it on the other.

But as a matter of fact, although the parallels of which Giolitti spoke were far from meeting, it was only five months after his enunciation that they swerved noticeably toward the same point. The immediate cause was the general strike of September 1904, the remote cause was the Catholic and Liberal-Conservative fear of the Socialist upsurge; the meeting point was the general election of November 6 and 13, 1904.

Pope Pius X was far from being as intransigent as Pio Nono had been in this matter. As Patriarch of Venice before his election he had been suspected of views differing from those of his illustrious predecessor on the *non expedit,* and had expressed a discreet inclination to modify its force.[14] The occasion presented itself in 1904, when his trusted friends from the province of Bergamo, among whom Gianforte Suardi, Paolo Bonomi, and Professor Rezzara, after consultation with Tommaso Tit-toni, Giolitti's Foreign Minister, hastened to advise the Pope that the stronghold of Catholic action and organization in their province was endangered by a Radical-Freemasonic incursion in the coming election, unless the *non expedit* were relaxed. The Pope, according to Suardi, listened attentively to Paolo Bonomi and, realizing the seriousness of the situation, told him: " 'Do, do as your conscience dictates.' " Bonomi asked:

---

accompanied and followed by the watchful suspicion and resentment of the Vatican. On April 28, a diplomatic note was forwarded by the Vatican Secretary of State, Cardinal Merry Del Val, to the Catholic Powers, in which it was stated that "any Head of a Catholic nation brings grave offense to the Holy Father by coming to pay homage in Rome, that is, in the very Pontifical Seat and in the same Catholic palace, *to him who against all rights retains his civil sovereignty . . .*" [italics added]. The note was made public by Jean Jaurès' Paris *Humanité* on May 17, 1904, and was fol-lowed by an explosion of protests, both in France and in Italy. The Milan *Corriere della Sera* (May 19, 1904) remarked that although Cardinal Merry Del Val spoke "four or five languages . . . there is, however, one language he seems to ignore: the lan-guage of diplomacy." For a good general account, see Saverio Cilibrizzi, *Storia parla-mentare*, III, 268–76.

[13] *Atti Parlamentari.* "Discussioni della Camera dei Deputati. Tornata del 30 maggio 1904." (Session 1902–04), VII, 13129.

[14] E. Vercesi, *op. cit.*, p. 122.

"Have we understood properly, Holiness? May we interpret that as 'yes'?"
"Do as your conscience dictates, I repeat,"

the Pope said.[15] In this manner, partial and limited as it was, the *non expedit* was lifted in those electoral districts where Catholic candidates were in danger, or where anticlerical candidates might win. Two deputies who were Catholics, Marchese Carlo Ottavio Cornaggia and Agostino Cameroni, were thus elected respectively at Milan and at Treviglio. The following year, the encyclical *Il fermo proposito* gave official sanction to modification of the *non expedit*.

A great step forward had thus been made toward a reconciliation of the two powerful antagonists, and they both benefited by it. It remained to be seen whether there would be a reversion to the *status quo ante* or a continuation on the road just cautiously and indirectly taken. But the years following the first partial lifting of the *non expedit* were years when some of the most tremendous problems of Church-state relations were raised once again, and they were rendered more acute by side issues of no less significance. The Church herself, in Italy as in other countries, was occupied with the Modernist movement, whose rationalistic interpretations she came to regard as counter to Catholic doctrine and dogma.[16] Many honest searchers for truth were condemned, together with the dilettanti of thought, by the encyclicals *Pascendi,* of September 8, 1907, and *Motu proprio,* of September 1, 1910.

The question of education, especially of religious teaching in the public schools, has always been one pregnant with explosive significance. The Church in Italy, fearful of what she regarded as the infiltration of anti-religious, Freemasonic doctrines in the Italian schools, made two insistent demands on the Italian state: that religious teaching be made compulsory in the primary schools, and that freedom of religious instruction be granted in the secondary schools.[17] Thus behind the great debate which took place in the Chamber of Deputies in February 1908, there stretched a long history of embattled animosities, of anticlerical agitation, of Free-masonic propaganda, of anti-religious programs, and, naturally, of Catholic and clerical reprisals.[18] As a climax to the controversies, in 1907 Ernesto Nathan, Past Grand Master of Italian freemasonry, had been elected mayor of Rome, and the Roman communal administration was openly suspected of anticlerical tendencies.[19]

From February 18 to 27, 1908, the Chamber was the scene of an important debate on the school question, following the presentation of a proposal for the elementary schools by Giolitti's Minister of Public In-

15 G. Suardi, "Quando e come i cattolici poterono partecipare alle elezioni politiche," *Nuova Antologia,* CCLVI (1927), 121.

16 On Modernism, see Ernesto Buonaiuti, *Le Modernisme catholique;* Giovanni Gentile, *Il Modernismo e i rapporti tra religione e filosofia;* L. Sturzo, *op. cit.,* pp. 463–64; and Antonio Fogazzaro's famous novel, *Il Santo.*

17 Barbagallo, *op. cit.,* p. 67.

18 T. Tittoni, *Nuovi scritti,* pp. 242–66, *passim.*

19 Cf. *La Civiltà Cattolica,* December 7, 1907, pp. 613 ff.

struction, Rava. The Reformist Socialist, Leonida Bissolati, by presenting a motion for the abolition of all religious teaching in the schools, started the long debate.[20] The best oratorical talents of the Chamber participated in the debate, which turned into a healthy occasion for the ventilation of repressed ideas and emotions. A close study of the parliamentary debates of those days reveals most interesting and significant material not only for the historian of Church-state relations, but also, and perhaps more, for the attentive student of class, religious, and pedagogical biases and theories. The country watched most attentively the actions in the Chamber.[21] There were, of course, some mutual recriminations, accusations of "Masonic conspiracy" and "theocratic tyranny," but on the whole the debate was kept on rather a high level of parliamentary practice by the sincerity of most of the participants.

Bissolati himself spoke of the distinction between morality and religion, and asserted that the Socialists believed only in a morality that expressed itself in terms of social relations. The Catholic deputy Agostino Cameroni launched into an attack against the "anti-patriotic premises" of freemasonry, a sect, he said, which since the Risorgimento had aimed to eradicate religion from Italy.[22] Sonnino made a semi-philosophical glorification of the religious spirit in man, saying that "religion will live as long as the unknown and the unknowable exist," [23] while Salandra saw the necessity of gathering every strength, whether Socialist or Catholic, around the Italian state, and he therefore condemned as "absurd, injurious, and inopportune" any form of persecution against either of these groups.[24] The great and salutary oratorical tourney in which men of practically all parties took part—the Republican Comandini, the Radicals Nitti and Ettore Sacchi, the Conservative Martini—was finally summarized by Giolitti himself, who said that the "open road of freedom" was that which corresponded to the sentiments of the majority of Italians and would most assuredly lead toward the true progress and prosperity of the country.[25] Bissolati's motion was subsequently rejected by a vote of 347 to 60, and the Chamber approved by a vote of 279 to 129 a motion acceptable to the Government. Thus once again the Chamber of Deputies had asserted itself as the heart of Italian political institutions under the benevolent sway of the master parliamentarian, Giovanni Giolitti.

The general elections of March 7 and 14, 1909, brought the question of *non expedit* once again to the fore. On this occasion, however, the Vatican, acting through the *Unione elettorale cattolica italiana*, laid down

[20] *Atti Parlamentari.* "Discussioni della Camera dei Deputati. Tornate del 18 al 27 febbraio 1908" (Session 1904–09), XVI, 19294 ff.

[21] Alberto Malatesta, *Il Parlamento italiano da Cavour a Mussolini*, pp. 161–66, *passim.*

[22] *Atti Parlamentari.* "Discussioni della Camera dei Deputati. Tornata del 18 febbraio 1908" (Session 1904–09), XVI, 19308.

[23] Sonnino, *Discorsi parlamentari*, III, 245.

[24] *Atti Parlamentari, supra,* p. 19337.

[25] *Ibid.*, p. 19634.

very precise instructions for the Catholic exercise of the franchise. The three principal conditions for the participation of Catholics in the elections were: (1) in an electoral district of their diocese there must be a militantly anti-Clerical candidate who was a member of the Popular bloc; (2) against such an anti-Clerical candidate there must be a candidate of the "forces of order," whether Catholic or not, who must give guarantee of not attacking religion; (3) in such an electoral district there must be great probability of victory for the anticlerical candidate should the Catholic voters abstain, while their participation would render his defeat certain.[26] The *Unione elettorale* circularized the rules. Besides, Don Margotti's old formula of *nè eletti nè elettori* was replaced by the other of *cattolici deputati, non deputati cattolici* (deputies who are Catholics, not Catholic deputies), a compromise between total abstention and the full participation of Catholics as a political party. The result was the election of twenty-one deputies who were Catholics, and a still greater step toward the practical and complete removal of the constraining *non expedit.*

Luigi Luzzatti's Ministry of one year (March 31, 1910 to March 30, 1911), following Sonnino's second Hundred Days, saw the Chamber return to the theme of Church-state relations. The Prime Minister himself, a scholar and philosopher of note, added his own to the long series of formulas. "Free religions in the sovereign state" was Luzzatti's counterpart of Giolitti's theory of the parallels.[27] Strongly contrasting to Romolo Murri's emotional attitude were the sober and mature tones of the Catholic deputy Filippo Meda. Meda pointed out, on April 29, 1910, that neither Giolitti's nor Luzzatti's formula was of great importance so long as the Government guaranteed freedom of conscience, the statutory rights of association for Catholics as well as for the other groups, and the educational functions of the school and of the family.[28] For his part, Meda reaffirmed the trust of the Catholics in the present and future of the Italian State.

Early in 1913, the Florentine review *La Voce* saw the possibility of a new outbreak of anticlericalism to be initiated perhaps by Giolitti himself, for, it said, the Vatican could "annoy the Italian Government more through Vienna, or even London, than through the twenty or fifty Cameroni [the Catholic deputy from Treviglio] whom the electoral districts of North Italy send to defend the Church in Parliament." [29] The general elections of October 26 and November 2, 1913, were to prove the bold prophecy of *La Voce* completely erroneous. Rather than a new period of persecutions, news of the Gentiloni Pact exploded upon the country. On November 8, 1913, less than a week after the general elec-

---

[26] A. Schiavi, "Programmi, voti ed eletti nei comizi politici del 1909," *La Riforma Sociale,* July–August 1909, p. 388.

[27] *Atti Parlamentari.* "Discussioni della Camera dei Deputati. Tornata del 28 aprile 1910" (Session 1909–13), VI, 6399.

[28] *Ibid.,* "Tornata del 29 aprile 1919," VI, 6351.

[29] Cf. *La Voce,* V (1913), 1005.

tions, Count Vincenzo Ottorino Gentiloni (1865–1916), president of the *Unione cattolica italiana,* granted an interview to the *Giornale d'Italia* in which he declared that in the elections he had tried to realize the directions of the Holy See, and he went on to give some details of the influence of the Catholic vote upon the results.[30] The rather open secret of a pact between Giolitti, the Liberal-Conservatives, and Count Gentiloni was thus confirmed.

In itself the Gentiloni Pact was nothing more than an expansion of the Catholic electoral directions of 1909. Catholics were permitted to vote for Liberal and Conservative candidates only upon the candidates' observance of a number of "rules": (1) defense of statutory institutions and guarantee of protection of liberty of conscience; therefore opposition to any act or law whose application might disturb the religious peace of the country; (2) no encroachment upon the jurisdiction of private schools; (3) guarantee of the right of parents to demand religious instruction for their children in the public schools; (4) opposition to any attempt to disrupt the unity of the family by the passage of a divorce law; (5) recognition of equal rights to economic and social organizations irrespective of social or religious principles; (6) support of a gradual and continuous program of tax reform based upon the application of the principles of justice in social relations; (7) support of a national and international policy tending to preserve and strengthen the economic and moral forces of the country.[31]

Thus there was hardly any dangerous new principle involved in the Catholic program. But the program was one thing and the underhand and occult maneuvers necessary to its acceptance and application by candidates was another. It was the maneuvers which aroused the country and in particular the extreme parties once it became a matter of certain knowledge. For it seemed as if the Government with Giolitti at its head had made an "alliance between bad faith and the sacristy" for the sole purpose of placing a barrier in the way of the democratic parties.[32] The Government, it was said, had shamelessly compromised the very basis of the moral and political life of the country.[33] Giolitti naturally became the object of a shower of philippics in the Chamber from the aroused members of the *Estrema.*[34]

By the Gentiloni Pact the Catholics came into the Chamber with thirty-three members, a fairly strong nucleus for the formation, when

30 A. Benedetti, "Intervista coll'altro presidente del Consiglio, il conte Gentiloni," *Giornale d'Italia,* November 8, 1913.

31 See Michele Rosi, *L'Italia odierna,* II, Tomo iii, 2150.

32 Cf. the speech of Carlo Altobelli in *Atti Parlamentari.* "Discussioni della Camera dei Deputati. Tornata del 5 dicembre 1913" (Session 1913–14), I, 154–66, especially p. 164.

33 Filippo Turati's comments on the Gentiloni Pact were extremely partisan and picturesque, *ibid.,* p. 145: "The Almighty placed at the services of the prefectures— the utilization of spiritual threats by parish priests—crucifixes given voters to kiss as sacrosanct engagements to vote for the Liberal candidate, for the Jew, for the Freemason, nay, for the Devil himself, were he a Government-sponsored candidate . . ."

34 See below in this work the chapter on *Giolittismo.*

needed, of a true Catholic party. The *Estrema,* with the exception of the Republicans (who lost six seats), rose from forty-one to seventy-eight for the Socialists, and from fifty-one to seventy for the Radicals.[35] The so-called Constitutional Liberals, of whom more than two hundred owed their election to the aid of the Catholics, seemed doubly shackled—to Giolitti's will and to Gentiloni's program. Giolitti had once again an apparently solid parliamentary majority. And yet, once the shouting and the recriminations were over, once the fact and the method were put in their true perspective, the extensive participation of the Catholic masses in the general elections of 1913 came to be viewed as the nation's gain, a strengthening of national unity just before its greatest ordeal came upon it with the First World War. There had been few steps greater than this toward the true moral unification of Italy since the breach of Porta Pia in 1870.

[35] "La prima prova del suffragio allargato," *Nuova Antologia,* CLXVIII (November 16, 1913), 334–38.

V

PROBLEMS OF ITALIAN SOCIALISM

Sono passati otto anni, il paese ha camminato innanzi,
il partito socialista ha moderato assai il suo programma,
*Carlo Marx è stato mandato in soffitta. . . .**

GIOLITTI

THE Italian Risorgimento, with its preoccupation with the problems of national unity and independence, had submerged the social and economic currents stirring within the complex of politics. It is true that some heroic and prophetic men had insisted on viewing the national struggle in terms not only of political freedom but also of the social and economic emancipation of the lower classes of the Italian people. One of these had been Carlo Pisacane, the fiery Neapolitan Socialist, for whom freedom was an indivisible and living faith not to be pawned at the counter of political and diplomatic exigencies, in whom the flame of patriotic fervor was to be made to feed the stronger fire of love and pity and selfless devotion to the greater cause of human justice. Poor, blundering, ineffectual Pisacane, who in 1857 was to be murdered by the very peasants for whose redemption he had given up wealth and career and easy glory! [1] Mazzini, too, after his dream of the Republic of Man had been measured against the practical structure Cavour was erecting in its place, had devoted his lessening energies to the question of the working classes. But, miserably disappointed and harassed by stronger antagonists even in his new mission, he had ended by confessing defeat in the present with hope reserved to the future. In 1871, the year before his death, he wrote: "I attempt to do the little I can for an ideal Italy and for men who are not yet. And if this religious sentiment had not fortunately remained in me, I would have killed myself." [2]

It was only when the country had left the problems of nationality and unity behind as pressing necessities that the social question was raised once again. But now the difficulty had changed its aspect. A contradiction inherent to the solution of the question itself faced those who attempted to canalize the Italian class struggle into the currents of orthodox revolutionary methodology. Italy was not a rich, highly industrialized nation like most of her neighbors to the north. If great progress had been made

---

* "Eight years have gone by, the country has gone on ahead, the Socialist party has much moderated its program, Karl Marx has been relegated to the attic. . . ." Giolitti, in a speech in the Chamber of Deputies on April 8, 1911.

[1] On this all too unknown precursor, see the definitive biography by N. Rosselli, *Carlo Pisacane nel Risorgimento italiano.*

[2] Quoted by N. Rosselli, *Mazzini e Bakounine,* p. 421.

and was being made in this respect, it was chiefly concentrated in small sections of the northern and central provinces, while the South was still, and was long to remain, a feudal region hardly to be conceived of in terms of capitalistic development. To be sure, the relation of master and worker was nowhere more general than in southern Italy, but it was not of the kind amenable to the ready-made ideology and programs of the scientific class struggle.

It was for this reason that the earliest currents of Italian revolutionary agitation which attained any measure of success were those which concentrated upon the realities of Italian economic and social conditions and of the already mentioned messianism of the first decades of unity. These in turn conditioned the forms of that agitation, its leaders, its method, and its achievements. The first twenty years of unity in this respect belonged to the violent and conspiratorial anarchism of Michael Bakunin and his group of Italian followers, from the noble and selfless Carlo Cafiero to the fiery and resolute Andrea Costa.[3] The next decade (1880–90), which coincided with a period of great industrial progress in the North, saw an accentuation of the struggle for revolutionary power between the remnants of the Mazzinian party concentrated in the Romagna including the Bakuninist-anarchist groups with followers in both the North and South and the Socialist adepts of the class struggle with their stronghold in Milan. The bone of contention was the Northern industrial proletariat, the fairly large class of urban artisans, and the unknown and unpredictable masses of the Southern peasantry.[4] This was the period of the rise of working-class associations through which the struggle for power among the factions was continued and further embittered. It was, so to speak, a period of preparation, one during which certain sections of Italy began to feel the breath of new revolutionary gospels of which the Marxist was no more than one among many.

The following decade (1890–1900) was to witness the extraordinary ascendancy of Marxism in Italy, the expulsion of the Anarchists from the ranks of orthodox socialism, the rise of the Italian Socialist party to a position of national and parliamentary importance, and the magnificent flowering of a cultural and intellectual renaissance which had its roots in the proselyting fervor of the Socialistic circles and their leaders.[5] Filippo Turati, editor of the greatest organ for the diffusion of Marxism in Italy, the *Critica Sociale* of Milan, in 1901 divided this decade of socialism into two distinct periods.[6] The first was a "period of assertion," marked by an

[3] For the abortive Bologna insurrection of July 1874 see the interesting historical novel by Riccardo Bacchelli, *Il diavolo al Pontelungo*.

[4] On all these developments and the achievements of the struggles, see Roberto Michels, *Storia critica del movimento socialista italiano*, pp. 17–100; also the commentaries in A. Angiolini and E. Ciacchi, *Socialismo e socialisti in Italia*.

[5] For a good synthesis of the cultural aspects of socialism in the decade, cf. Croce, *A History of Italy*, chap. vi, pp. 145–62.

[6] F. Turati, in the *Critica Sociale*, XI (1901), 209–15, reprinted in his *Trent'anni di "Critica Sociale,"* pp. 71–94, *passim*.

extraordinary verbal violence and by a simplicity of ideology equaled only by their weakness. The Genoa congress (1892) at which the Marxists had separated themselves from the Anarchists thus precipitating a schism between parliamentarians and antiparliamentarians, and the Reggio Emilia congress (1893) at which the victorious Marxians had adopted a name and a program for the new and "purified" party, were the culmination of the first period. The second period, that of defense, went from Reggio Emilia and the fall of Giolitti in 1893 to the Saracco Ministry of 1900. This was the time when Italian socialism was to learn, according to Turati, "to its cost, the inescapable necessity of liberty and the prudent tactics of alliances." [7]

The "inescapable necessity of liberty" referred to the *annus terribilis* with its *Fatti di Maggio* (May 3–8, 1898) and the subsequent regime of reaction under General Pelloux. The involved story of that complex of economic, political, and psychological frustrations which was to reach its climax early in May 1898, is not within the scope of this work.[8] It is sufficient to state here that following the outbreak of bread riots in southern Italy, an insurrection centering in Milan had broken out in the North which had resulted in the dispersal, imprisonment, or liquidation of the Socialist leaders suspected of having organized and directed the movement. Filippo Turati, his wife Anna Kuliscioff, Leonida Bissolati, Angiolo and Maria Cabrini, to mention only the more notable, belonged to a large phalanx of Socialist leaders who were arrested and condemned to prison terms; others escaped by crossing the borders or going into hiding. The military reaction was triumphant, but its triumph was soon lessened by the reaction of public opinion: organized meetings of protest and lengthy petitions demanding the pardon and release of the political prisoners. These means proved effective, for most of the condemned were released. Italy seemed to breathe again at this victory of the spreading spirit of freedom.

It was at this point that the "prudent tactics of alliances" of which Turati spoke were conceived as the best means for combating the reactionary tendencies and extreme measures of Pelloux's "barrack-room" Government.[9] The intransigent electoral and parliamentary tactics adopted by the Socialists at their Rome congress of 1897, a kind of policy of splendid isolation among the other parties, became impossible after the tumultuous events of 1898. The Socialist parliamentary group was forced to join forces with the other two extreme parties, the Republican and the Radical, to form the coalition known as the *Estrema Sinistra*. Under the leadership

---

[7] *Ibid.*, p. 71.

[8] Details of the events of 1898–1900 are to be found in Lodi, *Venticinque anni*, pp. 6–28; Okey, "United Italy," *Cambridge Modern History*, pp. 219–20; Michels, *op. cit.*, pp. 199–206; King and Okey, *Italy Today*, pp. 81–109; and particularly in N. Colajanni, *L'Italia nel 1898*.

[9] An interesting, if partially biased, account of the Pelloux regime is contained in the early chapters of Labriola, *Storia di dieci anni*.

of such able men as Cavallotti and Imbriani for the Radicals, Bovio and Barzilai for the Republicans, Andrea Costa, Enrico Ferri, Camillo Prampolini, Bissolati, and De Felice for the Socialists—the coalition held the reaction at bay for almost two years by the adoption of parliamentary tactics till then unknown in Italian politics, obstructionism. And it was an inspiring sight indeed to see the three parties which had been regarded as anti- or extra-constitutional defending the elementary constitutional rights of the nation—freedom of speech, freedom of association and of the press—against the men who were attempting to suppress them in the name of a "return to the Constitution." [10]

When Pelloux saw the impossibility of having his repressive measures passed by the Chamber because of the determination of the Extreme Left, he had recourse to the proclamation of a royal decree counter to all parliamentary usage. The decree included the laws already defeated in the Chamber and a date for dissolving the parliamentary session. On June 30, 1899, the Chamber of Deputies was the scene of a violence unknown in Italian parliamentary tradition: the Socialist deputies broke the voting urns, thus preventing the finishing of the balloting, which, given the reactionary majority in the Chamber, could only result in the complete defeat of their purpose. Four days later the ministry dissolved the Chamber. It seemed like a strategic retreat although it was actually an admission of defeat and a flight in the face of a small but compact minority behind whom stood the truly Liberal forces of the country. In February 1900, the Court of Cassation declared the infamous royal decree unconstitutional and null. The elections of June 3 and 10 of that year were a complete confirmation of the work of the Estrema, for the country returned a total of ninety-four of their members, of whom thirty-three were Socialists.[11]

For almost two years the Estrema, and especially the Socialist parliamentary group, had obstructed the Government in the realization of its reactionary measures. During that time the members of the coalition were the real arbiters of Italian parliamentary institutions and the defenders of the basic liberties of a modern people. They had gained the admiration of the whole Liberal element by their heroic stand in favor of the cause of political freedom and social justice. The Socialists had, moreover, made good their separation from the antiparliamentarian group in 1892 by showing that liberty could be defended within the very citadel of bourgeois political power, Parliament, and they had demonstrated to believers in the old Liberalism that a new Liberal democratic force had risen. For now looking back it seemed that from its birth in

[10] It will be remembered that Sonnino's notorious article "Torniano allo Statuto" was published in 1897 and that Sonnino himself was the majority leader under Pelloux. Cf. B. Croce, op. cit., p. 209.

[11] There is some disagreement about the number of Socialist deputies elected in 1900: Croce, op. cit., p. 211, gives 33; Lodi, op. cit., p. 25, also 33; Michels, op. cit., p. 208, says 33, while in his Il proletariato e la borghesia nel movimento socialista italiano, p. 90, he gives 32; Filippo Meda, Il Partito Socialista Italiano, p. 18, gives 32.

1892 to 1901 the Italian Socialist party had truly been a party of Liberal action with a Socialist banner.[12]

Having launched its career as the opponent of Liberalism and of the bourgeois Parliament in which all other parties could be viewed as of the same reactionary bloc, Italian socialism found itself at the beginning of the century the restorer of Liberal principles—the restoration achieved, moreover, by means of the same Liberal institutions it had formerly condemned.[13] When the last flicker of violence had died with the assassination of Humbert, and a new era of liberty had dawned with the accession of the new King and the formation of the Zanardelli-Giolitti Cabinet (February 15, 1901), Italian socialism was faced with the choice of either using the experience in fighting so recently gained or of returning to a position of intransigence, to revolutionary tactics. The majority of Socialists chose to see in the new era a period of "consolidation of liberty and respect for the law" (Turati); an irreconcilable minority saw in it the beginning of a new period of violent struggle. The subsequent history of Italian socialism was to be marked by this difference in point-of-view and method.

It was, by a paradox not unknown in Socialist history, a bourgeois and Piedmontese bureaucrat who came to rule as arbiter of the fate of Italian socialism at this time. From 1901 to 1914 behind the history of Italian socialism there looms a figure of no heroic stature, possessing no membership card in any of the myriad working-class clubs, unattached to any of the various political factions. And yet Socialist congresses resounded with his name, to curse or to defend; Socialist electoral campaigns were to be waged for or against him; Socialist newspapers and periodicals were to devote vast amounts of space to his personality and his policies; Socialist triumphs or defeats were to depend, in a large measure, on his disposition and desires; Socialist leaders were to be made and unmade because of his conduct or words. Turati, Bissolati, Labriola, Treves, Mussolini even, might choose to consider themselves independent leaders of Italian socialism, but behind them stood always the shadow of a prosaic administrator from the mountains of Piedmont: Giovanni Giolitti.

When Italian socialism was still only a scattering of local units unnoticed by most political leaders, Giolitti said that if statesmen and workers agreed upon a program, one had the certainty that that program answered the real needs of the country (1882).[14] Seven years later he had reached the point of injecting a quasi-Marxist note in a financial report (December 16, 1889) in which he said that in the modern world economic questions tend to gain the upper hand over all others; this was especially

[12] Salvemini, in *Critica Sociale*, March 1, 1907; see his *Tendenze vecchie e necessità nuove*, p. 48.

[13] I. Bonomi, *Leonida Bissolati*, p. 59. C. Curcio, *L'eredità del Risorgimento*, pp. 91–92, says: "Socialism, even if from a pessimistic point of view, was of the heritage of the Risorgimento."

[14] Letter to electors, October 15, 1882, see L. Salvatorelli, ed., *Giolitti*, p. ii.

true in countries like Italy, with democratic regimes, since upon the solution of such questions depended the welfare of those new classes of the people which had been called to participate in the government of the state, of the province, and of the communes.[15] Two years later (December 7, 1891) he said the social question was the sole test for the differentiation of political parties, and that its solution would be much more difficult than that of political questions.[16] Speaking against the Pelloux restrictive measures in the Chamber (December 18, 1898), Giolitti had taken a stand against the reaction when he said to the applause of the Left: "And should we after fifty years of free life restrict our liberties on account of tumults which had their first origin in an exceptional condition of misery?"[17]

Ten days before the formation of the Zanardelli cabinet, on February 4, 1901, Giolitti had exhorted the Conservatives in the Chamber to consider that "the Italian people do not have revolutionary tendencies; the Italian people tend, by a long tradition, to have trust in government, and no people have perhaps suffered through the centuries, with so much resignation, evils so grave as have the Italian people."[18] A period of social justice, he continued, inspired by government and the ruling classes, would draw the masses to established institutions in the rôle of a new Conservative force, a new element of prosperity and greatness, no longer a whirlwind that would overthrow the fortunes of the country.[19] But it was in his famous speech as Minister of the Interior in the Zanardelli cabinet (June 21, 1901) that Giolitti gained the name of a true Liberal democrat who set himself against the reactionary currents of the preceding years.[20] Answering the criticism of the Conservatives (among them Sonnino, Di San Giuliano and Gavazzi) he stated to the approval of the Left, his thesis that something more than reactionary measures was necessary to gain the affection of the people for free institutions. This he proposed to do not with words, but with deeds to show that the monarchy was not the government of the bourgeois class.[21] "It is my profound conviction," Giolitti continued, "that socialism can be fought against only on the field of liberty; the other road has been tried and you have seen the results!"[22] It was on this occasion that Giolitti made his geographic interpretation of Italian socialism—an interpretation in which some of the most eminent anti-Giolittian Socialists were to agree for a different reason. "The truth is," he said, "that the Socialist movement has an exclusively economic basis. A little study of parliamentary geography will prove it. Take away

[15] Ibid., p. 21.
[16] Ibid., p. 33.
[17] Ibid., p. 37.
[18] Ibid., p. 45.
[19] Ibid., p. 46.
[20] See Aldo Ferrari, *Principi e forme della lotta politica nella terza Italia*, p. 25: "During Giolitti's Liberal experiment (1900–11), the ascending march of the working classes continued uninterruptedly with a crescendo of triumph. . . ."
[21] Salvatorelli, *op. cit.*, pp. 39–40 *passim*.
[22] Ibid., p. 41.

from the Socialist party all those who are elected in the Emilia, at Mantua, at Rovigo, at Bologna, all those from that plain where the suffering of the peasants is greatest and then tell me what is left of the Socialist party. . . ." [23] That "little study of parliamentary geography" of which Giolitti spoke was to become a wide and deep question contributing not a little to the dilemma of Italian socialism.

No sooner, then, was Giolitti at the helm of the Ministry of the Interior than he initiated his policy of conciliation toward the Socialists. Braving the scandalized and frightened Conservatives, he began a policy of social reforms which was resented as an all-out concession to a party but lately risen against the state. The reaction came, and in March 1902 the Chamber of Deputies resounded with the Conservative cry against his Liberal policy. At the sitting of March 11, 1902, Gavazzi pointed out to the Government that the Socialists had formed within the framework of the state a state of their own, with their own armies, their own bureaucracy, their own generals, their own schools and universities, their own supreme court, their official newspapers. This Socialist state, said Gavazzi,

. . . has now invaded every province of northern and central Italy, except, they say, the province of Cuneo [Giolitti's province]. . . . During these days the grand strategists of the Socialist party are studying a plan for the conquest of southern and insular Italy. . . . I believe that you Socialists owe it in justice to grant a laurel crown and the title of honorary president to the Honorable Minister of the Interior [Giolitti] who, with such luck, has approved your designs. . . . Be bold, O Socialists, for nothing is denied you! Prefects, the police, carabineers, handcuffs, secret funds, have no power against you: you enjoy in every circumstance a beneficent impunity. (Comments. Interruption by the Deputy Prampolini.) [24]

The following day Riccio attacked the Government on the grounds that its policy of conciliation was a failure, and that the Socialists had remained what they were, that is, antimonarchical.[25]

It was the Socialist deputy from the Emilia, Camillo Prampolini, who took upon himself the task of answering these accusations. "We are an essentially Reformist party," he said, "our revolution is inherent in the final results of the reforms we advocate and not in the means we use to attain these reforms. . . ." [26] Prampolini closed with an exhortation to the Conservatives not to antagonize the Italian workers:

Do not insult them by calling them immature for freedom. . . . It would be cruelly unjust to attempt to stifle with violence the instinctive aspiration that spurs these poor people toward a more advanced form of social life! (Bravo! Bene! Prolonged applause on the Extreme Left.) [27]

23 Ibid.
24 Atti Parlamentari. "Discussioni della Camera dei Deputati. Tornata dell'11 marzo 1902" (Session 1902–04), I, 26.
25 Ibid., "Tornata del 12 marzo 1902," I, 49.
26 Ibid., "Tornata del 13 marzo 1902," I, 104.
27 Ibid., I, 108.

Among the many issues that determined the fall of Zanardelli in 1903, the Socialist threat to hiss the Czar out of Italy, should his proposed visit take place, played no small part.[28] Turati, upon being invited by Giolitti to join his cabinet, had answered through his friend Bissolati that the participation of a Socialist like himself in the Government seemed premature and that it would be misunderstood and condemned by the masses.[29] The formation of the Giolitti Ministry on November 3, 1903, found Enrico Ferri as editor of the *Avanti*.[30] It was Ferri who, by his campaign against the new Minister of Finance, the sensitive and artistic Pietro Rosano, caused Giolitti his first trouble with his new cabinet and succeeded in arousing the country against the Socialists.[31] Thus it was that Giolitti found himself with a majority whose general tendencies were conservative, but whose support he could neither refuse nor ignore and who, in their turn, sensed that the Piedmontese himself was not as revolutionary as they had at first suspected him of being.

The strengthening of the Conservative tendencies in the Government coincided with the vociferous ascendancy in the Socialist party of left-wingers inspired by the doctrines of syndicalism.[32] Led by an active group of irreconcilables, among whom were Enrico Leone, Walter Mocchi, Paolo Mantica, Agostino Lanzillo, Alceste De Ambris, Paolo Orano, and Costantino Lazzari, the Syndicalists were slowly becoming a source of preoccupation for the Reformist leaders. These extremists had assailed the very citadels of the Turatian and Bissolatian forces in the North and at Milan, where Arturo Labriola's *Avanguardia Socialista* was playing havoc with the Reformists. Labriola was a man to fear.[33] A Neapolitan professor who possessed an acute intellect, a forceful personality, a torrential, persuasive eloquence, reinforced by a solid mastery of economics and of revolutionary psychology, Labriola had moved to Milan after the congress of Imola (1902) and had there become a thorn in the side of the progressive, easy-going Milanese comrades. The victory of these revolutionaries over the Reformists at the regional Brescia congress (April 1904) had first given the Lombard Right-wingers cause both to suspect and to expect the worst. The chief point of the resolution which was approved at Brescia was a complete reversal of Reformist approach: [34] the congress,

[28] Cf. Lodi, *op. cit.*, pp. 62–64.

[29] See Giolitti, *Memorie*, I, 191–93.

[30] Labriola, *op. cit.*, p. 204: "Enrico Ferri is a Constitutional Radical become Socialist for the same reasons that make him a popular orator. He does not possess true eloquence. . . ."

[31] Giolitti, *op. cit.*, I, 186–88.

[32] On Syndicalist theory in Italy, see G. Prezzolini, *La teoria sindacalista;* E. Leone, *Il Sindacalismo;* A. Lanzillo, *La disfatta del Socialismo;* and A. Salucci, *Il crepuscolo del socialismo,* especially pp. 135–98.

[33] On Labriola's forceful personality, see S. Cilibrizzi, *Storia parlamentare*, III, 284: ". . . Arturo Labriola was not only gifted with a brilliant mind, but possessed also an extensive knowledge of economic affairs and a singular facility and impetuousness with the spoken word. In fact, tempestuous eloquence was Arturo Labriola's outstanding characteristic."

[34] The resolution is quoted in full by Michels, *op. cit.*, pp. 313–14.

while reaffirming the permanent and intransigent revolutionary character of proletarian action, asserted that the transformation of the political organization of the proletariat into a "parliamentary, opportunistic, constitutional and potentially monarchical" party was a degeneration of the Socialist spirit. It condemned any further collaboration with the "bourgeois Government," to whom it left the task of temporary reforms, while it reserved for the party the use of any means of attack or of defense against the state and the Government including the use of violence in cases where it might be necessary. Walter Mocchi, moreover, made the exegesis by giving a detailed account of the uses and potentialities of violent agitation whose ultimate aim should be the revolutionary expropriation of the bourgeoisie.[35]

The fearful day which Labriola and his comrades had predicted at the national Socialist congress of Bologna (April 8–11, 1904) and forcefully reiterated at the regional Brescia congress seemed to have dawned, not in a thousand years, as Mocchi had said but in September 1904, with the first successful general strike the world had ever witnessed.

As usual, the initial spark came from the South and the Islands. The South, as has been already pointed out, had been forsaken by almost everyone in the wave of prosperity and optimism and progress sweeping over the rest of the country. The promised reductions in taxes, the increase in wages, all aid so often spoken of had failed to materialize. It was therefore natural that the resentment of the exploited peasants should periodically find vent in violent agitation, directed as a rule against the nearest source of authority, the commune. The year 1904 was especially marked by such outbreaks. On May 17 a peasants' riot at Cerignola resulted in the killing of two demonstrators and the wounding of seven others by the police. On September 4, there was another riot at Buggerù, and more repressions. When the news of still another at Castelluzzo was received on September 16, the Milanese Chamber of Labor, carried by the turbulent eloquence of Labriola and Mocchi, proclaimed a general strike by acclamation.[36]

The strike spread like wildfire from Milan over all Italy. There were public protests and strikes interspersed with violence at Milan, Genoa, Turin, Venice, Verona, Brescia, Rome, Naples, and the smaller cities.[37] For four days, September 16–20, Italy seemed to have become a Syndicalist possession. The Reformists themselves had had to tolerate, if not actually advocate and approve the strike, although it was repugnant to their true inclination, in order not to antagonize the masses and especially their electors. The bourgeois and conservative classes took fright; the Govern-

[35] Ibid., p. 315.

[36] The text of the resolution was reported by the Corriere della Sera on September 16, 1904, as follows: "The Assembly of members of the Camera del Lavoro, faced with the new outrages caused by the sanguinary wantonness of ruffians of a homicidal Government, proclaims the general strike as a sign of protest and indignation."

[37] For Labriola's account of the Milan situation, see op. cit., pp. 245–52; another account is Marazio, Il Partito Socialista Italiano e il Governo, pp. 137–64.

ment hid behind promises of punishment for the agents responsible for the initial cause of the strike. On the twentieth of September the leaders called off the demonstration, most of them contented, as Labriola said, that they had proved to the masses that "five minutes of direct action were worth as many years of parliamentary chatter." [38]

The dissolution of the Chamber in October and the general elections of November 6 and 13 followed, in large measure, as a reaction to the insurrection. The frightened bourgeoisie and the Liberal-Conservatives determined to make a stand at the elections, and they were aided by the Vatican concern over the revolutionary character of the riots. It was against this background that Pius X issued his modification to the *non expedit* already described. The reaction to the excesses of the Socialists thus found expression in the result of the elections, in which the Socialist parliamentarians lost six seats.[39] Giolitti was contented, for, he said, the conservative character of the new Chamber would teach a lesson to socialism and to revolutionary theorists by showing that "the Italian people . . . did not intend to permit certain limits to be exceeded by any side." [40] The intellectual agility by which Giovanni Giolitti was able to rationalize and fit into a pattern all the various trends and events of the Italian social and political scene was a quality to fear or to admire, depending in whose favor that ability was practised.

The Reformist leaders, faced with a more complete reaction than they had deserved, hastened to show that their participation in the strike was not derived from profound conviction or policy but that it had been contingent upon the situation, the chief responsibility for which rested with the revolutionaries. The general strike, said Leonida Bissolati, as an insurrection could not be beneficial to the proletariat except upon condition that it have a well-determined and precise aim, without which it became only an abortive revolution serving merely to provoke and reinforce reaction. The leaders of the strike had not been able to give it an aim either in external circumstances or in the consciousness of the masses, and for that reason it had failed.[41] And Filippo Turati, himself pricked by a remark of Giolitti that the Socialists should learn not to throw stones at the soldiers, had burst out in the Chamber of Deputies with a disavowal of violence:

You know that we have always preached against violence; this is bad faith; it is not you [Giolitti] who should come to tell these lies, for you know that we have always maintained public order: for four years we have been your policemen for nothing.[42]

[38] Michels, *op. cit.*, p. 319. For Giolitti's opinion see his *Memorie*, I, 211–12.
[39] For the economic basis of the reaction to Socialist excesses, see E. Corbino, *Annali dell'economia italiana*, V, 27.
[40] Giolitti, *op. cit.*, I, 215.
[41] *Critica Sociale*, XIV (1904), 355.
[42] In the Chamber of Deputies, on December 15, 1904, quoted by Michels, *op. cit.*, p. 242.

Turati's words reëchoed, significantly, Labriola's verdict on the inefficacy of parliamentary action, and seemed at the same time a confession of resentful impotence on the part of the Reformists.

Could Turati's words be interpreted as a statement of democratic socialism's bankruptcy? The Extremists thought so, and many of the Reformists themselves were to begin to doubt the ultimate efficacy of Reformist philosophy and tactics. The next four years was the most confused period of internal party struggles in the history of Italian socialism. But it was also a period of consolidation of power on the part of the Reformists, who finally emerged triumphant at the Florence congress of 1908.

The Reformists received invaluable aid from the rise of the General Confederation of Labor (*Confederazione Generale del Lavoro*) in 1906. As in all countries, the Italian working-class movement was not identical with the Socialist movement, although its leaders had usually come from the Socialist intelligentsia.[43] It may be said that in general Italy possessed two main types of working-class organization: the working-class leagues and the trades federations.[44] These two types with their numerous ramifications and sub-types formed, during the first decade of the twentieth century, a splendid net of working-class associations throughout the peninsula and, even if thinly, in the Islands. When labor bureaus had begun to rise during the decade 1890–1900 they were naturally concentrated in the more industrialized section of Italy; their chief centers were in such northern cities as Milan, Turin, Piacenza, Bologna, Brescia, Cremona, Monza, Pavia, Parma, Padua, Genoa. The aim of the bureaus was to furnish a central local organization for the various trade leagues already in existence, taking over the functions of legal representation of the working classes. Their functions included also resistance and specific programs for the solution of practical problems. But as such they based their action on a purely economic basis, and were in some measure suspect to the Socialists, whose principles were founded on the efficacy of political action. In 1902 there rose at Milan a Central Office for Labor Bureaus and Resistance (*Segretariato centrale per la camere del lavoro e per la resistenza*), whose mission was to coördinate the forces of local workers' unions, represented by the bureaus, and of the national organizations, represented by the federations. *Pari passu* with the ascendancy of reformism in the Socialist party after 1904 there was the rise of Reformist exponents within the Central Office, and it was through their efforts that in 1906 that office was transformed into the General Confederation of Labor, with Reformist tendencies and under Reformist leaders: Rinaldo Rigola,

[43] There is as yet no definitive work on the Italian working-class movement. The following may be consulted for brief and limited treatment. A. Cabrini, "L'Organizzazione dei lavoratori," in A. Vallardi, ed., *Mezzo secolo di vita italiana,* pp. 112–17; Michels, *Il proletariato e la borghesia* and *Storia critica;* E. Lémonon, *L'Italie économique et sociale, 1861–1912;* V. Porri, *L'evoluzione economica italiana nell'ultimo cinquantennio,* pp. 72–354; also the *Annuario Statistico Italiano.*

[44] Lémonon, *op. cit.,* p. 380.

General Secretary; Pietro Chiesa, Ettore Reina, and Felice Quaglino.[45]

The Syndicalists, sensing what a powerful arm the newborn Confederation could be for their Reformist antagonists, had tried to organize a counter movement, the National Committee for Resistance (*Comitato nazionale della resistenza*) in Parma (1907), but with little measure of success. Not that the Confederation could be viewed as a political organ at the disposal of the Socialist party. As a matter of fact, the leaders of the party themselves realized that party and Confederation were two distinct organizations, the one to discipline and spur the masses, the other to prepare the paths through which the organized masses were to pass.[46] In other words, the Confederation was the economic organization through which the political mission of the party was to operate. Answering the criticism of the Syndicalists, who viewed the party as superfluous and parasitic, Rigola, the general secretary of the Confederation, pointed out that his organization did not try to influence and was not concerned with the political beliefs or party affiliation of its members.[47] Rigola asserted that the Confederation had definite anti-Syndicalist tendencies for, he said, "it is not true that the general strike is an instrument of conquest; nothing is gained with folded arms!"[48] Rigola and his companions by their organization and enlightened guidance of the Confederation [49] had furnished a great source of strength to the Reformists.

It was, however, this source of strength, which, finally triumphing at the Florence congress of 1908, was to present the Italian Socialist movement with one of its most fundamental problems, the extent and character of Socialist and working-class organizations. On June 20, 1901, the day before Giolitti's famous speech in the Chamber in which the Minister had given his geographic interpretation of Italian socialism, the *Avanti!* had written in glowing terms of the Socialist work of morale among the peasants.[50] For thirty years, said the great Socialist daily, the workers of the

[45] Cf. R. Rigola, *L'evoluzione della Confederazione Generale del Lavoro*, pp. 5–20.

[46] Turati, *op. cit.*, p. 140, reprinted from an article in the *Critica Sociale*, October 1, 1908.

[47] *Resoconto stenografico del X Congresso Nazionale: Firenze, 19–20–21–22 settembre 1908*, pp. 202–11, *passim*.

[48] *Ibid.*, p. 217.

[49] Statistics for membership in the Confederation are given as follows by Rigola, *op. cit.*, p. 23:

1907 ....190,422 members
1908 ....262,006 "
1909 ....307,925 "
1910 ....356,420 "
1911 ....383,770 "
1912 ....309,871 "
1913 ....327,302 "
1914 ....320,858 "
1915 ....233,963 "
1919 ....1,159,062 "
1920 ....2,320,163 "

[50] *Avanti!*, June 20, 1901, quoted by I. Bonomi, *op. cit.*, pp. 67–68.

field had been ignorant of the fact that the liberal revolution had broken political oppression and conquered liberty. For many years the new forms of government had remained a dead letter for them, and no breath of liberation had come to stir the monotonous tranquility of the Italian countryside. Parliament was far away, law was unknown. But now these forsaken masses of the peasantry, the *Avanti!* continued, were sweeping upon the stage of history and, having realized the meaning of political life, were coming to the Government and to Parliament demanding their right to be free. This was no mere episode; it was revolution.[51]

Giolitti and the *Avanti!* were thus in substantial agreement. The masses of the peasantry to which reference was made, however, were chiefly those in the northern zones, especially in the Emilia and Romagna. These represented at one time the most squalid sections in the North, but by strenuous efforts of organization and under able and devoted leadership they had gradually become powerful strongholds of peasants' leagues, associations of resistance, labor bureaus, and other proletarian organs. The organizational work done by men like the evangelical Socialist Camillo Prampolini among the mass of small peasants, day workers, and hired laborers of the Reggiano was as admirable as it was necessary.[52] The Socialists could rightfully be proud of these developments in their fight to raise the life of these workers to a civilized level.

There were, however, other factors to be taken into consideration in order to create a true picture of the organizational developments of the Italian peasantry. In 1910, for example, out of the eight million potentially organizable workers in Italy, only 843,811 were actually organized in the various labor bureaus, leagues, and federations.[53] Of those organized, about 390,000 belonged to peasants' organizations, and of them only about 100,000 were in the South and the Islands.[54] Even after allowance is made for the different levels of agricultural labor in the South and for the various other factors which may have discouraged attempts to organize the peasantry, the figure is very low considering the fact that Italy was hardly a land of peasant proprietors.[55]

Following the Bakuninist-Anarchist agitation of the eighties and the sporadic outbursts of the nineties of which the *Fasci siciliani* were the most significant, organized socialism can hardly be said to have made great inroads in the South. As late as 1904, for every 10,000 inhabitants the Emilia-Romagna furnished 201 members to the Socialist party, Tuscany 67, Piedmont 53, Lombardy 44, Latium 28, while the average for the South and the Islands was 10.7, with as low as 7 and 5 for Calabria and

[51] *Ibid.,* p. 68.
[52] On the Reggiano working-class movement, see the illuminating essay by G. Zibordi, *Saggio sulla storia del movimento operaio in Italia.*
[53] Cabrini, "L'organizzazione dei lavoratori," in Vallardi, *op. cit.,* p. 117.
[54] Cf. Salvemini, *op. cit.,* pp. x–xi, *passim.*
[55] Lémonon, *op. cit.,* p. 383, gives 400,000 families (1,300,000 individuals) as cultivating their own land (1913).

Sardinia respectively.[56] Moreover, although the phenomenon was by no means limited to the South alone, the members of the Socialist party from the South belonged chiefly to the urban intellectual centers and derived as a rule from middle-class and petit-bourgeois origins.[57] It was also by no mere coincidence that most of the leaders of the Extremist wing of Italian socialism, and especially syndicalism, were Southerners.

Given the different material, political, and social levels of culture in North and South, it became inevitable that the Socialist movement too was to be faced with deep problems arising from those differences. But just as the general question of the South had required years of devoted study and agitation on the part of the disinterested men who were first faced with the task of making the country conscious of the question, so too the Socialist version of the question of the South required hard work and persistent propaganda before it could become a live problem in the consciences of the more fortunate, therefore more optimistic, Socialists of the North.

The significance of Gaetano Salvemini in the Italian Socialist movement had its origins in the man's zeal and impassioned belief in the human dignity and in the potential value as citizens of his countrymen of the South. Born himself from among the disinherited of Apulia, Salvemini had devoted himself to the study of the class struggle in thirteenth-century Florence and later to that exemplar of uprightness and devotion to the principles of justice, Giuseppe Mazzini.[58] He had thrown himself early into the Socialist movement in the dark times of Adowa, when socialism was a mission of faith and the only promise of redemption. Salvemini's own faith in, and hope for, the fate of the brutalized masses of his country had been unbounded. But since he had become a part of the Northern movement he was struck by disillusionment of his fellow-workers. A profound abyss separated these Northern agitators and *duci* of socialism from the poor people he had left behind in the numerous Molfettas of the South. These Northerners would have to be made to understand and to act, they would have to be enlightened and spurred by being shown whole provinces where unbelievable poverty was the common, relentless daily fate of men.

Salvemini soon began his campaign of enlightenment. The pages of the *Critica Sociale,* of the *Avanti!,* of numerous other publications were filled with his pleas for understanding of the South. He lashed his Northern comrades for their complacency and smugness. He demanded moral aid and the joining of forces in the common fight for economic and social redemption. He spoke of freedom—political, social, economic, spiritual

[56] Roberto Michels, *Il proletariato e la borghesia,* p. 175, *passim.* Despite his statistics, Michels drew a very optimistic picture of Italian agrarian socialism. The Northern bias is very obvious in his treatment (pp. 175–87).

[57] Labriola, *Il Socialismo contemporaneo,* p. 280, note 1.

[58] *Magnati e popolani del comune di Firenze* (1900); *Mazzini* (1905). For a brief biography of Salvemini to 1918, see Destrée, *Figures italiènnes d'aujourd'hui,* pp. 135–58.

freedom—in accents so candid and sincere as to seem at once ingenuous
and noble. The political renovation of southern Italy, he wrote in 1903,
does not require the tutelage of the North, but only that the democratic
parties grant the progressive elements of the South a solid basis for
operation and work through universal suffrage, or at least to gain the
administrative franchise.[59] The economic phase of this renovation in the
South, however, required the aid of the state which, through the democratic parties, could alone discourage the northern protectionist magnates
from bleeding the South of its wealth. "Give us air to breathe politically,
give us the means to live economically, and then leave us alone, for we
shall know how to take care of ourselves": this was Salvemini's plea.[60]
Universal suffrage as a basic instrument of political reform was to become
his obsession. He returned again and again to the theme of 1903 in a
crescendo of exasperated hope until his final break with the party in 1910.

At the Florence congress of the Socialist party in 1908, when the Reformist forces to which he gave allegiance triumphed, Gaetano Salvemini
pounded once again on his themes, marring the excited and all-too-easy
optimism of his fellow victors. It was on this occasion that he most forcefully related the power, interference, pressures, and electoral corruption
of the Government (Giolitti) to the lack of universal suffrage. This ex-
plained, Salvemini said, the personal hatred of which Giolitti was the
object in the South, for "from 1860 to date we have had many ministers
who have trodden upon, who have corrupted southern Italy, but no one
has so systematically and so cynically trampled upon our honor and our
dignity!" [61] Only through universal suffrage could a real renovation
come.[62] And Salvemini closed his moving address with a reiteration of his
plea for the solidarity of the Northern comrades:

. . . It is your duty to make this sacrifice because you are Socialists, because you
should care not only for that part of the proletariat which is most developed and
powerful but also for the more backward part, that which is most in need of
your help! You can give us this solidarity, you must give it. It is the only help
worthy of free men: help us to become free, we shall do the rest! (*Bene! Bravo!
Great applause*).[63]

Upon being interrupted in the course of his Florence speech, Salvemini
had cried out that the uncivil interruptions were proof that "even in the
Socialist party there are two Italies." [64]

At the Milan congress of 1910 he made the initial speech which was to
dominate almost completely, with its fervid and sincere bluntness, the
entire proceedings.[65] The Italian Socialist party, Salvemini began, be-

[59] Under the pseudonym of "Rerum scriptor," *Critica Sociale*, XIII (1903), 35.
[60] *Ibid.*
[61] *Resoconto stenografico del X Congresso Nazionale (Socialista)*, p. 255.
[62] *Ibid.*, p. 256.
[63] *Ibid.*, p. 264.
[64] *Ibid.*, p. 257.
[65] *Resoconto stenografico dell'XI Congresso Nazionale del Partito Socialista Italiano: Milano, 21-22-23-24-25 ottobre 1910*, pp. 59-70.

tween 1900 and 1910 had done a magnificent work of organization among the advance guard of the movement in the North, but it was now high time that the promises made to the South began to be realized unless the party wanted to become just another Conservative party, a minority party.[66] The Northerners, instead, as their own strength grew, were becoming more indifferent and selfish: "That is why I can be quiet no longer: I protest against your indifference." [67] Salvemini then went on to make a profound analysis of the dilemma of the Italian Socialist party. The geographical triangle formed by Genoa-Milan-Ravenna had become a sort of privileged zone upon which all care and reforms and all forms of aid were lavished, while the great mass of workers outside that region were excluded from the benefits. The illusion had thus grown that a few nuclei conveniently situated geographically for economic and political action represented the entire working class. "We have believed a proletarian movement restricted to a few regions to be a national movement. Actually, the Italian proletariat, the real one today, is absent from our initiative." [68] With the growth of particularism, socialism had lost its original moral force as a party of impartial justice and freedom, and was thus losing all efficiency as the instrument for the emancipation of the entire working class: "Our party, instead, is slowly forsaking the class in order to become the instrument of partial conquests of a few groups. . . ." [69] He again demanded universal suffrage, but it must be as the result of proletarian activity, unsoiled by the hands of Giolitti, whom he called *"Il Ministro della mala vita"* (Minister of the Underworld).[70]

This proved to be Gaetano Salvemini's last public utterance as a member of the Italian Socialist party into which he had gone, as a young man, with such high hopes and such great expectations. It had been in truth a "disenchantment" for him, as Mario Vinciguerra has called it; another example of the class struggle between *magnati* and *popolani* this time within the Socialist party itself—a grim repetition of the fight between the *popolo grasso* and the humble plebs which Salvemini had studied in thirteenth- and fourteenth-century Florentine chronicles.[71] He broke with the party and soon after, with his *Unità*, returned to the battle almost alone. This ascetic of politics may with truth be called the anti-Machiavelli of contemporary society [72] who even in his long exile has never forsaken his great dream nor his fight for justice.

[66] *Ibid.,* p. 60.
[67] *Ibid.,* p. 61.
[68] *Ibid.,* p. 63.
[69] *Ibid.,* p. 68.
[70] *Ibid.,* p. 66: "There are moral necessities superior even to general reforms. Should universal suffrage be offered us by the Honorable Giolitti, but were the Honorable Giolitti to place it as a premise to the question of confidence in his Government, I would refuse to give my confidence and I would reject universal suffrage because, if granted on such a condition and by such a man, universal suffrage would come into the world dishonored. (*Signs of approval on the Left. Comments. Interruptions*)."
[71] Cf. M. Vinciguerra, *Un quarto di secolo, 1900–1925,* pp. 46, 48.
[72] E. Rota, *Una pagina di storia contemporanea—Gaetano Salvemini,* p. 15.

The very men who, within the party, had most strenuously combated Salvemini's general thesis were to return later to his theme with something like self-reproach and a sense of guilt. Turati, who since 1903 had tried to confute his friend's argument,[73] was to confess in 1911 that Salvemini's prediction in regard to universal suffrage as a mere grant from above was on its way to realization.[74] Other leaders also saw it. Oddino Morgari was to agree at Ancona in 1914, that, as Salvemini had said, there were two Italies, even for the Italian Socialist party.[75]

Salvemini had seen the party's problem of the South as no more than a part of the greater question of the relations between socialism and the Government, i.e., Giolitti. In a newspaper interview, Turati was reported to have said that the Socialists could have full trust in Giolitti since, although he fed "talk to his allies . . . to us, his adversaries, he gives positive facts." [76] It was exactly this grant of facts to the northern Socialists which caused the greatest doubts of Giolitti's motives. Had the shrewd Piedmontese really sensed the internal contradictions by which Italian socialism was torn? Was he playing on its double incapacity "to participate in government as well as to raise the barricades"? [77] There is little doubt that the attraction of socialism within the field of his power and influence was a point in Giolittian policy. Men as far apart as Arturo Labriola and Gaetano Salvemini agreed that Giolitti, by his flirtations with his concessions to certain sections of Northern socialism, had a double purpose: to temper, if not actually to tame, the revolutionary tendencies of those regions, and to assure himself the necessary Socialist votes to maintain his parliamentary majorities.[78]

Giolitti's own conduct and assertions and the continued support of the Reformist Socialists seemed to prove the success of his aims. In March 1911, with the fall of Luzzatti's ministry, Giolitti returned to the helm. He turned once again to the Socialists for support and invited Leonida Bissolati to accept a portfolio in his cabinet. But Bissolati, as in 1903 (this time in his own name), reiterated his belief that Italian socialism was

[73] Cf. *Critica Sociale*, XIII (1903), 3.

[74] *Resoconto stenografico del XII Congresso Nazionale del Partito Socialista Italiano: Modena, 15-16-17-18 ottobre 1911*, p. 208. Turati said: "The extension of the suffrage was demanded and advocated by us, but it is not, today, a Socialist and proletarian conquest. The value of every reform is always proportionate to the effort it requires for its realization."

[75] *Resoconto stenografico del XIV Congresso Nazionale del Partito Socialista Italiano: Ancona, 26-27-28-29 aprile 1914*, p. 90.

[76] *Nuovo Giornale* (Florence), March 9, 1908, quoted by Labriola, *Storia di dieci anni*, p. 306.

[77] This is the conclusion arrived at by "Spectator" in an essay, "Giovanni Giolitti," *Nuova Antologia*, CCLX (Ser. VII), 369. C. Barbagallo, *L'Italia dal 1870 ad oggi*, p. 71, tries to give the impression of a Socialist attempt to "dominate" Giolitti, "the stronger" of the two.

[78] Labriola, *Storia di dieci anni*, pp. 241-42, and p. 305: "The Honorable Giolitti ruled the Confederation of Labor and the Executive Committee (*Direzione*) of the Socialist party." See also Salvemini, *op. cit.*, pp. xiv-xvii, and pp. 123-24, *passim*.

too undeveloped to participate in government.[79] Once again Giolitti had succeeded in pointing up the Hamlet-like situation of Italian Socialist leaders—thereby indirectly contributing to the precipitation of another crisis within the party itself. As in 1904, he openly reproached the Socialists, when the Chamber convened, for their refusal to assume responsibility: "I believe that all who are in this Hall must, at certain moments, assume responsibilities. . . ." [80] In the same speech (April 8, 1911) he caused a pandemonium when he said: "Eight years have gone by, the country has gone ahead, the Socialist party has greatly moderated its program, Karl Marx has been relegated to the attic . . ." [81] An outburst of voices, protesting or approving, broke in upon Giolitti at that point, and the sentence remained forever suspended. But once again, it seemed, Giovanni Giolitti had shown himself as master of a certain ruthless logic in his characteristic manner which might be described as either casually intentional or intentionally casual.

It was Bissolati himself who, true to his promise to support the Government even while refusing participation in it,[82] made the apologia for Giolittian democracy. He predicted in the Chamber that by the realization of its proposal for universal suffrage Giolittian democracy would become the destroyer of *Giolittismo*.[83] For even after the country had gone through the tremendous events of the Libyan War, Bissolati, more than anyone else, could understand and appreciate Giolitti's reproach to the Socialists, as when Giolitti said:

The destinies of the proletariat are connected with those of the nation (*Bravo!*). The bitter economic competition among peoples finds its highest expression in the political struggle, and *the proletariat of a conquered people will never be a happy proletariat. (Signs of great approval and applause from all the benches, except those of the Extreme Left)*.[84]

But by 1911–12 new currents were agitating the country, and the Italian Socialist party was no longer merely a Liberal party with a Socialist banner. The congresses of Modena (October 1911) and Reggio Emilia (July 1912) had wrought a revolution within the party itself, and men with origins, passions, and aims that Giolitti and Bissolati had never fully understood and had, therefore, ignored or condemned had now come to positions of power within the ambit of Italian socialism.

[79] Cf. Giolitti, *op. cit.*, II, 288–90.

[80] *Atti Parlamentari*. "Discussioni della Camera dei Deputati. Tornata dell'8 aprile 1911" (Session 1909–13), XI, 13717.

[81] *Ibid.*

[82] Giolitti, *op. cit.*, II, 289, says: "Bissolati, however, told me that he thought he would be in a better position to help toward the realization of its program by not participating in the Government. This would facilitate his obtaining for the Government the positive, or at least the negative, support of his entire [Socialist] parliamentary bloc."

[83] L. Bissolati, "Sulla politica del Ministero," *L'Eloquenza*, I (1911), 270–84.

[84] *Atti Parlamentari*. "Discussioni della Camera dei Deputati. Tornata del 16 dicembre 1913" (Session of 1913–14), I, 486. Italics added.

In June 1914, when Giolitti was no longer officially in power, and the democratic socialism of which Bissolati had been the chief exponent was no longer the party policy, Italy witnessed a violent outburst of those political forces that had never been fully tamed. The tradition of mistrust was long, and the expressions of misgivings over the aim of the forces Giolitti had wanted to bring within the institutions of the state were many. The impotence of the state resulting from its policy of always giving in to extreme demands was an expression of fear and regret commonly spoken of,[85] and the growth of a state within the state, especially in the northern Socialist strongholds of Emilia-Romagna, had been noticed with misgivings.[86] Red Week of June 7 to 11 came as a terrible surprise to those who even until the end nourished the illusion that all Italian socialism had by now become a party of order within the state, as Giolitti had vowed to make it in 1901.[87]

Beginning as an anti-militarist protest at Ancona, on Sunday June 7, the Day of the *Statuto*, Red Week had grown into an insurrection spreading over all Italy from the "red" strongholds of the Romagna and the Marches. Enthusiastically supported by a man from the Romagna who was now editor of the powerful *Avanti!*—Mussolini—and led by men like Errico Malatesta who had had their revolutionary apprenticeship under Bakuninist anarchism, the insurrection finally assumed the aspect of another and more frightening general strike when the General Confederation of Labor gave it, if only reluctantly and for a short time, its powerful support. When the nightmare of a social upheaval had finally spent its full force and violence—an armistice, the *Avanti!* had called it on June 12—it was realized that the Italian Liberal state had passed successfully through one of the most dangerous moments in its history.[88]

On Monday, June 8, a group of Extremist deputies (including Turati, Morgari, Pietro Chiesa, Gaudenzi, Marangoni, and De Felice) had unsuccessfully attempted to have a request for adjournment passed by the Chamber as a protest "against the massacres of Ancona, the work of the public authorities." [89] The following day Prime Minister Salandra assumed full responsibility for the circular telegram he had sent out on

---

[85] Cf. R. De Cesare, *Mezzo secolo di storia italiana sino alla Pace di Losanna*, p. 170.

[86] For a description of the so-called Socialist "state within the state" in Emilia, see A. Ragghianti, *Gli uomini rossi all'arrembaggio dello Stato*. On p. 91, Ragghianti says: ". . . An entire region [Emilia] has drawn away from the control and authority of the state in such a way that quiet living must be contracted for in the offices of the [Socialist] Leagues; it cannot be guaranteed by law and authority. . . ."

[87] Cf. *La Voce*, VI (1914), No. 8, 35.

[88] *Avanti!*, June 12, 1914: "Armistice. The general strike that came to an end yesterday was the severest popular uprising that has shaken the Third Italy since 1870." The great Liberal-Conservative newspapers agreed; the *Giornale d'Italia*, June 16, 1914, going so far as speaking of "the bankruptcy of all confidence in the authority of the State," while the *Corriere della Sera*, June 13, 15, 1914, sarcastically described the bourgeois scare and the Government's weakness in the face of danger.

[89] *Atti Parlamentari*. "Discussioni della Camera dei Deputati. Tornata dell'8 giugno 1914" (Session of 1913–14), IV, 3857.

May 31 to all the prefects of the kingdom forbidding any public meetings designed as an antimilitaristic demonstration on June 7.[90] At the same meeting of the Chamber Deputy Modigliani condemned the Government and especially Salandra for their usurpation of the name of Liberals.[91] When, on June 10, the Socialist deputies again raised an uproar in the Chamber, it was President Marcora, himself coming from the *Estrema*, who told them: "But you do nothing but stir up continual violence: this is your condemnation!" [92]

The Socialist parliamentary group itself was to approve, on June 19, 1914, a motion presented by Filippo Turati in which it was asserted that the fundamental aim of socialism was not to be realized by "outbursts of disorganized mobs" whose failure succeeded only in loosening "the most savage and stupid currents of internal reaction." [93] Claudio Treves was to take up the same theme for lengthy discussion in the *Critica Sociale*, when he stated that *teppa* (hooliganism) was not to be confused with the orderly Socialist movement whose aim was a democratic revolution to be accomplished through propaganda, education, coöperation, parliamentary action, and organization rather than through the futile Republican, Anarchist, and Syndicalist uprisings poetically glorified and prosaically advocated by the fiery editor of the *Avanti!*, Benito Mussolini.[94]

From its first riotous appearance through its constructive Liberal phase during the years of Giolitti's power to its re-appearance on the eve of the First World War as a party of revolution, Italian socialism seemed to have come a full circle. All the problems it had faced throughout its involved career returned now to confront the old Socialist leaders who saw their creation of many years' toil once again take the road of violence which they hoped had long since been left behind. The stress and strain in Italian socialism had slowly become a torment, and its crisis a long convulsive agony.

[90] *Ibid.*, "Tornata del 9 giugno 1914," IV, 3864, for text of the circular telegram.
[91] *Ibid.*, p. 3887.
[92] *Ibid.*, "Tornata del 10 giugno 1914," IV, 3955.
[93] Quoted by Filippo Meda, *op. cit.*, p. 66.
[94] "Il Vice" (Claudio Treves), "Cause ed effetti," *Critica Sociale*, XXIV (1914), 178; "Il Vice," "La 'teppa' e la rivoluzione socialista," *Critica Sociale*, XXIV (1914), 193–95, *passim*.

VI

THE DAY OF THE REFORMISTS

SOCIALIST PARTY CONGRESSES, 1900–1910

*La libertà, questa grande redentrice, è, nel suo primo
sperimento, avviluppata da pericoli:* periculosa libertas.*

FILIPPO TURATI

THERE could be no greater mistake than to view the crisis of Italian
socialism as a unique or isolated phenomenon in the midst of a
smooth-running international movement. Italian socialism, despite its
significant national characteristics, was after all only a part and reflection
of the world Socialist movement. When Benedetto Croce, for example
asserted in 1911 that socialism was dead, he did not deem it necessary to
qualify his verdict by applying it to any particular nation.[1] He stated
simply and categorically that, in his opinion, socialism as an international
movement and ideal, having served its historic function as the poetry of
the working-class movement, and having contributed to the intellectual
and moral awakening and elevation of individuals and masses, was now
dead. True or false as Croce's verdict might be regarded, the Italian philosopher's opinion must nevertheless be accepted or refuted on an international and not any national basis.

Yet Italian socialism, as has already been described, must be studied in
its national and domestic developments in order to understand the course
and character its phase of the crisis took. Some of the problems it faced
and successfully or unsuccessfully attacked have already been treated, and
it will have been noticed that most of them originated outside the Socialist
party itself, that is, they arose and were viewed as being essentially inherent
in the environment and circumstances of the whole Italian scene. It
remains to be seen here how the leaders of Italian socialism themselves
reacted to the problems they faced, what they contributed to their solution, and how they themselves consciously or unconsciously contributed
to developments within their party to justify the last sentence of the preceding chapter. A methodical study of the official stenographic reports of
the Italian Socialist congresses has been made, of which certain developments will be described and some impressions and conclusions will be
given in this brief treatment.

As early as 1873, when his feud with Bakunin was at its height, Karl
Marx in one of his frequent moods of biliousness had passed a bitter judg-

* "Freedom, this great redeemer, is, in its first experiment, surrounded by dangers:
periculosa libertas." Filippo Turati in *Critica Sociale* (July 16, 1901).

[1] In an interview reprinted in Croce, *Cultura e vita morale*, pp. 150–59.

ment upon the leaders of the Italian International, whom he characterized as a troop of *declassés*, the refuse of the bourgeoisie.[2] Blinded by his envious anger at the success his antagonist, the "Holy Father," as he called Michael Bakunin, was having in Italy, Marx either did not see or preferred to ignore the social and professional origins and the mental caliber of such early leaders of Italian socialism as Carlo Cafiero, Emilio Covelli, Errico Malatesta, Giuseppe Fanelli, Francesco Saverio Merlino, Tito Zanardelli, and Andrea Costa. But while the facts were never examined, Marx's unjustified epithets stuck and, which is worse, were repeated with variations as applying to later leaders under other conditions.

As a rule, after its founding, the social and professional composition of the Socialist party and the character of the leaders of the movement in Italy followed the main lines of the international developments in so far as there was always a fairly large mass of party members from the working classes under the leadership of a rather small élite of intellectuals, and professional organizers, and men from other than the purely manual occupations. In 1903, for example, of 33,686 Italian Socialist party members actually enrolled who answered a questionnaire: 72.18% were urban or rural workers, 14.29% were petit bourgeois, 3.80% educated people, and the remainder unclassifiable.[3] Of a total of thirty-three Socialist deputies for the same year, on the other hand, there were: twenty-eight, or 84.84%, university graduates of bourgeois origins; three, or 9.09%, petit bourgeois; two, or 6.06%, authentic workers.[4] Two factors should, however, be kept in mind in appraising the last figures: that in Italy there was no parliamentary remuneration, and the Socialist party was, in contrast to the German and the French parties, very poor.[5]

In studying the reports of Socialist party congresses, the predominance of intellectual and professional men should be kept in mind. It is not infrequent to find occasional outbursts of anti-intellectual reaction within the party, the usual accusation being that it was dominated by lawyers. At the Florence congress (1908), the question of too many lawyers in the congress caused an uproar:

Gentile: Oh! dear friends, the truth is that we sent to the congresses too many lawyers and too many professors (*Loud protests. Epithets. Tumult*).
Voices: It is true! It is true!
A Voice: Lawyers or no lawyers, we are all Socialists.
Another Voice: Respect the workers then! You do not want the workers to speak (*Very loud shouts*).[6]

[2] Cf. R. Michels, *Il proletariato e la borghesia*, pp. 63, 64–76 for a rebuttal.
[3] *Ibid.*, p. 137.
[4] *Ibid.*, p. 98.
[5] Until 1908 not even Germany provided pay for members of the Reichstag, but the German Socialist party supplied most of the maintenance of the Socialist members. France had adequate pay for members of its Chamber of Deputies. In Italy pay for the deputies was provided for in 1912.
[6] *Resoconto stenografico del X Congresso Nazionale: Firenze, 19–20–21–22 settembre 1908*, p. 161.

At the Ancona congress (1914) the question of the lawyers came up again, and it was Giovanni Lerda, a self-educated intellectual and one of the most respected leaders of the party until his expulsion, who cried out:

> . . . We must get rid of all the lawyers, of all the professors, of all the doctors who now defile the Socialist party, just as we must get rid tomorrow of all the opportunists who come into the Socialist party in order the better to "succeed" . . .[7]

The last phrase was obviously aimed at Mussolini who had just made an anti-Masonic tirade which had hit Lerda.

It was unquestionably true that from its beginnings Italian socialism was dominated by intellectuals, but this had been inevitable and was perhaps not altogether a liability seen against the Italian political and social scene in the years immediately preceding Giolitti's rise to power.[8] The adherence of so many cultured young people, especially in the decade 1890-1900, had given the Italian Socialist movement the characteristics of an intellectual youth movement with all the faults and advantages of such movements in contradistinction to the older and more doctrinally solid developments in Germany and in France. Not that Italy lacked either leaders tried in the fire of revolutionary tradition or a Socialist doctrinal heritage, but in most cases the Italian natural and socio-political environment had tended to emphasize action and method more than doctrine, a tendency which left Italian socialism more susceptible to new currents. This could be considered the result either of a lack of firm principles or of Italian psychological plasticity, depending on the viewpoint. It was by no means, however, a fundamental limitation, becoming according to circumstances a virtue or a defect. Fundamentalism of any kind was always suspect in Italy.

Yet it was precisely the question of orthodoxy in principles and methods that was to be the predominant cause of numerous schisms, tendencies, and expulsions within Italian socialism during the period. It was at the Rome congress of September 8 to 11, 1900, that the Italian Socialist party, with the self-assurance the conquests of 1898-1900 had given it, adopted the very fountain-head of subsequent strife within it: a maximum program designed to keep alive the grand principles and final aims of the party, and a minimum program containing the principal features of goals immediately attainable within the framework of the existing social order in Italy.[9] The maximum program was a reassertion of the proletarian struggle whose ultimate achievement was to be the conquest of the bourgeois state in order to transform it from an instrument of oppression into an instrument for the economic and political expropriation of the ruling

[7] Resoconto stenografico del XIV Congresso Nazionale del Partito Socialista Italiano: Ancona, 26-27-28-29 aprile 1914, p. 138.

[8] Cf. I. Bonomi, "Il Congresso Socialista di Bologna," Nuova Antologia, CXL (1904), 129-30, passim.

[9] Roberto Michels, Storia critica, pp. 212-22, gives in full both the programs and the reports upon them.

class.[10] The minimum program consists of such immediate aims as: (1) universal suffrage and the referendum; (2) assumption of full responsibility for their actions by all governmental offices; (3) abolition of the Senate, but salaries for deputies; (4) freedom of speech and assembly; (5) the absolute neutrality of the state in all conflicts between capital and labor.[11] These essentially political demands were further reinforced by the demand for numerous economic, financial, educational, and administrative reforms aiming at a complete transformation of the Italian social structure.

The Italian Socialist movement was from this time forward to oscillate between the limits marked by "maximum" and "minimum." Practically all the tendencies by which it was to be harassed were nothing but variations of the opposing motives of revolution and evolution, of radical as opposed to democratic methods. Henceforth individual Italian Socialist leaders were to bring all their intellectual, moral, and psychological resources to the rationalization of the ideas and methods their personal origins, idiosyncrasies, and outlook made inevitable for them. The test question was this: were the Italian people remiss, and therefore in need of continual spur to action, or were they impulsive, and therefore in need of restraint? [12] The recrimination that broke out after Red Week in 1914 between the *Avanti!* and the *Critica Sociale,* i.e., between reformists who were a step removed from bourgeois radicalism and revolutionists who were a pace away from anarchism, had a long history which through Turati the democrat and Labriola the Syndicalist harked back to Jean Jaurès and Georges Sorel, to Karl Marx and Michael Bakunin. The nemesis of history lay heavy upon Italian socialism.

At the next congress (Imola, 1902), it was Filippo Turati (1857–1932) who won the day. Born of respectable Milanese parentage, elegantly educated, inclined in his youth to write bad Italian verse, Turati became, nevertheless, the dean of Italian Reformist socialism. It was he who had spread the seeds of Marxism in Italy through the pages of the *Critica Sociale* which he had founded and, since 1891, had edited with Anna Kuliscioff. A speaker who combined volubility and wit, he enlivened his discussions of serious issues with an irony which was as pleasant to listen to as it was incapable of probing deeply or of permanently solving the questions he so dexterously treated. As a writer he had a surface facility in both language and ideas. But Turati was frequently formidable, usually effective, always sincere. His inexhaustible fund of *spirito* (irony and wit), his elegant style, his fluent tones were valuable qualities in an environment that was often oppressively sober. Turati has been called an artist

---

[10] *Ibid.,* p. 213.

[11] *Ibid.,* p. 219.

[12] *Ibid.,* pp. 238–34, for an analytic summary of the origins and premises of Italian reformism and revolutionary tendencies. The polemic was synthesized during the period by characterizing the aim of socialism to be either *eccitatori dei torpidi* (exciters of the phlegmatic) or *moderatore degli impulsivi* (moderator of the impulsive).

of socialism, a description truer than most such phrases.[13] He had a strain of solid Milanese Liberal conservatism which all his Socialist education and agitation never completely managed to suppress. Socialism, he said at Imola, should be a middle course between anarchism and radicalism, for had not democracy—Giolittian democracy it was now—rendered less violent the class conflicts and had it not, by its grant of the suffrage, of political education, of civil arms to the people, relegated to the museum uprisings, pronunciamentos, and the barricades? [14]

At the Imola congress Turati's reformism triumphed over the revolutionary tendency represented by Arturo Labriola and Enrico Ferri, but the formal and immediate unity of the party seemed to have been preserved by a resolution which frankly recognized the existence of the two uncompatible tendencies.[15] When the Socialist leaders met again at Bologna (April 8–11, 1904), the unity established at Imola at first hung in the balance. The Reformist forces were still led by Turati and Bissolati, the revolutionary wing by Labriola, Leone, and Marangoni, but a new group, the Center, led by Ferri, had made its appearance. Turati expressed the fear that the congresses of the Socialist party were becoming conferences of parties where discussions were "carried on academically while millions of proletarians expect us to show results." [16] But Labriola, even while extending his hand cordially toward Turati in a show of solidarity of views, did not forget to reiterate his own thesis:

I believe that the Socialist party, and not only that of our country, will remain in a state of permanent crisis until it succeeds in renouncing two illusions: that socialism is the result of an addition of reforms, and that these must be accomplished through parliaments. . . . *Reformism is not a manner of substantiating socialism, it is rather its most violent negation.*[17]

Enrico Ferri introduced a motion which was aimed at maintaining unity; it won the day by a majority of 16,304 votes out of 32,225 members represented at the congress.[18] Ferri's motion granted a respite to both forces, but the struggle was by no means definitely decided.[19]

---

[13] A. Salucci, *Il crepuscolo del Socialismo*, p. 302. For a short critical biography of Turati, see the sketch by his close friend and collaborator Claudio Treves, *Un Socialista: Filippo Turati;* also Salvemini, "Filippo Turati," in *Encyclopedia of the Social Sciences* (New York, 1937), VIII, 130–31.

[14] Quoted in F. Meda, *Il Partito Socialista Italiano*, p. 23.

[15] The revolutionary leader himself, Arturo Labriola, *Storia di dieci anni*, p. 137, characterized Imola as a *guazzabuglio indemoniato*, a mad-house situation, in which his adversary Turati with the full resources of his superficial genius had consciously confused the issues. Labriola's characterization of Turati and his friends (p. 138) was extremely partisan: "Turati and his friends—who had pledged themselves to the Government—wished only to assure the Government of the continuation of their parliamentary support and of a very remiss policy on the part of the Socialist groups. The rest was talk (*letteratura*)."

[16] *Rendiconto dell'VIII Congresso Nazionale: Bologna, 8–9–10–11 aprile 1908*, p. 106.

[17] *Ibid.*, pp. 143, 147, in bold type in the stenographic report.

[18] This was on a second ballot; *ibid.*, pp. 160–61.

[19] Meda, *op. cit.*, p. 25, asserts that Turati had been so discouraged by the apparent failure of his unitary dream that he had been prepared to break from the party before Ferri introduced his winning motion.

One of the younger Reformists, Ivanoe Bonomi, soon after the Bologna congress had publicly predicted great things for the revolutionary forces of Arturo Labriola; [20] before the year was out his prediction had come true—truer perhaps than he had intended, for, as has already been seen, in September 1904 the first general strike broke out in Italy. Syndicalism was in the ascendancy. When the Rome congress assembled (October 7–10, 1906) under the presidency of the venerable Andrea Costa, the party's Pandora's box was finally opened. The meeting became so tumultuous that on October 9 Costa offered his resignation as presiding officer, but he was restrained by a great demonstration of esteem by all the members. [21]

Enrico Ferri's Center, become by now a full-grown tendency known as integralism, wanted to be something to everybody. "Integralist thought," said Oddino Morgari, one of the exponents, "affirms that there is no antithesis between the concept of violence as such and that of the gradual development of socialism within the very bosom of bourgeois society." [22] The successful Integralist order of the day, with its delicate balancing ("integration") of the Reformist and the revolutionary Syndicalist programs seemed proof once again that logic could be stronger than passions. It approved revolutionary aims and advocated evolutionary methods; it affirmed the use of legal means and held in abeyance the use of violence; it admitted the efficacy of direct action and approved the utility of social legislation. [23] It was in fact a restatement of issues, not their solution, and as such its only positive result was to furnish all factions with material for arguments for the next two years. Sensing the popularity of the Integralist's appeal for a middle course, the Reformists joined forces with Ferri. [24] The Syndicalists struggled on alone taking whatever consolation they could from Labriola's apostrophe to the Reformists: "You will be left alone, but the crisis will automatically recur again among you. The Socialist party is condemned to a permanent and inescapable crisis. *We* [the Syndicalists] are the health of socialism." [25]

The anti-intellectualist note was injected by Enrico Leone who said that it was very strange indeed to see a party which was supposedly that of the workers send "a representation composed exclusively of professional men" into the national parliament. [26] Leone then aroused the laughter of the Reformists when he stated that workingmen were not sent to Parliament because the Socialists feared that their ungrammatical language

---

20 I. Bonomi, *op. cit.*, p. 129.

21 Cf. *Resoconto stenografico del IX Congresso Nazionale: Roma, 7–8–9–10 ottobre 1906*, pp. 177–79.

22 *Ibid.*, p. 60.

23 *Ibid.*, p. 276, for Integralist motion.

24 *Ibid.*, p. 281, for results of voting:

Integralist motion	26,943 votes
Syndicalist "	5,279 votes
Intransigent "	1,101 votes
Abstained	753 votes

25 *Ibid.*, p. 129.

26 *Ibid.*, p. 244.

might discredit them before the bourgeoisie.[27] Turati, on the other hand, called the Syndicalists "mystics, messianics, who await a kind of apocalypse" in which they would lead "an army of underfed, hungry, uncouth and coarse people, an army of slaves, to realize the complete liberty of the world!"[28]

By the time the Florence congress had assembled in 1908 the "mystics, messianics and esthetes" of socialism, the Syndicalists, had gone their separate way. Between 1906 and 1908 the Syndicalists had reached the height of their power and had consolidated their forces. There was a systematization of their doctrines and their organs of propaganda, with the help of such powerful Syndicalist periodicals as *Il Divenire Sociale* (Rome), *L'Avanguardia Socialista* (Milan), *La Lotta Proletaria, Sindacalista, Socialista, Rivoluzionaria* (Mirandola), *La Lotta del Lavoro* (Florence), and later *Pagine Libere* (Lugano), had continued their criticism of reformism. In the summer of 1908, the Syndicalists once again had their day with the agrarian strike in the province of Parma. Directed this time by a genial organizer, Alceste De Ambris, the Parma strike had resulted in great disorder, but the Confederation of Labor and the Reformists openly fought the strike. After two months the strike languished and the suspicions and hatreds of Syndicalists and Reformists came to a head.

The Florence congress (September 19–22, 1908) was an overwhelming Reformist victory. Presided over once again by the old leader Andrea Costa, the man most representative of Italian socialism, the congress culminated in a solemn and explicit condemnation of the Syndicalists, an anathema whose force was blunted by being directed against men who had already broken away from the party. The so-called *concordato* resolution which was approved, declared on one hand, that the doctrine and practice of revolutionary syndicalism was incompatible with the principles and methods of the Socialist party and, on the other, affirmed that the closest relations should be established between the party and Confederation.[29] It was, in other words, a double move against the Syndicalists and toward the Confederation.

The Reformist position was further consolidated at Florence by a restatement of gradualist policies—social legislation, maternity aid, sickness and old-age insurance, abolition of tax on grain, progressive taxation, reduction of military service, opposition to and condemnation of the general strike in general and of strikes in the public services in particular—and by a reassertion of the benefits of ministerialism.[30] Pure socialism, said Turati on September 22, 1908, had returned to its own: "Revolutionary [Syndicalist] tendencies having disappeared from the party, integralism being transformed, only socialism remains. It once

27 *Ibid.*, p. 248.

28 *Ibid.*, p. 206.

29 Cf. *Resoconto stenografico del X Congresso Nazionale: Firenze, 19–20–21–22 settembre 1908*, pp. 334–36, for the "kilometric" resolution approved.

30 *Ibid.*, pp. 335–36, *passim*. See also Michels, *Storia critica*, pp. 342–43.

again finds itself, it returns to its normal and hard-working way, it becomes once again fused with the only substantially genuine Socialist forces, the working class." [31] But even in the midst of the celebrations of victory, Gaetano Salvemini had lashed at the "boneless and resigned" within reformism who, by placing the great question of universal suffrage last on the agenda of the congress, had again given proof of their inclination to postpone even their compromises:

When we ask for something we always take care to say that we shall be satisfied with a half, a quarter or an eighth of it, and we make renunciations . . . in the very moment when a wholesome program is needed. Thus, in practice, we do not make a compromise, but the compromise of a compromise of the compromise. (*Some applause. Hilarity. Comment.*) [32]

The Syndicalists were now satisfied that reformism had revealed its true features, for, as Leone said, by having expelled the radicals it could celebrate its complete divorce from socialism.[33] It was true, however, that with the Florence congress Italian socialism assumed the general character and direction it was to retain until the First World War. Bissolati took over the editorship of the *Avanti!*, the relations of party and Government were established, even if vaguely, on a workable basis, and the democratic elements seemed definitely triumphant.

Before the next Socialist congress assembled at Milan in 1910, Giolitti's long ministry (1906–1909) had fallen, Sonnino's second "Hundred Days" were over (December 1909–March 1910), and Luigi Luzzatti's cabinet was already eight months old. The Chamber of Deputies had voted (in May) the thorny Maritime Conventions and had approved the Daneo-Credaro law for primary educational instruction. Senator Giorgio Arcoleo's attempt to reform the Senate had come to nothing, and Luzzatti himself was considering the failure of his modest electoral reform.[34] The Socialists had taken part in most of this legislation and had given their support to Luzzatti even while realizing that the fine old scholar, as the Republican Barzilai was to say in the Chamber, had only the "scepter of the regency" while the majority looked elsewhere—to Giolitti—for the true "imperial purple." [35] It was strange indeed that so few of these great problems that agitated the country found so little echo in the Milan congress of the Socialist party.

[31] F. Turati, *Le vie maestre del socialismo*, p. 110.

[32] *Resoconto stenografico . . . Firenze*, p. 252.

[33] Michels, *Storia critica*, p. 344. For another Syndicalist reaction see Roberto Forges-Davanzati, "Dopo i Congressi di Modena e di Firenze," *Rassegna Contemparanea*, IV (1908), 168–74.

[34] Cf. Salvatore Barzilai's speech in the Chamber in *Atti Parlamentari*. "Discussioni della Camera dei Deputati. Tornata del 18 marzo 1911" (Session 1909–1913), IX, 13539–13545. Barzilai was to characterize Luzzatti's project for electoral reform in musical phraseology as *allargato ma non troppo* and "too little and too early."

[35] *Ibid.*, p. 13543. Meda, *op. cit.*, p. 36, calls the Socialist support of Luzzatti illogical, since "Luzzatti's cabinet was born and lived only by the approval and direct participation of the true and greater friends of the Honorable Giolitti."

The Reformists naturally dominated the congress (October 21–25, 1910), but the rumblings of old and new dissident groups and tendencies were not altogether absent from the harmonious chorus. There was first of all Salvemini, the irrepressible idealist, with his thesis of universal suffrage freely won, as the instrument of redemption for the poor derelicts of his forsaken South.[36] The Northern Reformists through Angiolo Cabrini answered Salvemini's point by a detailed review of Reformist achievements—the coöperation of the powerful Confederation of Labor won, the establishment of labor banks, and maternity and unemployment funds, the passage of labor laws affecting women and children, the use of arbitration in industrial disputes.[37] But an apology of reformism itself seemed small argument against those who, with Salvemini, did not quarrel with its general principles and practical accomplishments so far as they went but rather with its essentially sectional character and preoccupation. Filippo Turati, with his flare for the paradoxical and with his ability to reduce his opponents' arguments to the absurd, attacked Salvemini's thesis directly. Said the shrewd Milanese:

When Salvemini, with his love for paradox, declares that he would renounce even universal suffrage should it be offered by a Giolitti ministry, I can answer him that we, after having prepared it with our strength and with our sacrifices, have already accepted the freedom of association and the freedom of strike from Giolitti. As far as I am concerned, being convinced of the utility of universal suffrage for the proletariat, I would accept it not only from Giolitti, but, if necessary, from the Pope himself.[38]

At the morning sitting of October 23, another dissident voice was heard, that of Benito Mussolini who rose to speak in favor of Costantino Lazzari's Leftist resolution.[39] "I shall make a few telegraphic declarations," Mussolini began, "first of all not to prolong this discussion, which savors a good deal of an academy or of an ecumenical council, and then also to heed the recommendations made by our chairman." [40] He then went on in an attempt to demolish reformism "telegraphically" by pointing out that while Austria and Germany had universal suffrage, and while England was well advanced in social legislation, those countries were not even near socialism. Mussolini continued:

I say that if the Italian proletariat were no longer represented by deputies in Parliament, the harm would be slight. And last of all I say that this matter of the fatherland, this old cliché of the fatherland in danger, is the ideological cliché of all bourgeois democracies, with which cliché for the past thirty years the blood has been pumped from the poverty-ridden proletariat (Some applause).

[36] Salvemini's entire speech at the Milan congress is reprinted in his book Tendenze vecchie e necessità nuove, pp. 109–22.
[37] Resoconto stenografico dello XI Congresso, p. 159.
[38] Ibid., p. 270.
[39] On Mussolini's life prior to the First World War, see G. Megaro, Mussolini in the Making.
[40] Resoconto stenografico . . . Milano, p. 140.

Then, with more truth than was at the time realized, Mussolini told the congress:

Italian Socialists have understood nothing about the conflict in the Romagna (*Uuuh! Uuuh!*). You have always given us a kind of wailing solidarity, you have always talked about brotherhood, but that is nonsense! *There* people live in full revolution: and this is what you have not understood (*Mutterings. Some applause*).[41]

In the end, however, a resolution presented by Turati was approved. It stated, among other things, that the political action of the Italian Socialist party was to be based upon four cornerstones: the demand for universal suffrage for both sexes; absolute freezing of the military budget, and its subsequent diminution; widespread development of local, communal and provincial organizations, through the founding of schools, libraries, and other works of "proletarian education"; the establishment by the State of overall social insurance, beginning with old-age and unemployment insurance as a minimum.[42] The editorship of the *Avanti!* went from Bissolati to Claudio Treves. Another congress was to be called, as was the custom, two years hence, in the fall of 1912. Socialist reformism was triumphant and its popularity seemed to be at its greatest heights.

[41] *Ibid.*, pp. 40–41; see also Megaro, *op. cit.*, pp. 299–301, for a report of Mussolini's speech and for contemporary press comments.

[42] *Resoconto stenografico . . . Milano*, pp. 361–62, *passim*, and p. 380 for results of balloting: of 34,413 votes cast:

Turati (Reformist) motion	13,006
Modigliani (Dissident Socialist) motion	4,547
Lazzari (Revolutionary Left) motion	5,928
Abstaining	932

VII

THE INTIMATE HISTORY OF A CRISIS

SOCIALIST PARTY CONGRESSES, 1911–1914

Il partito è un distruttore di uomini . . . *
MUSSOLINI

WITH typical Milanese precision and foresight everything seemed to have been provided for the forthcoming Socialist party congress at Milan. Everything but the unexpected.

One day in March 1911, two of the trusted friends of Italian reformism, one in and the other outside the Socialist party, met and amicably discussed important affairs of state, disagreed on one very basic point (official collaboration), and parted with mutual admiration strengthened. Bissolati had met Giolitti and refused a post in his new cabinet. But the consequence was a tremendous uproar in the Socialist ranks: the next congress was advanced a year in order to discuss the implications of Bissolati's talk with Giolitti, and—*horribile dictu*—his visit, although in soft hat, to the King of Italy. The congress was to settle once and for all the official Socialist position on such actions. But before the Socialist congress actually met (October 15–18, 1911) even the Bissolati case had dwindled into comparative insignificance, for Giovanni Giolitti had precipitated a vastly more important crisis. On September 29, a state of war was declared to exist between Italy and Turkey. The Libyan conquest had begun, the nation was in arms, the Socialist party at the crossroads.[1]

When the twelfth congress of the Italian Socialist party met at Modena (October 15–18, 1911), it was Bissolati who was to bear the brunt of attacks for the crime of being himself. A Reformist of character, a man who followed through his actions to almost the very final step of giving his convictions practical application, Bissolati had been and still was the well-beloved of Italian socialism. Born of Cremonese parents, Leonida Bissolati (1857–1920) had received his legal training at the University of Bologna, where he met Filippo Turati, his twin soul. He had passed early through an intellectual crisis, due in part to the essentially literary and philosophic background of his first studies. He had been drawn more to the republicanism of Cattaneo and Alberto Mario than to the mystical republicanism of Mazzini. When he was thirty years old, after the death of his father, Bissolati had joined the Socialist party (*ca.*1886–87).[2] From

---

* "The party is a destroyer of men . . ." Mussolini, on April 27, 1914, at the Ancona congress of the Socialist party.

[1] The Libyan War of 1911 will be discussed elsewhere in another connection. See below, chapter viii.

[2] Cf. Destrée, *Figures italiènnes*, pp. 115–16, *passim*.

72

then on his Socialist career had been active and very constructive. He organized leagues of resistance (*Leghe di resistenza*), he had spread the Marxist gospel among the northern peasantry, he had contributed to Turati's *Critica Sociale*. When, in 1896, the *Avanti!* was founded at Rome, he became its first editor.[3] From an intransigent position during the hectic days of obstructionism, Bissolati had gradually been transformed into an exponent of democratic, gradualist socialism and, with Turati, became one of the high priests of reformism.

Bissolati was a gentleman in the best sense of the word. There was an element of chivalry in him, an aristocratic reserve, an inherent uprightness that kept him unperturbed in the midst of even the greatest agitation. But his high moral character was at times a hindrance to the great promise of his career, giving him an appearance of quixotism among those whose realism consisted, more often than not, of a great ability in compromising. In April 1911, when calumny, as a result of his meeting with Giolitti, was beginning to injure his friend's reputation, Turati said:

Where Bissolati appears, hypocrisy vanishes. No one has ever doubted him. In the savage political world full of compromise and vulgar scepticism, no one has ever suspected him. Men have smiled; they have deplored; they have shaken their heads; they have feigned surprise or scorn. Nothing else.[4]

Bissolati's political philosophy was simple and clear: conciliation with the democratic state, acceptance by the Socialists of the rules and responsibilities of representative government, recognition of the superior interests of the nation and solidarity with the national community and readiness to defend it in its honor, in its freedom, in its rights.[5] At the Milan congress of 1910, Bissolati had given a "scandalous" interpretation of the functions of the Socialist party:

I do not believe the function of the Socialist party to be over, I believe, however, that it must change. Its composition has changed. . . . The phase of the struggle for freedom being over, today the party is a dead branch, an old organism which must leave the way free for the blossoming of authentic proletarian life. . . . The time must come when the working class will itself formulate its needs and lay out the way of its own destiny.[6]

Speaking in support of Giolitti's proposal for universal suffrage, he said in the Chamber (April 8, 1911) that universal suffrage, the "civil arm of the multitudes," would render unnecessary a recurrence of the "Turati bill for the prevention of proletarian massacres." [7] He had an unbounded trust in Giolitti's aims. When, on October 17, at Modena, he was being reproached for his subservient attitude toward the Government, Bisso-

[3] See Michels, *Storia critica*, pp. 175–76, *passim*, on the *Avanti!* in the early period.

[4] Turati, "Dura salita," *Critica Sociale*, XX (1911), 97–99; also his *Trent'anni di "Critica Sociale,"* p. 158.

[5] I. Bonomi, *Leonida Bissolati*, p. x.

[6] F. Rubbiani, *Il pensiero politico di Leonida Bissolati*, p. 107.

[7] Bissolati, "Sulla politica del Ministero," *Eloquenza*, I (1911), 283. The last reference was to Turati's motion of 1906 in the Chamber, during the first Sonnino ministry.

lati simply said: "You may break me before I will pass to the opposition against the Government of Giolitti." [8]

This was not *ministerialismo,* it was *ministeriabilismo* in flagrance, it was the Socialist original sin which the Modena congress was called to judge—to condemn or to absolve. Condemnation, however, was a foregone conclusion, since only a small group of Reformists on the Right (Bissolati, Cabrini, Berenini, Bonomi, Reina) were prepared to fight for absolution. But the other groups (revolutionary Intransigents: Ciccotti, Lazzari, Lerda; Integralists: Colasanti, Paoloni, Pescetti; Reformists on the Left: Turati, Treves, Modigliani, Rigola), while they disagreed as to its form, agreed to the necessity for the adoption of an antiministerial Socialist policy at the congress.[9] The Treves motion was adopted by a very slim margin and that only on the second ballot: "The [Socialist] congress . . . *expresses the opinion* that the Socialist parliamentary group cannot and must not *(non potere e non dovere)* further *systematically* support, with its votes, the present cabinet." [10]

Ministerialismo seemed to stand condemned, but that phrase "expresses the opinion" and the word "systematically" in the motion betrayed completely the congress' doubt and vacillation. Was the motion an order or a request, was it a way of saying no when yes was meant, or was it simply a confession that Italian socialism was no longer confident of its own position? Turati himself put his finger on the vicious circle when he said: "We call our congresses together in order to repair the vices and weaknesses of the party, and our congresses are so fully immersed in the same vices that they do not even succeed in clearly formulating a diagnosis." [11]

But Turati himself had favored the antiministerial motion, not because he doubted his friend Bissolati's motives in his pro-Government attitude, but because he had begun to believe that the Government was no longer master of its own fate. Upon declaring war on Turkey, Giolitti had created the famous phrase, "historical fatality." Turati's reaction was that if Giolitti

today asserts that he was dragged reluctantly into the Tripolitan enterprise, if he invokes as his excuse historical fatality, a concept and a phrase so much beyond and unlike his usual bureaucratic thought and style, I am inclined to believe him sincere because I cannot conceive Africa in the petit-bourgeois geography of his program of Government. *(Laughter).*[12]

Ivanoe Bonomi, on the other hand, spoke in defense of the Right Reformist support of the Government, asserting that while it was difficult to draw the line between a policy of sustained support of the Government and actual participation in it, it was inevitable that

[8] *Resoconto stenografico del XII Congress Nazionale del Partito Socialista Italiano: Modena, 15–16–17–18 ottobre 1911,* p. 149.

[9] *Ibid.,* pp. 36, 156, 184–87, 242, 244, for the various motions.

[10] *Ibid.,* p. 187; for results of balloting, pp. 249, 318–20.

[11] *Ibid.,* p. 189.

[12] *Ibid.,* p. 195.

parties that refuse consistently to accept their responsibility after having succeeded in incorporating a part of their ideas and programs in the Government
are destined to become sterile because they will no longer have the right of directly influencing the political directives of their country. (*Bravo!*) [13]

When Bissolati rose to speak there was a triple outburst of applause in
spite of the generally hostile atmosphere. Although he felt like a defendant before a court, Bissolati said he would not exploit his position by
assuming "heroic or gladiatorial poses," but would rather "enhance the
responsibility of what I have done." He had gone to see the King, he
continued, like any deputy who has been consulted by his Sovereign as
to the best method of solving a ministerial crisis:

I was invited. I did not go like a deserter who leaves his ideals on the threshold
in order to seize power. I went like a man who brought and had to bring even
there the entire patrimony of his convictions. (*Bravo! Applause.*) I went to the
Sovereign and I indicated men and programs—I indicated universal suffrage as
the absolute necessity of Italian political life. And it seems to me, no matter how
you might judge my action, it seems that I was right, as a Socialist, in being
pleased that the Head of the State had recognized the political power now held
by the Italian proletariat. Then, I did not accept the invitation to be a minister.
But as I said a while ago, my not having accepted should not be in your judgment an extenuating circumstance. And why? Because I did not motivate my refusal by pointing out to the Honorable Giolitti any incompatibility of Socialist
faith and participation in power. I did not accept (I must give an account even of
the reasons for my refusal) because of a weakness: I did not accept because, let me
say it, my untamed temperament shrinks not so much from the external forms
as from the very exercise of power.[14]

The great outburst of applause that greeted the end of Bissolati's speech
at Modena was more testimony to his personal uprightness and sincerity
than to the ideas he had advanced. But Modena was only the first phase
of a great public trial, and the prosecution merely rested its case. Would
the defendant prove to be merely a penitent sinner or an unregenerate
heretic?

For from now on the council-complex whose symptoms have appeared
throughout the whole history of the Italian Socialist party became an
almost irrepressible mania. The unknown delegate from the Romagna
who had spoken at Milan in 1910 had said that the discussion there
savored "a good deal of an academy or an ecumenical council." Sensing
the course of the malady at Modena, Turati had mentioned the absurdity
of excommunication.

Excommunication [Turati said] is not only uncivil and Jacobin, it is also lacking
in seriousness and, at the bottom, attests to a very tepid faith in the principle it
wishes to defend. . . . A party like ours, itself heretical, cannot fear heresies; it
must rather welcome them and gain light from them when they arise; otherwise
it must conquer them by persuasion.[15]

13 *Ibid.*, p. 64.
14 *Ibid.*, p. 236.
15 *Ibid.*, p. 204.

The last two congresses of the Socialist party before the First World War were testimony that Turati's words had been sown to the wind.

The Libyan War was meanwhile proceeding with a great display of bravery despite mediocre military leadership. The people at home followed developments with great hope and applause, if without actual enthusiasm. At its outbreak, the Socialists had attempted a protest by the proclamation of a general strike, but protest was of no avail and the strike was from the start a dismal failure. They had then had recourse to a rather futile pacifistic campaign of low vilification, stressing the most pathetic and sordid (and inevitable) aspects of war (the tortures, the open wounds, the sorrow of the poor mothers, etc.).[16] When, however, the Chamber of Deputies resumed its sessions in February 1912, and the Government issued its Decree of Sovereignty over all Libya, the approval given it was overwhelming, only 38 out of 420 deputies voting against it. Many of the Socialist deputies seemed to have been forced by the logic of circumstances to approve the colonial measure.[17]

On March 14, 1912, a certain D'Alba made an unsuccessful attempt upon the life of the King Victor Emmanuel, and the Chamber of Deputies moved to suspend the sitting and to go in a body to the Quirinal to congratulate the King upon his escape. Among the great crowd who went were three Reformist Socialists: Leonida Bissolati, Angiolo Cabrini, and Ivanoe Bonomi.

The Reggio Emilia congress (July 7–10, 1912) found the Italian Socialist party dominated by a revolutionary intransigent group more powerful than syndicalism had ever been because it was directed by more forceful and resourceful leaders. Among them were Costantino Lazzari, the old revolutionist, Francesco Ciccotti, an able journalist, G. M. Serrati, Angelica Balabanoff, Elia Musatti, and Giovanni Lerda. But their official spokesman was Benito Mussolini who had confirmed his anti-militaristic faith by writing venomous articles against the Libyan War and the Fatherland and had spent some time in jail as a result of his activities and publications.[18] The Reformists of the Left, a sort of Center now, were led by Turati and Modigliani, while on the Right were the defendants and their sympathizers: Bissolati, Cabrini, Bonomi, Guido Podrecca, Berenini, and Pietro Chiesa. Broadly viewed, two antithetical conceptions of socialism never more clearly confronted each other than at Reggio Emilia: the uncompromising, fundamentalist, revolutionary tendency and the mild, democratically inspired, evolutionary Reformist tendency. The antithesis could not be better personified than in the principal defendant, Leonida Bissolati, and the chief of the prosecution, Benito Mussolini.

Mussolini's speech, delivered in the afternoon of the second day of the

16 As late as the fall of 1913, during the general elections, a pictorial show was put on at Empoli, Tuscany, depicting the sufferings of the soldiers during the Libyan War. Cf. Lodi, *Venticinque anni*, p. 163.

17 *Resoconto stenografico . . . Modena*, p. 154.

18 Cf. G. Megaro, *Mussolini in the Making*, pp. 246–73, for a detailed account of Mussolini's activities and writings during the Libyan War.

congress, July 8, 1912—a fierce but self-assured attack on democratic government in general, reformism in particular, and Bissolati personally—dominated the proceedings of the congress.[19] It had none of the rational, logical argument of the debater—it was aimed at the passions and sentiments—not to persuade the mind, but to conquer the heart. Only a brief textual summary can be given here:

I have sometimes asked myself—through intellectual curiosity—the reasons for the slight success of abstentionist propaganda in Italy. Italy is certainly the nation in which parliamentary cretinism—that indeterminable disease so acutely diagnosed by Marx—has attained the gravest and most deadly forms. It is obvious that we have been a political people for so long a time that, despite all disillusions, we always return to the old sins. Italian parliamentarianism is already exhausted. Do you want the proof of it? The almost universal suffrage granted by Giovanni Giolitti is an able attempt made with the aim of giving some content, another period of life (funzionalità) to the parliamentary regime. The parliamentary regime is not absolutely necessary to socialism inasmuch as an anti-parliamentary or a-parliamentary socialism can and has been conceived, but, on the contrary, it is necessary to the bourgeoisie as a justification and perpetuation of its political rule.[20]

Universal suffrage, Mussolini continued, was merely the oxygen pump administered to the dying parliamentary regime in order to prolong its life a while, but it could not be the instrument for the complete emancipation of the proletariat.

The bourgeoisie, as it must complete its economic cycle, must also complete its political parabola—that is, it must realize all the desiderata of the democracies—until the day when the possibility of further transformations of its political institutions having vanished, another problem, the fundamental problem, that of justice in the economic field, must be solved, and its solution can only be Socialistic. . . .[21]

Having thus disposed of the democratic and Reformist illusions, Mussolini proceeded to attack Bissolati for his part in the Chamber's visit of congratulation to the King. The duty of Bissolati, Bonomi, and Cabrini was not to tender congratulations, but rather

. . . to consider the happening as an accident of the trade of kings. (Bravo! Applause!) Why be touched and weep for the King, only for the King? Why this excessive, hysterical sensibility in the case of crowned heads? Who is the King? He is the useless citizen by definition.[22]

[19] Resoconto stenografico . . . Reggio Emilia, pp. 69–78, for the complete text of Mussolini's speech.
[20] Ibid., p. 69. For other violent anti-democratic tirades see Francesco Ciccotti's speech, pp. 208–14, especially p. 211: "We believe the Socialist party to be an eminently anti-democratic party. . . . Democracy is a bourgeois expedient. Democracy is the negation of the triumph of the social antithesis, it is the negation of the triumph of the proletariat."
[21] Ibid., p. 70.
[22] Ibid., p. 73.

Turning to Bissolati, Mussolini told him that he stood condemned by his own words. *"Ex ore, tuo te judico,"* Mussolini told Bissolati and then proceeded to read from an antimonarchical essay published by Bissolati following the assassination of King Humbert in 1900.[23] At last Mussolini thundered forth his condemnation of the Reformists:

> You, indicted deputies, have for some time been awaiting our execution; for you it means liberation. Freed from all formal encumbrance and from all moral ties, you will be able to follow your path with greater dispatch. At its end you will not find the fiery pit, but the flower-decked steps of power. We have a precise duty: that of leaving you henceforward to your own destiny. Bissolati, Cabrini, Bonomi, and the other candidates may go to the Quirinal, even to the Vatican if they so desire, but let the Socialist party declare that it is not disposed to follow them, either today or tomorrow, or ever. (*Prolonged and spirited applause. Many congratulations.*).[24]

Thus ended the oration of the young man who only two years before had feared that the congress was degenerating into an ecumenical council. Now he himself seemed to have adopted the manner of a grand inquisitor hurling anathemas from sheer heights of orthodoxy upon those who had defiled their faith by contact with the sordid realities of the world. The motion Mussolini presented was to precipitate the greatest schism in the Italian Socialist party. Expulsion was demanded for the offenders.[25]

The defense was eloquent but weak since the outcome was inevitable. Cabrini wanted to know whether there was proof of a single deviation in the defendants' faith in, and fight for, the cause of the working classes.[26] Bonomi in attempting to justify the group's visit to the King as an act of courtesy forthrightedly pointed out that the Reformist and revolutionary conceptions of socialism were irreconcilably at war. The Extremists, he told them, were merely preoccupied with dogmas, formulas, and rites aiming to make proselytes maintain their faith in its original purity.[27] Reformist socialism, on the other hand, was a realistic movement which recognized that the needs of any and every class must be reconciled with those of the nation, and the rights of the workers with those of the whole community.[28] Guido Podrecca, the editor of the satirical and anti-Clerical Roman newspaper *L'Asino,* who was also hit by the Mussolini motion for his warmongering attitudes, pointed out the contradictions of Social-

---

[23] *Ibid.,* pp. 74–77, *passim.*

[24] *Ibid.,* p. 78.

[25] *Ibid.,* p. 230. Three motions were presented at the congress, with the following results (p. 234):

Mussolini's for expulsion	12,556 votes.
Modigliani's for declaration of incompatibility because of Rightists' action	3,250 votes.
Reina's for condemnation only	5,633 votes.
Abstained	2,027 votes.

[26] *Ibid.,* pp. 81–89, for Angliolo Cabrini's speech.

[27] *Ibid.,* p. 101, *passim.*

[28] *Ibid.,* p. 103.

ists who found it convenient to be Nationalists (Irredentists) at Trento, but pacifists at Tripoli.[29]

Bissolati, the chief defendant, spoke with courage, even with pride in his "heretical" convictions.[30] He once again reviewed his past position and beliefs to justify the consistency of his present action. He looked back with regret at the great opportunity the Italian proletariat had failed to utilize when it had been invited to participate in the Government: "But if the Italian proletariat had wished, with me or with another person, to be inside the citadel of executive power, perhaps we should not have gone to Libya, or the developments of the war would have been different." [31] The Italian Socialist party, said Bissolati, had for too long ignored national organisms which, he shrewdly added, could not be dispersed by the resolutions of congresses, and the fact that the clash of armed nations was over and above the class struggle.[32] The continuance of the Socialist opposition to the war had been based on the false premise that something positive could be accomplished by combating the Giolittian ministry; but, said Bissolati, it had merely succeeded in compromising the social reforms promised by the Government: "Even if you could have another Government it would be more warmongering than that of Giolitti because they are all more warmongering than he, and you would not have either universal suffrage or the monopoly. And you will still have war." [33] As to Mussolini's *"ex ore tuo, te iudico,"* Bissolati said that under similar circumstances he would still act and write as he had; so now he gave back his membership card to the party, knowing that that would constitute his greatest merit in the eyes of the Italian proletariat.[34]

This marked the official end of Bissolati's career in the Italian Socialist party. On the night of the vote of expulsion a group of Right Reformists founded the Reformist Socialist party. They formulated a program and launched an appeal.[35] The Confederation of Labor, facing the dilemma of choosing either the official party or the new Reformists, declared itself autonomous, an act which was equivalent to a declaration of support for the Bissolati party. But the Reformist party was not destined to succeed, losing itself during the war (1917) in the radical wing of the parliamentary scene.[36] Bissolati, however, always remained a figure apart. His last speech

[29] *Ibid.*, p. 130, *passim.*

[30] *Ibid.*, pp. 151–65, for full text of Bissolati's speech. There is a fairly long excerpt from the speech in the posthumous collection of his writings and speeches, *La politica estera dell'Italia dal 1897 al 1920,* pp. 255–67.

[31] *Resoconto stenografico . . . Modena,* p. 163.

[32] *Ibid.*, pp. 160–61, *passim.*

[33] *Ibid.*, pp. 163–64.

[34] *Ibid.*, p. 165.

[35] Cf. Meda, *Il Partito Socialista Italiano,* pp. 56–57, for the founding and program of the Reformist Socialist party.

[36] For a sympathetic exposition of reformism, see L. Granone, *La crisi socialista;* for a Nationalist's reaction to reformism, G. Bellonci, "Il Riformismo: Ivanoe Bonomi," *L'Eloquenza,* II (1912), 127–41. Angelica Balabanoff, *My Life as a Rebel,* pp. 90–102. treats of the Reggio Emilia congress in which she was an active participant in Mussolini's camp; her account, however, is undocumented and anecdotal though interesting, and seems to have been drawn entirely from memory.

at the congress of Reggio Emilia had been a magnificent expression of his personality and of his thought, of his Socialist faith as well as of his patriotic fervor: a kind of nostalgic backward look to a light called "Socialism" and an idealistic looking forward to a vision called "Country." That light and that vision symbolizes Leonida Bissolati's significance in the Italy of his day.

After Reggio Emilia practically all the key positions in the party were taken over by the revolutionary group, including the editorship of the *Avanti!* which devolved upon Mussolini on December 1, 1912. When the last pre-war Italian Socialist party congress assembled at Ancona on April 26, 27, 28, 29, 1914, the revolutionary wing was the complete master of the party's affairs.

Ancona, in the Marches, a pretty and industrious little seaport on the Adriatic, fabled for the siege of Barbarossa, the papal stand against the Turks, the French and Russian occupations of Napoleonic memory, the fight against the Austrians in 1849, was also to be remembered for the spark that set afire Red Week in June, and for this fourteenth congress of the Italian Socialist party in 1914. When the Socialists assembled there on Sunday morning, April 26, there were already among them forebodings of things to come. Comrade Ellenbogen brought the greetings and "embrace" of the Austrian Socialists to their Italian brothers; Comrade Pittoni, the salute of the Socialists of Trieste; Comrade Skatula, the greetings of the faraway Bohemian brothers.[37] Before the congress ended, militarism was to be condemned in two resolutions.[38]

Membership had grown in the party by about 20,000 since Reggio Emilia, being now, as Zerbini reported, 49,148.[39] Mussolini, making his report on his seventeen-month editorship of the *Avanti!*, stated that the policy he had followed and would continue to follow was "intransigence on all lines, fight against kindred parties, especially the democratic. Italian democracy can never be fought sufficiently."[40] And, as if to confirm the death of reformism among them, and all that Reformists had stood for with their democratic inclination to form coalitions of popular parties, the Ancona congress approved, by a vote of 22,591 out of 34,389 ballots cast, C. Ratti's motion for absolute intransigence in administrative elections.[41] This was by far the most important result of the congress of 1914

---

[37] *Resoconto stenografico . . . Ancona*, pp. 11–15, *passim*.

[38] *Ibid.*, pp. 273–77, *passim*.

[39] *Ibid.*, p. 25. The figures by provinces were given as follows: Piedmont, 8,331; Lombardy, 7,189; Veneto, 2,455; Liguria, 1,885; Emilia and Romagna, 12,860; Tuscany, 6,818; Marches and Umbria, 3,023; Latium, 1,106; Abruzzi, 464; Apulia and Basilicata, 1,299; Calabria, 290; Sicily, 491; Sardinia, 278.

[40] *Ibid.*, p. 28.

[41] *Ibid.*, p. 234; cf. pp. 191–232 for the heated debate on this question. The northern delegates to the congress inclined for intransigence, while the Southerners favored transigence, or at least local autonomy and "special conditions." Verbal skirmishes on this important question became so bitter that the chairman saw the necessity of reminding the delegates that "there is no North and South, but the Socialist party" (p. 206).

since it set a line of official Socialist policy that was to be followed during and after the war, but it was obscured at the time by the more popular discussion and more dramatic motion of expulsion of Freemasonic Socialists.

The history of Italian freemasonry since 1870, and its relations with socialism, is still to be written. The contribution of freemasonry to the work of unification is a debatable question, although it is probably true that freemasonry was of some help during the early Risorgimento.[42] After the attainment of national unity, Italian freemasonry still attracted many men, prominent and otherwise. The attraction seems to have been due, among other things, to the vague democratic and humanitarian-positivistic outlook it represented, its conventional anticlerical attitudes, and the secrecy with which it surrounded its activities and influence.[43] The general political character of Italian freemasonry must, however, be firmly kept in mind for an understanding of the controversies it aroused in Italy. Italian freemasonry was always much more than the merely social Anglo-Saxon organization.

Italian Socialists had entered into Masonic lodges, especially during the years of obstructionism, but from the beginning there had been opposition and agitation within the Socialist party against the infiltration of freemasonry. During the years 1900–14 the anti-Masonic question was insistently raised by Socialists in articles and discussions, but it was never completely solved. In an article in the *Avanti!* on February 17, 1904, the historian and Socialist Ettore Ciccotti had called freemasonry "a lay congregation" (*una congregazione senza tonaca*) and the epithet, with numerous variations, stuck.[44] Soon afterward the *Critica Sociale* took up the question with an anonymous article declaring that Freemasonic socialism was a moral inconsistency and stressing the contradiction between the "dark and secret machination" of the order and the open work of the party.[45] The question was brought up at the Bologna congress (April 11, 1904) but no extended discussion took place.[46] Gaetano Salvemini had

[42] For freemasonry during the Risorgimento see A. Luzio, *La massoneria e il Risorgimento italiano;* G. Leti, *Carboneria e massoneria nel Risorgimento italiano;* Salvemini, "L'Italia politica nel secolo XIX," in *L'Europa nel secolo XIX,* I, 325–50; and the very biased article by A. Cavacciocchi, "La massoneria italiana attraverso il risorgimento nazionale," *Gerarchia,* III (1924), 624–33. A. M. Ghisalberti, "Massoneria," in *Enciclopedia Italiana,* XX, 537: "The thesis of an absolutely negative and irrelevant participation of freemasonry in the struggle of the Risorgimento cannot be altogether accepted."

[43] Leti, *op. cit.,* pp. 393–95, *passim,* reports the following as Freemasons: A. C. De Meis, political thinker; the poets Carducci, Stecchetti (O. Guerrini), M. Rapisardi, and Giovanni Pascoli; the historian Pasquale Villari; the Socialist Andrea Costa; the Radicals Giovanni Bovio, Ettore Socci, Felice Cavallotti, Ettore Sacchi, and Napoleone Colajanni; the littérateur G. Chiarini. Alberto Cavacciocchi, "La Massoneria italiana dal 1870 ai giorni nostri," *Gerarchia* (Fascist source), III (1924), 744–56, *passim,* gives as Freemasons: Depretis, Nicotera, Crispi, Zanardelli, Nitti, Bonomi, and even Giolitti! (p. 755).

[44] Cf. "V," "La Massoneria," *Critica Sociale,* XIV (1904), 124.

[45] *Ibid.,* p. 125.

[46] *Rendiconto dell'VIII Congresso Nazionale: Bologna,* p. 161.

always viewed the fight against freemasonry as a work of moral regeneration, especially in the South. His uncompromising attitude toward all
manifestations of dogmatic and occult forces was aimed equally against
anarchism and freemasonry. At Naples, in 1907, at a teachers' convention,
he introduced a motion openly condemning both "black priests" and
"green priests," but it was defeated.[47]

The ascendancy of reformism during the decade 1900–10 and the alliances it had sponsored in many electoral districts had opened the way for
further Masonic infiltrations, or at least it had prevented a decisive discussion of the question at a Socialist congress.[48] But the year 1910 was to
be critical in the relations of freemasonry and socialism. Benedetto Croce
published a scathing philosophical attack upon the "Masonization" of
Italian socialism, in which he viewed freemasonry and socialism as antithetical in philosophical derivations, in developments, in intellectual outlook, and in aims.[49] He directed his bitterest shafts against what he called
the Masonic mentality, with its all-inclusive faith in reason, its tendency
to simplify the most complex problems of history, science, philosophy,
and morality, and its love for fine words such as liberty, humanity, brotherhood, tolerance. A fine culture for shopkeepers, elementary school teachers, lawyers, and quacks because it was cheap culture, freemasonry, according to Croce, was at the same time a wretched culture for those who wished
to delve deeply into the great problems of the human soul, and of society.[50]

During the course of the year 1910 the Masonic question was discussed
everywhere in Socialist circles [51] finally reaching the floor of the Milan
congress through Salvemini who, on the last day of the congress (October
25), proposed that it discuss the relations between socialism and freemasonry.[52] Despite the protests of an old Socialist and professed Freemason, Giovanni Lerda, a resolution signed by Mondolfo, Mastracchi,
Balabanoff, and Salvemini was presented at the congress restating in detail
the antithesis between socialism and freemasonry and inviting all Socialists who were non-Masons not to join freemasonry and those who did belong to leave it.[53] At the same time the congress instructed the Executive
Committee to conduct a referendum upon the question of socialism and
freemasonry.

At the Reggio Emilia congress (July 1912) the Masonic question, brought
forward by the revolutionary wing, assumed a definite anti-democratic

[47] Cf. E. Rota, *Una pagina di storia contemporanea—Gaetano Salvemini*, p. 7; also
Salvemini, *Tendenze vecchie e necessità muove*, chap. iv, pp. 20–21.

[48] Cf. Meda, *op. cit.*, p. 40.

[49] Cf. Croce, *Cultura e vita morale*, pp. 143–50.

[50] *Ibid.*, p. 145.

[51] See an interesting pamphlet by a young Socialist, G. Feroci, *Socialismo e Massoneria*.

[52] *Resoconto stenografico . . . Milano*, p. 289; Salvemini defined (p. 347) freemasonry
as "a secret malady against which there is no remedy."

[53] *Ibid.*, pp. 338–39, for the full text of the resolution. Giovanni Lerda (p. 295), a
Freemason, said that the Socialist party was childishly seeking in freemasonry "the
reasons and causes for its profound decadence and for its imminent decomposition."

aspect. Nino Mazzoni, insisting that it was high time that the question be solved, presented a resolution (signed also by Mastracchi, Serrati, Zibordi, Capri, and Modigliani) in which the democratizing influence and the "deceitful and dangerous penetration" of freemasonry among the workers were condemned and proposed for mature consideration of the problem by the Executive Committee.[54] The Right Reformist Berenini, however, warned the congress that the Socialist party had become prey to a mania for schisms and expulsions, expelling first the Anarchists, then the Syndicalists, the Right Reformists, and next the Freemasons.[55]

This, in its main lines, was the background of the Socialist-Masonic question before it came before the Ancona congress. The revolutionary Executive Committee of the party, as Mazzoni had insisted at Reggio Emilia, seemed to have given it mature consideration, for four resolutions for the solution of the vexatious question were presented. There was an attempt to put off the discussion on grounds of non-competency of a national Socialist party to pass on a question of international interest, such as the relation between socialism and freemasonry was supposed to be.[56] But Giovanni Zibordi replied that every country had the right to discuss the Masonic question upon the terms in which it developed and thrived in its peculiar environment, and that, Italian freemasonry being actively and profoundly political, it must be discussed upon that level.[57] Thereupon three speakers for each side were chosen to participate in the discussion. Zibordi, Mussolini, and Nino Mazzoni for the anti-Masons; Poggi, Lerda, and Orazio Raimondo for the Masons.

The sitting of April 27, 1914, was a tempestuous session lasting well into the night. The six speakers enjoyed the confidence of the congress. Zibordi, a secondary school professor and a member of the Executive Committee of the party, lashed at the corrupting and class-leveling influence of freemasonry and its sectarian anti-Marxistic premises and aims.[58] Poggi replied for the Masons by trying to prove the common philosophic origins of socialism and freemasonry in nineteenth-century German idealism, but his arguments, given the attitude of the meeting, only brought cries of "Down with freemasonry!" from the audience.[59] Nino Mazzoni developed the thesis that in a country like Italy, freemasonry weakened the morale of the workers whom it threw together with high personages of state inside the lodges! [60] Mussolini rose to make a change in the resolution presented by Zibordi. Instead of "the congress . . . invites the Socialists to cease

[54] *Resoconto stenografico . . . Reggio Emilia*, pp. 294–97, *passim*.
[55] *Ibid.*, p. 224.
[56] *Resoconto stenografico . . . Ancona*, p. 107. It was Valsecchi who presented the *pregiudiziale*.
[57] *Ibid.*
[58] *Ibid.*, pp. 110–13, *passim*. For his further reactions to the congress, see G. Zibordi, "Un Congresso di transizione," *Critica Sociale*, XXIV (1914), 147–49.
[59] *Resoconto stenografico . . . Ancona*, pp. 114–19, and especially p. 117.
[60] *Ibid.*, p. 145.

their affiliation . . ." it was to read: "the congress . . . declares in the most explicit form the incompatibility of Socialists' entering and remaining in freemasonry, and invites the [local] clubs to expel those comrades who in the future do not regulate their conduct according to the principles expressed in this resolution. . . ." [61] The resolution was thereafter known by both Zibordi's and Mussolini's names. Mussolini's own anti-Masonic harangue was based on the premises that whereas individuals were important in freemasonry they count for nothing where the life of the party is concerned, and that as such the party was a destroyer of men.[62] His anti-Masonic sentiments were one with his anti-democratic biases. Mussolini ended his speech amid the thunderous applause of his colleagues and a good part of the audience with the cry: "We Socialists say: Enough of shadows! More light! Always! Today we want to fight our battles in the streets, under the light of the sun, looking one another well in the eyes." [63]

Giovanni Lerda and Orazio Raimondo, one of the greatest public orators of his day, both Freemasons, warned the congress that the inquisitorial mentality and method of the Socialist party did not speak well for the future of Italian socialism. They spoke with courage, dignity, and intelligence. Lerda said that Socialists should not accept the new function being forced upon it—that of determining "who is baptized and who is circumcised, because you will come to this: that you will have to pass upon how a group thinks or even how an individual in the bosom of his family thinks (Groans), because it will no longer be Socialistic to think in a way that is not dictated by the decalogue of the Socialist party." [64] Orazio Raimondo, who only a few months earlier had shaken the Chamber of Deputies with an anti-Giolittian declamation and had thus become the hero of Italian socialism, now himself accused, tried to vindicate the rights of Socialists to seek their moral growth wherever they wanted to, whether, coming from a bourgeois environment, they sought it in socialism, or being Socialists they sought it in freemasonry. Raimondo then continued: "But be warned, friends, that a truth does not cease to be truth and falsehood does not become true in moral and political questions because it is thus affirmed or denied in a majority vote." [65]

The die, however, was cast and the anti-Masonic majority at the congress asserted itself in an unquestionable manner. Of the four motions that had been presented, the following were the results out of 34,152 ballots cast: [66]

[61] Ibid., p. 134.

[62] Ibid. See Megaro, op. cit., pp. 214-17, for Mussolini's anti-Masonic background. In reading Megaro's account it should be kept in mind that Mussolini was perhaps unique only in the violence with which he expressed his anti-Masonic sentiments, but by no means in the sentiments themselves.

[63] Resoconto stenografico . . . Ancona, p. 137.

[64] Ibid., p. 141. When Lerda turned to Mussolini himself with the apostrophe: ". . . You, Mussolini, are not absolute truth, and you are not God," Mussolini interrupted him with: "Perhaps the devil!"

[65] Ibid., pp. 127-28.

[66] Ibid., p. 164.

Mussolini-Zibordi motion for incompatibility and expulsion............27,378
Poggi motion for compatibility...................................... 1,819
Montanari's motion for neutrality on the Masonic question.............. 2,485
Matteotti motion for declaration of incompatibility alone (no expulsion).. 2,296

The machinery for the expulsion of Freemasonic Socialists was to reside in the local Socialist clubs. The revolutionary Socialists, under the able leadership of Mussolini, had once again asserted their will and power. And yet this very year of 1914 was not to end before that dominating figure of two Socialist congresses, the energetic editor of the *Avanti!*, the supporter and poet of Red Week was himself to be expelled from his Milan club and from the Socialist party itself (November 1914). Contrary, however, to his assertion at Ancona, the Socialist party by its action did not destroy him; rather it had made him even more of a figure to reckon with.

The crisis of the Italian Socialist party, however, having reached its height in 1910–12, with Modena and Reggio Emilia, had long since drawn to an end.[67] The party which had risen as the voice of Italian freedom and justice had now become a mere inquisitorial and authoritarian instrument of repression and partisanship. The party which had fought the battles of modern civil and political freedom against the reaction in the bright days of obstructionism had at length become a council of the elect in which common belief was more important than common action. It had enjoyed the widest liberty under Giolitti to organize and coördinate its forces, to establish organs of popular education and mutual aid, to found workers' unions and peasants' leagues, to proclaim strikes and make protests, to see some of its fundamental demands incorporated into programs of government and, which is more, to see them realized. But when it had been called to assume part of its responsibility in the government of the country in which its voice had grown so strong, it had vacillated and at length taken refuge behind its myths, as if afraid to soil itself by contact with reality. Thus socialism, and not only in Italy, had proved incapable of positive action, uncertain of itself, and yet afraid to collaborate with others. Clearly, the cycle of Italian socialism, in the spring of 1914, was in its declining phase soon to be submerged in the fiery pit of war, to emerge ghostlike only after many years of civil strife and fascism.

[67] For other comments and interpretations of the crisis of socialism, see Salvemini's articles in his periodical *L'Unità*, May 2, 1913, especially p. 291: "The Socialist party is not sick; it is dead, and now it is only a ghost"; Croce, "La Morte del socialismo" in *Cultura e vita morale*, pp. 150–59; the article "Il compito del Partito Socialista," *La Voce*, IV (1914), 55–56; C. Treves, "Involuzione rivoluzionaria. Revisione e riaffermazione della dottrina socialista," *Critica Sociale*, XXIV (1914), 209–11; I. Bonomi, *op. cit.*, especially pp. 87–88.

VIII

NATIONALIST CROSS CURRENTS

*Questa Italia, senza unità di visione sua, senza pro-
gramma di azione sua, ha bisogno di qualcuno che la
batta perchè si risvegli e che l'inciti perchè agisca.**

PAPINI

THE purpose of the present chapter is neither to present a complete
history of Italian nationalism nor to delve into the complex phenomenon of imperialism and its manifestations. It is rather to trace briefly
the origins and the course of certain currents of national consciousness in
the varied forms and expressions it assumed in Italy during the era of
Giolitti.

The Italian Risorgimento had, ideologically, been the child of liberalism and nationalism. As has already been pointed out elsewhere, after the
achievement of unity Italian liberalism underwent such profound transformations that it was hardly recognizable. But, strangely enough, what
liberalism had lost as an ideal it had gradually regained in practice.[1]
Nationalism, on the other hand, seemed to have lost its very raison d'être
when the object of its struggles and aims had been attained. For almost a
century Italy had been the most tangible expression of a new principle:
the right of a nation to govern itself. The cry of Garibaldi's men to the
Austrians had epitomized their mission and Italy's position: *"Passate
l'Alpi e tornerem fratelli"* ("Return across the Alps and once again we shall
be brothers").[2] When that principle and that mission had been at least
partially realized (for there was always an Irredenta), the heritage of the
Risorgimento took the form of an abhorrence equally of being oppressed
and of oppressing, of subjection and of conquest. Thus irredentism,
Cairoli's policy of clean hands, and Mancini's idealistic trust in the principles of international justice and equity were all branches of a same
trunk. Strangely enough, however, the statesmen who insisted in seeing
Oberdan's Irredentist dream and "act of madness" as vain sacrifices that
hurt the cause of peace did not seem to consider that, in a world where
Bismarckism, imperialism, and world-politics were becoming a new trinity
of power, their own idealism might be an anachronistic and ephemeral
instrument with which to stem international violence and injustice.[3]

* "This Italy, without a unity of vision of her own, without a program of action of
her own, needs some one to beat her that she may awake, and to incite her that she
may act." Giovanni Papini, in a speech of February 21, 1904, reported in Giovanni
Papini and Giuseppe Prezzolini, *Vecchio e nuovo nazionalismo*, p. 7.

[1] See Chapters i and ii of present work, *passim*.

[2] Cf. R. Michels, *L'Imperialismo italiano*, pp. 1-3, *passim*.

[3] For summaries of Italian attitudes and bases of foreign policies during the period

What seemed to have its bases in idealism and belief in the principle of self-determination for all peoples might also be seen to have had roots in the negative aspects of Italian political reality after the Risorgimento. The unity itself was more an administrative and bureaucratic fact than that social and spiritual fusion without which no truly national consciousness was possible. The negative attitude of the Church, the debased state of the national culture, the weakness of the new state's economics and finances were all parts from the Risorgimento inheritances. The framework of the nation was pacifistic—socialism in the latter part of the century became a part and a reinforcement of this framework. Without sharing in the idealistic ideology of the Risorgimento heritage, socialism attempted by itself to canalize the already existent currents into a definite program. For it too preached the principles of international justice, but its premises were other than the rights of a national community within a structure of international equity—they were based rather on class rights in a world community, transcending all national boundaries. In socialism, idealism and social discontent, repressed hopes and passions, messianism and opportunism, were to find a movement whose final aim was none other than the total transformation of the world, the abolition of national boundaries, the achievement of an earthly paradise for the poor and the disinherited.[4] It was to be a long time before the Italian ruling classes came to see that the beauty (or danger) of the Socialist ideal was not at all proportionate to the possibility of its ever becoming an actuality—or even to the Socialists' desire that it should become such. The failure of Francesco Crispi—from the explosion of the *Fasci siciliani* (1893–94) to the tragedy of Adowa (1896)—was in no small measure due to the old Sicilian's blindness to the deeper significance and inherent limitations of the new movement.[5] The relative good fortune of Giovanni Giolitti—from his policy of liberty for all within the limits of the law to the success of the Tripolitan War—was to a great degree facilitated by the shrewd Piedmontese' conscious realization that there is perhaps nothing better to spoil or to blunt the force of an ideal than to grant it its minimum demands and then to invite it to share the sordid exercise of active power.

It was by no means coincidental that when, during the first decade of the century, a new Italian Nationalist movement began to take shape among the older political currents, it attempted to juxtapose in sharpest

---

1870–90, see Croce, *A History of Italy*, chap. iv, pp. 106–25; and M. Hentze, *Pre-Fascist Italy*, pp. 137–60.

[4] Carducci, the classic poet of *italianità*, was to dedicate to his pupil Andrea Costa, the pioneering Socialist, some verses in which he revealed a passionate admiration for the aims of socialism:

> Ell'è un'altra Madonna, ell'è un'idea
> Fulgente di giustizia e di pietà.
> Io benedico chi per lei cadea,
> Io benedico chi per lei vivrà.

Cf. R. Michels, *Storia critica*, p. 59.

[5] On Crispi and socialism see A. C. Jemolo, *Crispi*, pp. 54–66.

outline an ideal past against a sordid present. Modern Italian Nationalism, that which became a school and a party, built a superstructure of anti-Liberal, antidemocratic, anti-Masonic, imperialistic theories upon an anti-Socialistic basis.[6] Nothing, however, could successfully obscure the literary-rhetorical origins of the movement, even though it tried to translate its vague formulas into the cold figures of statistical science, especially in relation to Italian emigration.[7]

Towering, demon-like, above all other Nationalists stood the figure of Gabriele D'Annunzio. Poet and dramatist, novelist and artist, impostor and thaumaturge, are mere names that describe the outer manifestations of this man's genius but not the genius itself. For a generation he ruled Italian minds with a completeness hardly equaled by the most ruthless political tyrant. He translated the currents of thought of his time into novels and poems which by the music, the beauty and fascination of his words seized upon the imagination. D'Annunzio declaimed upon the beauty of fire and destruction, the voluptuous attractions of power and glory, he sang of the Nietzschian superman.[8] Was he a creator or merely a symbol and symptom of the new currents of Italian intellectual and emotional life? Few seemed to know or care, for all felt him as a reality, an influence, a ruler to be loved or feared, to be accepted or denied.[9] Perhaps no other modern poet has been more read, more admired, hated, despised, and written about than D'Annunzio in Italy. Men who could say, with G. A. Borgese, in 1904: "Yes, we love and admire Gabriele D'Annunzio more than any other modern poet of ours, living or dead, and from him we begin our art. We are disciples of D'Annunzio . . . ,"[10] could with perfect naturalness write, again with Borgese, five years later: D'Annunzio, "a barbarity overburdened and oppressed by culture" (una barbarie gravata ed oppressa di cultura),[11] for such were the violent contrasts of attraction and abhorrence D'Annunzio's genius could inspire.

There was in his work a lustful vision of life that dominated even the

6 E. Corradini, L'unità e la potenza dele nazioni, p. 93: "The decadence of the bourgeoisie and the triumph of socialism determined the origins of nationalism in Italy." See also S. Cilibrizzi, Storia parlamentare, IV, 140.

7 E. Corradini, La rinascita nazionale, p. 310: "The action of Italian nationalism took its spur from the real historical conditions of the Third Italy, from that [condition] which was the effect and symbol of emigration." In an article entitled "Italy Is Born Again" ("L'Italia rinasce") published in the Nationalist review Il Regno, January 23, 1904, No. 9, Giovanni Papini said that the period of the philosophic nationalism of the Risorgimento (Mazzini, Gioberti, etc.) being over, Italy was entering a period of economic nationalism which best expressed itself in terms of figures, machinery, exports, imports, etc.

8 The very titles of some of D'Annunzio's works are indicative of the temper of the man: Pleasure (1889), Naval Odes (1892), The Triumph of Death (1894), The Virgins of the Rocks (1896), The Dead City (1898), Glory (1899), Fire (1900), The Ship (1908), Praises of the Sky, of the Sea, of the Earth, and of the Heroes (1899-1904).

9 On D'Annunzio, Fogazzaro, and Pascoli as symbols and symptons of the new age, see the illuminating essay of Croce, "Di un carattere della più recente letteratura italiana" (1907), reprinted in his La letteratura della nuova Italia, IV, 187-204.

10 G. A. Borgese, in the first editorial of his short-lived review Hermes, I (1904).

11 Borgese, Gabriele D'Annunzio, p. 163.

purest aspects of the reality he tried to capture in them. Lust and violence, all-embracing and inescapable, are the central themes of D'Annunzian literature: men and nature, history and thought, are all simply variations of those themes.[12] If he sang of heroes like Garibaldi, he exalted their actions but never penetrated the spirit that animated these actions. When he wrote of the Fatherland and of the nation there was no sign of any consciousness of transcendent human values or moral dignity; only pure force and the demonic moments in which it had expressed itself in the nation's history were the motives of his Nationalist art. "Open the gates of future dominions to our strength!" D'Annunzio apostrophized the new king, Victor Emmanuel III, in 1900.[13] "Arm the prow and set sail toward the world!" he told his country in his semi-orgiastic play *La Nave* (1908). "Paradise lies in the shadow of the sword," he cried during the Libyan War.[14]

D'Annunzio is regarded as the anti-Giolittian par excellence.[15] Where the one was scintillating poetry and often empty rhetoric, the other was solid fact itself; where the one excited the passionate imagination of Italians, the other attempted to keep them within the bounds of prosaic reason. D'Annunzio wanted to bring Italy to the starry firmament of glory, Giolitti to the workaday reality of productive labor. They might have been of different races of men, so dissimilar were they in temperament, in outlook, in aims. It was not at all strange that when Italy in 1915 was herself at the parting of the ways she found D'Annunzio urging her toward the fire and Giolitti toward an escape. Both were dangerous but the temper of that day being what it was the poet from the Abruzzi was more attuned to it than was the old Piedmontese.[16]

D'Annunzianism was among the most powerful of the Nationalist cross currents in which the Nationalism of Enrico Corradini and his colleagues had its origin. Corradini, who during the period of their review *Il Regno* (1903–1905) was to have as his chief collaborators Giovanni Papini and Giuseppe Prezzolini, came more completely than the others under the spell of the poet's lyrical nationalism.[17] It was through the group that con-

12 See F. Flora, *D'Annunzio*, pp. 85–96, for an interpretation of D'Annunzio's conception of war.

13 See the poem "Al Re Giovine," in E. Palmieri, ed., *Crestomazia della lirica di Gabriele D'Annunzio*, p. 172.

14 In the famous "Canzone d'Oltremare." *Ibid.*, p. 315.

15 G. Prezzolini, *La coltura italiana*, p. 82: "The Italian loves D'Annunzio, whom he feels closer to his own weaknesses, but he is shrewd enough to let himself be guided rather by Giolitti. In the former he enjoys the pleasures of poetry while in the latter he feels the solidity and satisfaction of prose. Thus, albeit reluctantly, he accepts Giolitti with an obedience that resembles discipline."

16 On Giolitti and D'Annunzio in 1915, see the none too objective book by G. Dàuli, *L'Italia nella Grande Guerra*, pp. 57–65, *passim;* also, and especially on Giolitti during the grave period of neutrality, the memoirs of an old antagonist from the Right, A. Salandra, *L'Intervento*, especially pp. 247–67, *passim;* finally Giolitti, *Memorie*, II, 509–51.

17 Cf. an article by Corradini himself on the D'Annunzian origins of nationalism in *Il Regno*, 1903, No. 3; see also Croce, *op. cit.*, pp. 248, 321.

tributed to Corradini's review that the creation of a Nationalist myth was undertaken and was hammered with violent insistence into the consciousness of its limited circle of readers.[18]

This movement, allegedly a reaction against the negations of Italian life, was itself rooted in negations: it was anti-Socialist, antiliberal, antidemocratic, antiparliamentarian, antipacifistic, anti-Giolittian. In the very first editorial of *Il Regno* Corradini stated that the new review wanted to be a voice crying out against the "cowardice of the present hour." [19] In May 1904, Papini lashed the "politician" Giolitti and invoked against him another "great statesman," a "second Crispi." [20] The program of the Nationalists was expounded in detail by Papini himself when he said that they wanted a resurgence of the bourgeoisie, that they wanted to fight the democratic mentality of the French Revolutionary catchwords, that they wanted a reassertion of the principle of authority.[21] The D'Annunzian motives in Papini's position were evident:

Let all those who want a vaster, larger, more heroic, more glorious life for our country, all those who hate the melancholy of resignation, the policy of stay-at-home, cowardice, all those, finally, who are for an intense and heroic life against a narrow and vulgar life, let them be with us and for us and let them bring us the spur of their enthusiasm and the power of their actions.[22]

Some of the antiparliamentary ideas already studied in the second chapter of the present work were reiterated by the writers of *Il Regno*. Prezzolini attempted to vindicate the purely Italian origins of the new nationalism when he said that it did not need to go to the ideology of foreign nationalists and imperialists such as Barrès, Chamberlain, and Kipling, since it possessed its own Gaetano Mosca and Vilfredo Pareto.[23] To these last-named writers could be traced Prezzolini's antiparliamentary criticism. In an article entitled "The Parliamentary Lie" (June 5, 1904), he predicted the removal of the fetish of a parliamentary regime and proposed to substitute workers' syndicates.[24] For, according to Prezzolini, there were two Italies, the Italy of Montecitorio (Parliament), full of vain talk, and the Italy of farm and factory.[25] This was a new note in the Nationalist

[18] From 1900 to 1915 there was in Italy a sort of literary renaissance which found expression through a great number of reviews and periodicals, among the most important being Croce's *La Critica* (Bari), *La Voce*, *Lacerba*, and *Leonardo*, with marked literary and artistic tendencies, and Salvemini's more political *L'Unità*, all in Florence. On the Florentine reviews, see the critical book by A. Bobbio, *Le riviste fiorentine del principio del secolo, 1903–1916*. On Papini and Prezzolini, see the enthusiastic thesis expounded by P. M. Riccio, *On the Threshold of Fascism*.

[19] Cf. M. Maffi, "Corradini e il Regno," *Politica*, XVI (1937), 81.

[20] G. Papini and G. Prezzolini, *Vecchio e nuovo nazionalismo*, pp. 102–05. The book is a collection of the writers' Nationalist articles of the *Il Regno* period.

[21] *Ibid.*, pp. 8–19, *passim*.

[22] *Ibid.*, p. 35.

[23] *Ibid.*, p. 38, from article "L' aristocrazia dei briganti."

[24] *Ibid.*, pp. 80–81, *passim*.

[25] *Ibid.*, pp. 71–73, *passim*; article "Le due Italie" (May 22, 1904).

ideology and, while it was to mark one of the first steps toward the con-ciliation of the two extremes of Nationalism and syndicalism, it separated Prezzolini from some of his friends for whom the resurrection of the middle class was the most imperative need of Italy.[26]

War as an end in itself, or at least as an instrument of discipline, was invoked by the Nationalists. Papini said (February 21, 1904):

When lives have to be sacrificed we are not saddened if before our minds shines the magnificant harvest of a superior life that will rise from those deaths. And while the lowly democrats cry out against war as a barbaric residue of ferocious ages, we believe it to be the greatest awakener of the weak, a quick and heroic instrument of power and wealth.[27]

Corradini made the main character of his novel *La Patria lontana* (1911) celebrate war as the "supreme act of a nation," "the supreme sacred act of national incarnation"; [28] elsewhere he asserted that the "essential duty of nationalism is the formation of a warlike conscience to oppose the pacifist conscience." [29] The enthusiastic admiration expressed for Japan after her victory over Russia in 1905 was derived in the Italian Nationalists from their belief that the Japanese were a virile people greatly contrasting to the pacifistic Italians.[30]

The collaboration of Corradini, Papini, and Prezzolini established on *Il Regno* lasted only for a brief period of two years. When the review itself ceased publication in 1906, the Nationalist trio parted ways, Cor-radini to continue and expand his original themes, the other two, after a brief separation during which Papini had dedicated himself to literary and philosophical studies and Prezzolini had been immersed in the Mod-ernist and Syndicalist movements, to meet again in the latter's serious anti-Nationalist review, *La Voce*. What had they contributed to Italian intellectual life during their Nationalist collaboration? If they had been personally moved by ideal motives they had failed signally to demonstrate them in their writings. They had demanded a more robust national life— for materialistic ends. They had asserted the need of power, energy, au-thority, war,—as goals unto themselves. They had, in fact, contributed nothing and in the process had made themselves the outstanding symbols of the moral malady they affirmed Italy was prey to.[31]

[26] G. Prezzolini, *La teoria sindacalista*, was to be one of the most thoughtful works on syndicalism.

[27] Papini and Prezzolini, *op. cit.*, p. 13.

[28] *La Patria lontana*, p. 244.

[29] E. Corradini, *Discorsi politici, 1902–1923*, p. 175.

[30] *Ibid.*, p. 49.

[31] Croce, "Di un carattere della più recente letteratura italiana" (1907), reprinted in his *La letteratura della nuova Italia*, p. 194. In the same article, and on the same page, Croce thus characterized the Italian imperialist: "The imperialist wants to lead Italy to a great destiny. He wants to crush the 'democratic beast.' He wants to conquer, wage war, destroy, spill rivers of blood. But if he is asked against whom he wishes to raise such a commotion, and why and with what means and for what purpose, he gets into a rage and immediately turns his cannonades of words against the inopportune

It was at least to the merit of Papini and especially of Prezzolini that they soon realized the futility of their Nationalist effort and thereupon abandoned it for more constructive work in moral and cultural education. The great Florentine review, *La Voce* (founded in 1908), was to start from different and more solid premises than *Il Regno* had in that its editor, Prezzolini, and his chief contributors (Papini, Gaetano Salvemini, Luigi Ambrosini, Giovanni Amendola, Antonio Anzilotti, and Bendetto Croce himself) realized that political, economic, and social progress, the acquisition and spread of a sane and solid culture, the possession of true moral and spiritual values and goals, could be the only lasting foundations for the national renewal of the Italian people.[32] As a result, *La Voce* became one of the most influential organs in the field of contemporary Italian culture.

The "spiritual nationalism" advocated by *La Voce* after 1908 by no means supplanted the older nationalism of Corradini. In fact, when nationalism seemed to be slowly dying, it partly sought, partly spontaneously received strength from two apparently antithetical sources—irredentism and syndicalism.

Since the attainment of partial unity, the Irredentists had never ceased their agitation which was a source of frequent diplomatic tension between Italy and Austria.[33] The rise of nationalism in Italy furnished the Irredentists with an outlet in the fatherland itself. This was especially welcome since some of them felt that they could hope for little from Liberals like Luzzatti, Tittoni, and Giolitti, and still less from the influential Clerical and Socialist parties in the Irredentist regions themselves, especially in the Trentino.[34] Thus, as the result of the sociologist Scipio Sighele's bringing the old irredentism into the Nationalist movement, and the journalist Luigi Federzoni's (Giulio De Frenzi) carrying on his own Irredentist campaign against German (not Austrian) infiltration around the Lake Garda region,[35] nationalism took a new lease on life. And when such a public figure as Luigi Luzzatti asserted, in an article in the *Corriere della Sera* (January 24, 1909), that: "All those who love their country must for some time divert their mind as much as possible from foreign policy,"

---

questioner. He feels that, were an attempt made to determine them historically, his programs of domination and devastation would forthwith lose their grandiosity and soon vanish into thin air."

[32] For a comparison and contrast of the two periods, see Prezzolini's Introduction to *Vecchio e nuovo nazionalismo*, pp. vi–x.

[33] How serious the Irredentist question could become may be gathered from reading Giolitti's account of the agitation over the University of Trieste (1909) and its national and international repercussions, in Giolitti, *op. cit.*, II, 256–61, and on the same topic, S. Sighele, *Pagine nazionaliste*, pp. 77–101. For a general account of Irredentist quèstions see G. Volpe, *L'Italia in cammino*, pp. 120–33.

[34] Cf. Sighele, *op. cit.*, p. 71, for a description of the influence of priests and Socialists in the Trentino; also his *Il nazionalismo e i partiti politici*.

[35] Cf. L. Federzoni ("Giulio De Frenzi") *Per l'italianità del "Gardasee,"* a collection of the author's journalistic writings on the Garda question.

the response from the re-invigorated Nationalist and especially Irredentist-Nationalist quarters was sharp and sustained.[36] It was useless for men like G. A. Borgese to demand a definition of program from the Nationalists and to take them to task for their attempt to monopolize old-fashioned patriotism.[37] For the Nationalists, Sighele's cryptical Cartesian formula: "They fight us, therefore we exist," [38] was sufficient answer.

By 1910 the Nationalists deemed they were sufficiently strong and important to warrant the calling of a Nationalist congress at Florence (December 3–5, 1910). The congress, under the chairmanship of Scipio Sighele, assembled in the ancient Hall of the Dugento in the Palazzo Vecchio, and there proceeded to discuss in detail questions of national and Nationalist importance.[39] The leading Nationalists, among the two hundred and thirty persons [40] assembled, were Corradini (who reported on the nation and the proletariat), Federzoni (on the policy of alliances), Sighele (Nationalism and irredentism), Maurizio Maraviglia (Nationalism and political parties), and Luigi Villari (Nationalism and emigration).[41] There was a brief moment of discord when democratic Nationalists (led by Sighele and Ercole Rivalta) and young Liberal Nationalists (led by Giovanni Borelli and Alberto Caroncini) suggested that the movement gather allies wherever it could,[42] meaning even in such extreme parties as the Republican. But the general atmosphere of the congress was characterized by the reassertion of Nationalist principles of power and authority. A strong foreign policy with definite anti-Triplice tones was advocated in the party program approved.[43] *Il Regno's* themes were voiced once again; the necessity of war as an instrument of national power was reaffirmed by Maraviglia; [44] Giovanni Pascoli, the mild Romagnuole Socialist poet, sent a telegram telling the Nationalists: "It is time to take up once again the

---

[36] Sighele, *Pagine nazionaliste*, pp. 144–45, answered Luzzatti's advice with: "To tell a country of thirty-four million inhabitants not to occupy itself with questions of foreign affairs is equivalent to a recommendation of suicide."

[37] Cf. G. A. Borgese, "Nazionalismo," in *La Vita e il Libro*, II (1911), 314–22, *passim*.

[38] Sighele, *op. cit.*, p. 324.

[39] For complete details on the reports presented see *Il nazionalismo italiano: Atti del Congresso di Firenze*.

[40] P. L. Occhini, *Enrico Corradini e la nuova coscienza nazionale*, p. 191.

[41] Nationalists of Jewish origin were as prominent in their party as others were in the Liberal and Socialist parties. While the Liberals had Luzzatti and Sonnino, and the Socialists Treves, Modigliani, Musatti, Sarfatti, Norlenghi, and A. O. Olivetti (Syndicalist), there were three Jews among the seven organizers of the Nationalist convention in Florence: R. Luzzatto, E. Rivalta, and the publisher E. Treves. Sighele, *op. cit.*, p. 218, had taken pride in the fact that, unlike its French counterpart of the *Action Française*, Italian Nationalism was not synonymous with a retrograde, clerical, anti-Semitic, Legitimist party.

[42] Occhini, *op. cit.*, pp. 195, 217–18, for the sources of the schism that eventually took place between the authoritarians and the liberals and democrats within the party.

[43] *Il nazionalismo italiano*, pp. 129 ff. For a contemporary Syndicalist viewpoint of foreign policy, see Labriola, *Storia di dieci anni*, p. 174: "Italy is regarded with diffidence and suspicion by her allies, and is left helpless by the other nations!"

[44] Cf. the citation of M. Maraviglia's speech as reported in Cilibrizzi, *op. cit.*, IV, 133.

heroic work: it is time that we set out to reconquer Italy for Italy!" [45]

The substantial results of the Nationalist congress of Florence, however, were the founding of the Italian Nationalist party (*Associazione nazionalista italiana*); the founding, on March 1, 1911, of a weekly Nationalist organ at Rome, the *Idea Nazionale* (transformed into a daily in October 1914); and the assertion of nationalism and imperialism as the socialism of a proletarian people.[46] Corradini, who claimed to have originated this imperialism of the poor, thus synthesized his theory: "Just as socialism was the method utilized for the redemption of the proletariat from the bourgeois classes, so nationalism shall be for us Italians the method of redemption from the French, the Germans, the British, and the North and South Americans who are our bourgeois." [47] During the course of the Libyan War, the Syndicalist Arturo Labriola wrote in the Neapolitan *La Scintilla*, October 11, 1911, that perhaps the Italians were not only fighting the Turks and Arabs, but also "against the intrigues, the threats, the snares, the money, and the arms of a plutocratic Europe that does not tolerate the smaller nations to dare endanger by word or action its iron-like hegemony." [48] The theme of a proletarian nation like Italy fighting against the plutocratic nations with their monopoly of the world's wealth was to prove very successful not only at the time it was being promulgated by Italian Nationalists and Syndicalists, but also at later times and in other countries.

The outbreak of the Italian-Turkish War might have seemed like the long-invoked and anxiously awaited answer to the Nationalist prayers. Had not Corradini himself shouted "Tripoli's hour has come!" (*L'ora di Tripoli*), Gualtiero Castellini "Tunis and Tripoli" (*Tunisi e Tripoli*), Giuseppe Piazza "Our promised land!" (*La nostra terra promessa*) earlier in that same year 1911? Had not their newspapers and reviews, from *Il Carroccio* (Florence) and *Il Tricolore* (Turin), to the Roman *La Grande Italia* and *L'Idea Nazionale* and the Neapolitan *La Nave* demand a victorious war and an Italian colony where the poor could go and thrive under Italian care rather than emigrate to unknown shores? But "to ascribe to the Nationalists the seizure of Tripoli would be excessive," says Professor Foerster,[49] and it might be added that it would be unfair, if credit or blame is to be taken, to history and to the Italian people and its government. For while the contribution of the Nationalists to the preparation of a state of mind receptive to the war can hardly be denied, the Libyan War itself, diplomatically and psychologically, had deeper roots and achieved more far-reaching results than any mere Nationalist conquest could have given it. Unquestionably the war had been maturing in the consciousness of Italian statesmen and of the majority of the Italian people

---

[45] Occhini, *op. cit.*, p. 192.

[46] See E. Corradini, *Il nazionalismo italiano*, pp. 67–69, for his speech of December 3, 1910, at the Florence congress where he first publicly advanced the new theory.

[47] *Idem*, *Il volere d'Italia*, p. 206.

[48] Quoted by Michels, *L'Imperialismo italiano*, p. 92, note 4.

[49] R. F. Foerster, *The Italian Emigration of Our Times*, p. 496.

since the dark days of Adowa, or at least since the beginning of the century.[50]

Behind the Libyan War there was, too, the half-century of national unity and progress that had been celebrated in the spring of 1911. That celebration had been a kind of national stock-taking in which the economic, political, and spiritual growth of Italy and her people had been assessed and found, on the whole, not wanting. This progress was especially characteristic of the years following Adowa and the advent of Giolitti. "The development of Italian economy in the thirteen years preceding the outbreak of the World War," says Corbino, "had been effected with such an intense rhythm of progress as to make one believe in miracles" if one did not know that the rest of western Europe had made proportionate advance.[51]

Population had increased from 26,801,154 in 1872 to 32,475,253 in 1901, and to 35,845,048 in 1911.[52] There had been an immense industrial growth, especially in the North, where the iron and steel industries, cotton production, sugar refineries, chemical factories, automobile plants, and hydro-electrical works rendered Piedmont, Lombardy, Liguria, and Tuscany one of the most highly industrialized regions of Europe.[53] Italian foreign trade during the twenty-year period from 1890 to 1910 made greater advance than that of any other European nation, rising from some two billion lire to over four billions during the decade 1890–1900 and close to six billions by 1910, although the margin of unfavorable balance continued to be decried by both Nationalists and free-traders.[54] Agriculture, too, showed

[50] For the diplomatic and military history of the Libyan War, see Giolitti, *op. cit.*, II, 327–473; G. Mondaini, *Manuale di storia e legislazione coloniale del Regno d'Italia. Storia coloniale*, pp. 261–99; *La Libia negli atti del Parlamento e nei provvedimenti del Governo*, issued by the Collegio di Scienze Politiche e Coloniali and edited by Emilio Pagliano. W. C. Askew, *Europe and Italy's Acquisition of Libya*, is an excellent and thorough diplomatic history of the Libyan War based on a study of original sources.

[51] E. Corbino, *Annali dell'economia italiana*, V, 1. D. Russo, "Hommes du Jour: M. Giolitti," *Le Correspondant* (Paris), July 10, 1920, says: "Les dix ans qui s'écoulerent de 1904 a 1913, la période de la dictature giolittiènne, furent les années grosses de l'économie italiènne, si grosses qu'elles purent donner l'illusion qu'on était assez riche et assez fort pour pouvoir se conceder le luxe de la guèrre de Libye."

[52] *Annuario statistico italiano*, Second Series, Vol. I (1911), p. 4; Corbino, *Annali*, V, 2.

[53] Cf. G. Volpe, *L'Italia in cammino*, pp. 80–81; Croce, *A History of Italy*, pp. 227–28. On the "invasion of Italy by foreign capital" during the period, see G. Preziosi, *La Germania alla conquista dell'Italia*; F. S. Nitti, *Il capitale straniero in Italia* (Bari, 1915); I. Silone, *Der Fascismus*, p. 27, note 7. Besides R. Bachi's annual publications *L'Italia economica*, other reliable economic studies are N. Colajanni, *Il progresso economico*; E. Messeri, *Cinquanta anni di vita economica e fianziaria italiana*; and particularly the monumental anniversary publication *Cinquanta anni di storia italiana (1860–1910)* published under the auspices of the Reale Accademia dei Lincei. The *Annuario statistico italiano* for these years is basic.

[54] Croce, *op. cit.*, pp. 227–28; Volpe, *op. cit.*, p. 85. See also A. de Viti de Marco, *Per un programma d'azione democratica*. E. Giretti, *I trivellatori della nazione italiana*, and Labriola, *Storia di dieci anni*, argued that by sponsoring and "imposing" protectionist policies upon the government, the iron, steel, sugar, and agrarian magnates were perpetuating the economic plight of the rest of Italy.

marked improvements, agricultural production having more than doubled since the attainment of unity in 1861. Moreover, vast land reclamation projects had been finished or were still in progress in marshy lands of the Po Valley in Romagna and Venetia, in the malarial Pontine Marshes, in the sandy regions of the Marches and Abruzzi, in the arid plateau of Apulia, in the Tuscan Maremma, and, to a lesser extent, in the forsaken areas of Sicily and Sardinia.[55] The credit of the Italian government was in excellent conditions and the conversion of the national debt had been accomplished in 1906 amid national enthusiasm and without even a shadow of the panic generally attendant upon such maneuvers.[56]

The increase of both the number of industrial and agrarian strikes [57] and emigration [58] during the Giolittian period may be variously interpreted, but fundamentally they testified to a social ferment and to the expansion of a freedom of action in direct contrast to the preceding period. Emigration, moreover, from being a source of shame, had slowly become a means of national and personal rehabilitation, especially in southern Italy. The growth of savings banks (*Casse di Risparmio*), of the Banca Commerciale, of the Credito Italiano and other such agencies bespoke, among other things, a wholesome relative increase of security among lower-income groups as well as more widespread investments in national enterprises.[59] At the same time illiteracy was steadily being reduced (although it still formed one of the gravest national problems).[60] State action, legislation, and appropriations, the strenuous efforts of local communities, the admirable educational crusade of such organizations as the *Opera nazionale per il Mezzogiorno* (founded to aid the South after the earthquake of 1908), the opening of evening schools and public libraries in provincial towns and municipalities, the self-sacrifice of numerous teachers who volunteered to bring the alphabet to the countryside without

[55] Cf. *Inchiesta parlamentare sulle condizioni nelle provincie meridionali e nella Sicilia, 1910–1911.* Volpe, *op. cit.*, p. 82.

[56] Cf. Giolitti, *op. cit.*, I, 240–48, for an authoritative account of the conversion.

[57] Corbino, *op. cit.*, V, 466, gives the following statistics:

Year	Agriculture		Industry	
	No. of strikes	Strikers	No. of strikes	Strikers
1900	27	13,000	383	81,000
1901	629	223,000	1042	197,000
1902	221	147,000	810	197,000
1904	208	95,000	631	125,000
1906	350	118,000	1299	264,000
1907	377	254,000	1891	327,000
1908	257	136,000	1417	188,000
1909	140	47,000	931	142,000
1910	88	26,000	1021	173,000
1911	148	133,000	1107	253,000

[58] From 1901 to 1912 Italian emigration averaged about 600,000 annually. Cf. Foerster, *op. cit.*, and Michels, *L'imperialismo italiano.*

[59] Cf. Volpe, *op. cit.*, pp. 83–84.

[60] In 1871, the percentage of illiteracy was 68.8, in 1901, 48.5, in 1911, 43.1. Cf. "Analfabetismo" in *Enciclopedia Italiana*, III, 80.

remuneration, these and many other means helped to remove the veil of ignorance and illiteracy from large areas of the Italian peninsula.[61] Great organs of public opinion such as the *Corriere della Sera,* the *Giornale d'Italia,* the *Stampa,* and many others during this period achieved a European and world-wide reputation and significance.[62] At the same time social legislation in Italy had kept pace with the more advanced European nations, laws having been passed and enforced enjoining Sunday rest, strengthening old-age and unemployment funds, regulating woman and child labor, providing for the construction of low-rent working-class homes (*case popolari*), for poor relief and sickness insurance, and special measures for the rehabilitation of the poverty-stricken Southern provinces, Sicily and Sardinia.[63] Thus there is a great measure of truth and justified pride in Giolitti's assertion that these provisions were consonant with a policy of peace, freedom, work, and social justice if Italy was destined to reach "that high goal which was and still is the ideal of all those who love" her.[64]

Unquestionably, economic, social, cultural, intellectual, and scientific advancement had brought Italy once again into the vanguard of European civilization. It had been a difficult ascendancy, but a true national resurgence unnoticed by most men because they had been unconsciously absorbed in it—Liberals and Socialists, capital and labor, workers and farmers, cultured men and illiterates, financiers and emigrants. Not all had shared equally in the work or in its fruits and there was still much to be done. But the achievements after fifty years of unity were nevertheless solid and gave great promise for the future of the nation.

The psychological significance of the Libyan War in Giolittian Italy must therefore be viewed in the perspective of this growth and progress to be properly understood. Those who, before and after the war, attempted to gauge the extent and intensity of the national consciousness of Italians in terms of nationalistic sentiments and ideology alone were bound to be disappointed.[65] Given the complexity of the Italian ideological and political scene it was to be expected that the war would reveal a lack of unanimity of opinion which (except perhaps from a nationalist point of

[61] Cf. Cilibrizzi, *op. cit.,* Vol. IV.

[62] L. Piccioni, *Il Giornalismo* is an enlightening bibliographical guide to Italian journalism, national and local.

[63] Cf. Giolitti, *op. cit.,* I, 269–70. Angiolo Cabrini, *La legislazione sociale, 1859–1913,* is an excellent short study of social legislation in Italy from Cavour to Giolitti.

[64] Giolitti, *op. cit.,* I, 271: "Il complesso di quei provvedimenti, rispondeva ad una politica di pace, di libertà, di lavoro, di giustizia sociale, che io ritenevo dovesse continuare con sempre crescente fermezza ed energia, se si voleva che il nostro paese si avvicinasse rapidamente a quell'alta mèta che fu ed è l'ideale di quanti amano l'Italia. Che questo ideale si potesse raggiungere perseverando nella via seguita lo dimostrava in modo evidente il grande progresso compiuto dall'Italia in quegli ultimi anni."

[65] See Paolo Arcari, *La coscienza nazionale in Italia* for the results of a poll of public opinion conducted on the subject of national (or nationalistic) sentiment in Italy on the eve of the Libyan War. See also Paola Maria Arcari, *Le elaborazioni della dottrina politica nazionale fra l'unità e l'intervento.*

view) was not altogether a liability and, when it did not originate in mere petty partisanship, might act as a source of restraint to the passions all wars so easily let loose. Thus the negative attitude of the majority of Socialists, and their organs, the *Avanti!* and the *Critica Sociale,* the opposition of the group of *La Voce,* and of Salvemini's new review *L'Unità* could be easily understood.[66] How far the temper and attitude of the people in general and of the Socialists in particular had changed since Adowa could be seen in the lack of concerted opposition, in the failure of the general strike called in the early days of the war by the Italian Confederation of Labor, in the failure of all positive attempts to arouse anti-militarist feeling.[67]

On the other hand, the prevailing sentiment of the people toward the war was perhaps best expressed by Giovanni Pascoli, when he exclaimed: "The great proletarian has stirred itself!" (*La grande Proletaria si è mossa!*),[68] and by the Tuscan Conservative, Ferdinando Martini, who cried on December 28, 1911: "Blessed through the centuries be the brothers who perished, and those who live and fight at Tripoli, at Derna, and at Bengasi, who not only give back to Italy the place she deserves in the world, but also give us back our lost [national] conscience! . . ." [69] The bourgeois press, from the Giolittian *La Stampa* to the anti-Giolittian *Il Corriere della Sera,* supported the war enthusiastically, and even part of the Syndicalist press, from Paolo Orano's *La Lupa* (Florence) to A. O. Olivetti's *Pagine Libere* (Lugano), was favorable to it. All political groups, all shades of political opinion during and after the Libyan War, vied with one another to demonstrate their support of, and their direct participation in, the enterprise. The Nationalists, of course, tried to arrogate to themselves the credit of having imposed the war. "We Nationalists," said Luigi Federzoni, "accused of imperialist and warlike infatuations, succeeded in rousing public spirit, and it was through our propaganda that the will of the nation was able to impose conquest on Libya." [70] The Conservatives, with Sonnino and Salandra, also claimed their share. It was not a matter of confidence in Giolitti, said Sonnino, but rather of confidence in Libya and in the mission of Italy in the Mediterranean that had spurred him to vote in favor of Giolitti's Cabinet.[71] Salandra asserted that it was "well known that we helped to impel the Government toward the Libyan conquest." [72] The Republican party was split on the question

[66] Cf. Volpe, *op. cit.,* pp. 160–61, *passim.*

[67] On the activities of Mussolini during the period of the Libyan War see G. Megaro, *Mussolini in the Making,* pp. 246–73.

[68] G. Pascoli, Barga speech (November 27, 1911), *La grande Proletaria.*

[69] For full text of Martini's speech commemorating Tuscan officers fallen in Libya, see *La Stampa* (Turin), XLV (1911), No. 360. See also Croce, *A History of Italy,* pp. 323–24, and Michels, *L'imperialismo italiano,* pp. 166–67.

[70] L. Federzoni, electoral speech of October 25, 1913, in his *Presagi alla Nazione,* p. 39.

[71] *Atti Parlamentari.* "Discussioni della Camera dei Deputati. Tornata del 10 dicembre 1913," (Session 1913–1914), I, 281.

[72] A. Salandra, "Il partito liberale nell'ora presente," *L'Eloquenza,* III (1913), Nos. 9–10, 325.

of support of the war, but Salvatore Barzilai, its leader, had tried to justify
his own approval by stating that even Mazzini and Carlo Cattaneo would
have supported Italy's attempt to break the chains that were slowly en-
closing her in the Mediterranean.[73] "There are certain moments in the
noontide of history," he said, "in which it is impossible to forsake the
interests of the fatherland in the hope that party fortunes may some day
come to restore them!"[74] The undoubtedly significant Catholic and
clerical support of war was naturally ascribed to religious fanaticism (a
Catholic country versus Islam), when it was not imputed to their interest
in protecting their financial stake in the Banco di Roma![75]

The havoc wrought in the Socialist party by the Libyan War has already
been described. That the official Italian Socialist party had never completely succumbed to the out and out pacifism (Hervéisme) of some of its
more extremist leaders was attested as early as 1909 by Turati.[76] The outbreak of the Libyan War, however, revealed how wide was the gap in the
party between the lack of Hervéisme and a positive Socialist support of "a
sign of Nationalist self-conceit and awkward piracy," as Turati styled the
war.[77] Fortunately, the violence of the Socialist epithets against the war
was never proportionate to the actions they could arouse. Socialism as a
whole, moreover, sustained a profound shock when it was realized that
the masses did not respond to its reasoned anti-Nationalist appeals as
readily as they did to the poetical expressions of Pascoli and Martini.
And Turati in his speech in the Chamber against the Decree of Annexation
of the whole of Libya (February 23, 1912), as if to pay tribute to the new
temper of the times, had contented himself with a merely formal protest.[78]

The actions and words of the Reformists of the Right had shown, moreover, that patriotism had made great inroads among the democrats of the
Socialist party. Cabrini, Bonomi, Bissolati, Giuseppe Canepa, De Felice-
Giuffrida (the old leader of the Fasci siciliani), recognized that the rights
of a class could not and should not stand in the way of an endangered
fatherland. Speaking in the Chamber on April 8, 1911, Bissolati had asserted that he was a Nationalist in so far as he wished patriotism to be
fostered among the masses of the people by giving them the sense of responsible action in the community.[79] At the Modena congress (October
1911), Ivanoe Bonomi said:

73 For his speech in the Chamber of March 3, 1912, see S. Barzilai, Luci ed ombre
del passato, pp. 127–29, passim.

74 Ibid., pp. 127–29.

75 Cf. Volpe, op. cit., pp. 160–61, passim.

76 F. Turati, Trent'anni, p. 150: "In Italy today we do not have a true militant
Hervéisme that has any influence on the state, and, much less, on Parliament" (April
16, 1909). For Socialist attitude toward the military budget, see Turati's speech in
Atti Parlamentari. "Discussioni della Camera dei Deputati. Tornata del 12 giugno
1909" (Session 1909–1913), II, 2303–14.

77 Resoconto stenografico del XII Congresso: Modena, p. 207.

78 Turati, op. cit., pp. 109–99 for his speech.

79 Cf. Atti Parlamentari. "Discussioni della Camera dei Deputati: Tornata dell' 8
aprile 1911," (Session, 1909–1913), XI, 13706–07, for Bissolati's entire speech.

There is a national solidarity that is not opposed to, but rather complements, class solidarity [in so far as it] asserts the necessity of a great social discipline without which there is no strong people, whether it be governed by bourgeois or by Socialist laws. (*Approval on the Right. Groans and interruptions on the Left.*) [80]

Angiolo Cabrini let loose pandemonium in the congress when he said that it was the duty of the Italian Socialists, while wishing for a quick return of peace, to wish also that "victory smile upon the banner of our people" in Libya.[81] Bissolati, both at the Modena and at the Reggio Emilia congresses (July 1912), justified his conduct toward the Libyan War by pointing out that the Government had been impelled to war in order to prevent Italy's being strangled by a siege-belt in the Mediterranean.[82] It should have been the duty of the Socialists, Bissolati said, to oppose by concrete and positive actions the monopoly of Italian patriotism the reactionary Nationalists were establishing. He, too, referred to the disciplinary value of war for a democratic people:

Our country, which today is the equal of England and I think even surpasses her in matters of liberty and in political institutions, tomorrow may become the forge of great democratic movements. . . . It may have to bring its help to international movements the goal of whose struggles may be the attainment of social justice. I make the vow that then Italian soldiers will fight with the same energy, with greater energy even than they used against Arabs and Turks.[83]

Indeed, while in its military phase the war against Turkey was proceeding in the slow normal course of all colonial adventures, in Italy it seemed to have become a great mould into which the various currents and cross currents of Italian life flowed to be fused into a unity of purpose that resembled a popular Risorgimento. Despite the diplomatic correctness of their official attitude, most of the European Powers gave evidence of hostility or blindness to the deeper significance for Italians of the Libyan War.[84] It is true that by the course of the war and by the peace treaty of Lausanne (October 18, 1912) Italy contributed an irreparable shock to the already precarious European balance of power and a violent pull at the dangerous diplomatic net enveloping the Ottoman Empire. But the sources for this lay with Italy as much as they were inherent in the long-standing insecurity of international relations, and with the Powers that had long abetted for their own particular interests Italian ambitions and designs on the last remaining unoccupied zone of North Africa.[85] As it

[80] *Resoconto stenografico . . . Modena*, p. 69.

[81] *Ibid.*, p. 162.

[82] *Resoconto stenografico . . . Reggio Emilia*, pp. 157–58, *passim*.

[83] *Ibid.*, p. 161.

[84] Cf. Giolitti, *op. cit.*, II, 345–68, 377–81; Askew, *op. cit.*, pp. 64–81, for European reactions to the outbreak of the war.

[85] Europe was hardly out of the most acute phase of the second Moroccan crisis when Italy declared war on Turkey. Perhaps more than the declaration of war itself its timing burst like a bomb-shell upon the European chancellories. In a way, by going to Tripoli, Italy was merely cashing a diplomatic check guaranteed by Germany (1887), France (1900, 1902), Austria (1902), England (1902), and Russia at Racconigi (1909). Cf. Askew, *op. cit.*, pp. 11–22, 266–74.

was, hostile reactions and expressions of diffidence abroad came to be viewed by Italians as plots to discredit their character and to rob their country of its rightful place in the sun.[86] But despite the sordid aspects inherent in the war as such and the inevitable disappointments and disillusions it was expected to bring in its train, the Libyan War found the majority of Italians rallied around their government in an amazing show of solidarity.

"Giolitti," commented the anti-Libyan *La Voce*, "the anti-Nationalist par excellence, the stay-at-home Piedmontese, the evil hypnotist, by going to Tripoli has changed the course and tenor of Italian life and has stolen the thunder from the Nationalists." [87] Was this man Giolitti perhaps another Cavour, an artificer capable of molding the complex elements at work in war into a sturdy new democratic unity for Italy's ascendancy in peace?

[86] Even Bissolati felt compelled to assert at the Reggio Emilia Socialist congress that he had participated in a demonstration in favor of Jean Carrère because this French journalist had been courageous enough to want "to vindicate the dignity and integrity of our people" at a moment when "all capitalistic Europe" was trying to discredit Italian soldiers by calling them "cold-blooded torturers and killers of Arabs." Cf. *Resoconto stenografico . . . Reggio Emilia*, p. 158.

[87] "La fine del nazionalismo," *La Voce*, IV 1912, No. 19, p. 87.

IX

GIOLITTI AND *GIOLITTISMO*

L'onorevole Giolitti è stato un uomo molto discusso.
In un certo senso egli è stato un uomo
*più vituperato che lodato. . . .**

ARTURO LABRIOLA

HAD anyone expected Italy's premier, Giovanni Giolitti, to epitomize the inner meaning of the Libyan War by an inspired Cavourian gesture or word, he would have been sadly disappointed. There was, of course, hardly anything in the man's past to justify such an expectation. Enthusiasm, passion, poetry were as foreign to his nature as calculation, reason, and prose were its most apparent characteristics. There might be more complexity in him than appearances presented, but, as is the fate of all men in similar public positions, he could only be known and appraised for what he seemed.[1]

During and immediately after the Libyan War the Italian psychological situation seemed prepared for the sowing of the seeds of idealism. A statesman who was also a political artist, or at least a rhetorician, would have rejoiced at such an opportunity to steal the thunder from the Nationalists, from the D'Annunzios mouthing poetical generalities, the Mussolinis with their semi-anarchical invectives. Not so Giolitti. When the war was only a few days old and enthusiasm and expectation running high, in a long-awaited speech at Turin (October 8, 1911) Giolitti hardly referred to the war perhaps thinking it better or wiser to ignore the sentiments of his people rather than to fan them beyond control (as a demagogue would have done), or to try to master them and make them his own in a noble fusion of passion and reason (as Cavour had done).[2] It was his characteristic way of being exasperatingly sober since soberness was his usual demeanor and the situation seemed to demand a cautious fervor and a warm wariness. A year after the conclusion of the peace, in 1913, his soberness was more understandable since by then the initial enthusiasm had cooled to the critical self-analysis of all post-war periods:

* "The Honorable Giolitti has been a much-discussed man. In a certain sense, he has been more abused than praised. . . ." Arturo Labriola, *Storia di dieci anni, 1899–1909*, p. 230.

[1] On the sentimental aspects of Giolitti's so-called skeptical character, see Lodi, *Venticinque anni*, p. 69; Croce, *A History of Italy*, p. 261; and C. Sforza, *The Real Italians*, p. 134. All three writers were at one time or another close associates of Giolitti.

[2] Cf. Giolitti, *Memorie*, II, 470–71: "I was of the opinion and I am now convinced that the success of an enterprise ought not to be gauged at all by the theatrical grandiosity of the ways and means through which it is achieved. It should rather be measured by the sober use made of the means adapted for its attainment." Contrast the editorial "La pace giolittiana," in *La Voce*, IV (1912), 915.

I have declared it on other occasions and I do not hesitate to repeat it: I did not undertake the Libyan War out of enthusiasm—quite the contrary! (*Comments. Interruptions.*) It is the truth and I must confess it. I undertook it, however, after having carefully calculated on the one hand the great advantage of possessing a vast colony in the Mediterranean, and, on the other, the disaster to which we should have exposed ourselves had we not undertaken it. (*Warm approval. Applause from many sides. Interruptions on the Extreme Left.*) [3]

The dispassionate politico who has been impelled by a necessity stronger than his will (had he not called the Libyan War an historical fatality at its outbreak?) to an action foreign to his usual calculations speaks in those words. Who was this man who made a passion of dispassion, and what was his significance in the Italy of his time?

Perhaps no other modern Italian political figure has been the source of more controversy than Giovanni Giolitti. A kind of Giolittiana has been in the making almost since his appearance on the public scene. The most violent passions have raged about this man without passion, and the extensive vocabulary of political invective does not seem yet to have exhausted its possibilities where Giolitti is concerned. His mind, his public character, his policies, his methods, his aims, his achievements, have been variously diagnosed and catalogued. And yet the impartial student who approaches this Giolittian literature afresh—through Giolitti himself—cannot fail to sense such an air of partisanship, of factiousness, of insufficiency in it, that he is impelled to review the case and to try to achieve an understanding that is beyond the clash of personalities, beyond class, beyond political, and psychological preconceptions.

One thing was certain about Giolitti: there was nothing of the Alexander or Napoleon in or about him. He was not a *condottiere*, either *quattrocento* or *novecento* style. Tall, sturdy, broad-shouldered, this solid man from the mountains of Piedmont looked like "a clergyman disguised as a carabineer in plain clothes." [4] He was truly a man of peace for whom war was a distraction of destiny or a matter of geography. Tripoli seemed merely a brief parenthesis between the law for state monopoly of life insurance (June 1911) and the law for electoral reform (June 1912). A man interested only in domestic affairs and politics, for whom foreign relations were the inescapable burden and necessity of government, Giolitti must be approached and appraised as such.[5] It is apparent from a study of his administrations, of his policies, and of his speeches that he was more at home in Parliament than in the Libyan Desert or at Fiume.[6] The Na-

[3] *Atti Parlamentari.* "Discussioni della Camera dei Deputati. Tornata del 16 dicembre 1913," (Session 1913–14), I, 480.

[4] The description is attributed to the Conservative F. Martini. See S. Barzilai, *Luci ed ombre del passato*, p. 293, for a variation of the characterization.

[5] For an authoritative study of Giolitti's foreign policies, see L. Salvatorelli, "Giolitti und seine auswärtige Politik," in *Europäische Gespräche*, VII (1929), 117–37.

[6] For sustained studies of Giolittian ministries, see S. Cilibrizzi, *Storia parlamentare*, Vols. III–IV; F. Quintavalle, *Storia dell'unità italiana*; Lodi, *op. cit.* For an intelligent attempt in English to present the Giolittian regimes, see Hentze, *Pre-Fascist Italy*, chaps. vii–viii.

tionalists who abused him for this might just as well have reproached him for his Piedmontese birth or for his massive shoulders.

In the problems of Italian political life examined in the preceding chapters of this work, whenever he has made an appearance Giolitti has been allowed to speak for himself. No amount of exegesis can properly recapture the tone of that staid Giolittian prose. It was as much a part of his personality as were his policies, and if his manner of speaking is examined here it is because it may furnish a key to his political character as a whole. During his long tenure of power, the Chamber of Deputies heard some of the most brilliant Italian luminaries of the spoken word, among whom were Barzilai, Turati, Martini, Fradeletto, Altobelli, and Raimondo. Pure eloquence was a national characteristic, as rhetoric was a national vice. Yet Giolitti never varied his laconic eloquence which was without apparent artifice or search for effect, cold, factual, analytical. Once Felice Cavallotti, the Radical leader and bard of democracy, had reproached Giolitti for the brevity of his remarks in the Chamber. Giolitti apologized by saying that "when I have said what I have to say, I find it impossible to continue to speak." [7] In his speech of June 21, 1901, while describing the center of North Italian working-class agitation, Giolitti had had recourse to a Dantesque allusion, but the Chamber bursting out with "Oooohs!" he stopped, and then simply added he would never quote Dante again.[8] Despite the popular legend to the contrary, he is reputed, by men who knew him intimately, to have been a man of wide culture who even kept abreast of modern literature.[9] Yet Giolitti made pure reason his main oratorical weapon.[10] He seldom quoted or appealed to authority in his speeches, and seemed to avoid consciously the rules of classic oratory by hitting first at the strongest rather than at the weakest points of an opponent's argument. His wit and irony were most effective when most commonplace, as his "Marx-in-the-attic" speech revealed. Unquestionably his speech lacked warmth and feeling and displayed no purely lyrical outbursts; this conspired to make it more bureaucratic and impersonal than it need have been.

His career had flowed on as unimpressively as his prose. Born at Mondovì in Piedmont, on October 27, 1842, Giolitti had studied law at the University of Turin and immediately after graduation entered government employment through which he had risen from the lowest grades.[11] In 1882 he was on the Council of State and was thereby elected deputy

---

[7] See L. Salvatorelli, ed., *Giolitti*, p. xxvi.

[8] *Ibid.*, pp. 38–42, *passim*.

[9] Cf. C. Sforza, "Giolitti," in *Makers of Modern Europe*, pp. 236–54.

[10] V. E. Orlando, "L'Oratoria di Giovanni Giolitti," *L'Eloquenza*, I (1911), 288. Cf. T. Palamenghi-Crispi, *Giovanni Giolitti*, p. 4, for a contrary view of Giolitti's character and oratory; Crispi's whole book, however, is highly polemical and his opinions must be accepted with great caution.

[11] Palamenghi-Crispi, *op. cit.*, pp. 2–3, seems to make much of the fact that Giolitti, a Piedmontese, did not participate directly in the stirring events of 1860, 1866, and 1870.

from the electoral district of Cuneo, from which he was returned until his death in 1928. He participated in important parliamentary committees, and in 1888 made a debut in the Chamber with a cutting speech against the financial policy of Magliani. Minister of the Treasury in the Crispi cabinet (March 1889 to November 1890), Giolitti himself became Prime Minister after the fall of Di Rudinì (May 10, 1892 to November 1893). It was from this time, and especially after the general elections of 1892, that *Giolittismo* came to be identified with the worst kind of governmental interference in political elections.[12] Then came the turbulent period of the Banca Romana scandals and the deadly feud with Crispi.[13] Following a period of political eclipse, Giolitti returned to public life during the days of obstructionism, and was Minister of the Interior in the Zanardelli cabinet from February 1901 to October 1903.[14] On November 3, 1903, he formed his own cabinet, and from that time until the fall of his last prewar cabinet on March 31, 1914, the Government was associated with his name, whether he was officially in power or not.[15] His long tenure of power came to be viewed as a dictatorship: parliamentary at its best, total at its worst.[16] His was called a typical form of the spoils system,[17] and the views of his aims and achievements varied from their non-existence to their destruction of the national soul.[18]

The most noteworthy characteristics of practically all the literature of *Giolittismo* may be separated into two main categories: that of purely political opposition, and that of personal sympathy or antipathy.[19] These two currents are never mutually exclusive, but either the one or the other, or both together, throw light upon the otherwise sometimes obscure sources of Giolittian and anti-Giolittian contemporary and historical literature. Perhaps the most conspicuous example of the first of those currents was the Conservative (or so-called Liberal and Liberal-Conserva-

[12] *Ibid.*, pp. 36–37. Cf. King and Okey, *Italy Today*, pp. 5–6.

[13] For a brief and authoritative account of the Banca Romana, see Cilibrizzi, *op. cit.*, II, 450–93. For two points of view on the notorious Crispi-Giolitti Affair, see Giolitti, *op. cit.*, I, 99–129, and Palamenghi-Crispi, *op. cit.*, as a whole. Both accounts are naturally apologetic.

[14] On the controversial issue of Giolitti's having abandoned Zanardelli's "sinking ship" in 1903, in order to hasten his succession, see Giolitti, *op. cit.*, I, 182–84. Labriola, *op. cit.*, pp. 221–24, has some interesting comments on this point.

[15] During the period 1903–14 only Giolitti's own ministries lasted more than a year. For a rather brilliant critical analysis of Giolittian ministerial ubiquity in other than his own cabinets, see S. Barzilai's significant speech against Luzzatti in *Atti Parlamentari*. "Discussioni della Camera dei Deputati. Tornata del 18 marzo 1909" (Session 1909–13), IX, 13539–13545.

[16] M. Claar, "Giovanni Giolitti (1842–1928) und die liberale Parlamentsdiktatur in Italien," in *Zeitschrift für Politik*, XVIII (1928), 231–39, is a concise and clear summary of the issues and antecedents of the Giolittian dictatorship as contrasted with the Fascist.

[17] A. De Viti De Marco, *Un trentennio di lotte politiche*, p. 383.

[18] M. Missiroli, *La monarchia socialista*, p. 123: "In ten years he has killed the national soul, by suppressing all oppositions, but he has saved the monarchy."

[19] There is a penetrating post-war essay on Giolitti's character and political personality in Filippo Burzio, *Politica demiurgica*, pp. 41–79.

tive) opposition to Giolitti during most of the period—an opposition
which had its roots in mistrust of his popular tendencies on the part of
large agrarian, industrial, and capitalistic interests.[20] In Parliament this
opposition usually found its political expression in the Right and Center.
In the North, the powerful Milanese Liberal newspaper *Il Corriere della
Sera,* and throughout the country those ideological and political currents
whose chief spokesmen were Sonnino and Salandra, also commonly reflected that opposition. Giolitti's policy of liberty for all within the limits
of the law, his apparent infatuation with the extreme parties, his flirtations with the Socialists, his utilization of the clericals as an electoral
weapon, his attitude of official neutrality in the clashes between capital
and labor, his demagogic financial policies, perhaps even his up-to-date
social and political vocabulary, seemed all to be sources of deep suspicion
for those who still conceived of the Italian state in terms of nineteenth-
century Liberal-conservatism, *Staatsrecht,* and social statics rather than
social dynamics.[21] The Conservative criticism of Giolittian policy was often
reinforced by political Conservatism of quite different origins. Thus it
happened that a Republican like Salvatore Barzilai, a Radical like Antonio Fradeletto, and a real Conservative like Ferdinando Martini found
themselves in agreement in their anti-Giolittian censure. Barzilai's analysis
of Giolitti and Giolittian policy is often acute and always enlightening.
Speaking in the Chamber of Deputies on December 2, 1903, he contributed
the following to Giolittian exegesis:

> Undoubtedly the Honorable Giolitti has in his mind certain formulas, pre-
> cise, lucid, almost geometric, to regulate the relations between the Government
> and the various classes of citizens, and in the application of these formulas he
> has a swift perception, a remarkable rapidity. The Honorable Giolitti, however,
> I believe does not possess the inspired and passionate conception of those things
> which are the complex necessities, both material and spiritual, of the life of a
> great country, [and] he does not see what the destiny of this country may, or
> should, be in the world. The Honorable Giolitti loves liberty, yes, but not with
> a deep spiritual feeling; it, too, is a geometrical calculation inspired by utilitari-
> anism of an economic kind, by considerations of public order. . . . He does not
> see Italy as she has manifested herself during the last years, he does not seek
> out the traditional, historical, and philosophical sources for her being. He is
> modern . . . even in his vocabulary. . . . For instance, I say "popular classes,"
> the Honorable Giolitti says "proletariat"; I say "better their conditions," he
> says "elevate their tenor of life." Above all even his vocabulary is modern. (*Hilar-
> ity. Comments.*) [22]

In April 1911, upon Giolitti's presenting his third cabinet and program of
Government, both the Radical Fradeletto and the Conservative Martini

---

[20] Cf. Labriola, *op. cit.,* pp. 229–30, for a Syndicalist's view that Giolitti represented
a transfer of the government of the country from a "political" to a bourgeois Italy.

[21] See V. Saporito, *Trenta unni,* for a presentation of the Conservative attitude
toward Giolitti. Saporito had sat in the Center.

[22] *Atti Parlamentari.* "Discussioni della Camera dei Deputati. Tornata del 2 dicembre 1903" (Session II, 1902–04), X, 9246.

reproached him for his lack of fixed programs and high ideals, and for his arbitrary methods. Both seemed to agree that Giolitti's practice of a "pendulum-like" policy (Martini) and his "amorphous" political programs (Fradeletto) were weakening the authority and the prestige of the state.[23] Fradeletto thus criticized Giolitti's program:

Having followed its reading attentively, I have not heard one word that bespoke a feeling of the pressing, imperative necessity which all good citizens of all parties recognize and assert. I mean, gentlemen, the necessity of restoring the prestige of the state. (*Approval on the Right.*) I believe that the antithesis [between private energy and initiative and the exercise of the public authority] must be done away with . . . especially now on the eve of the enlargement of the suffrage; since the equilibrium within a democracy depends upon the strengthening of the power of the state in proportion to the spread of reforms among the lower classes.[24]

The "limpid and righteous consciences" in the Chamber were exhorted by Fradeletto to prevent the further separation and dissension (*dissidio*) between the "honest soul of the country" and parliamentary activity.[25] Leonida Bissolati, speaking in the name of the Socialist parliamentary group, agreed with Fradeletto that the feeling for the state was weakened, but, he asked:

Do you want to restore it by force, with blows of authority? You must have recourse to the democratic way, because democracy ever demands an increase of itself! You must restore it by enlarging the bases of authority in order to impose real social discipline.[26]

It was on that occasion that Giolitti attempted to defend himself against both the charges of possessing no policy and of having a demagogic and State-destroying policy.[27] He reviewed his policy of extending liberty to all, including the lower classes, in order to demonstrate the continuity of his policy since 1889. The charge of the Conservatives he answered with: "Fortunately the results have shown that my system, semi-revolutionary in appearance, was the only one really conservative." [28] This assertion of Giolitti's constitutes one of the invaluable keys to an understanding of his

[23] The chief items on Giolitti's program were the enlargement of the suffrage and a proposal for State monopoly of life insurance; see *Atti Parlamentari*. "Discussioni della Camera dei Deputati. Tornata del 6 aprile 1911." (Session 1909–13), XI, 13572–13574.

[24] *Ibid.*, p. 13588.

[25] *Ibid.*, p. 13592.

[26] *Atti Parlamentari*. "Discussioni della Camera dei Deputati. Tornata dell'8 aprile 1911" (Session 1909–13), XI, 13709.

[27] *Ibid.*, pp. 13714–13717, *passim.*

[28] *Ibid.*, p. 13714. After the election of 1909, upon being accused of Clerical leanings by the Socialist deputy Guido Podrecca, editor of the Roman satiric, anti-Clerical *L'Asino*, Giolitti reiterated his policy of liberty for all, but he said: "I deny that there can be any power in Italy with greater authority than that of the State, because the State represents the entire nation which is above all religions, all sects, and all political parties. (*Very warm approval. Great Applause. Many deputies go to congratulate the orator.*)" See *Atti Parlamentari*. "Discussioni della Camera dei Deputati. Tornata del 28 maggio 1909" (Session 1909–13), VI, 1524.

aims and achievements. Its value is attested by most of the developments and currents of Italian political and social life described in the present work. With good or questionable motives, through praiseworthy or reproachable methods, Giovanni Giolitti seemed to have conciliated and continued to conciliate antagonistic or indifferent masses of people and currents of Italian life within the great organism that was the Italian nation.

But it was precisely in that question of motives and methods that the opponents of Giolittian politics found the rallying points for their attacks on the entire Giolittian scheme of things. It was here that the elements of opposition to Giolitti fused—the purely political being sometimes inextricably intermingled with personal (psychological, spiritual, moral) antipathy to the man as a politico, as a type, as a symbol.[29] Personalities as different and contrasting as Gaetano Salvemini, Arturo Labriola, Ettore Ciccotti, Napoleone Colajanni, Carlo Altobelli, Innocenzo Cappa, Leonida Bissolati, Mario Missiroli, Tancredi Galimberti—men of all classes and all political creeds were in agreement that *Giolittismo* as a method of government must be uprooted.[30] What were the chief characteristics of this so-called Giolittian method or system? Both his contemporaries and historians still diverge widely in their emphasis on the various characteristics involved, but in one thing they are in accord: the basis of the system lay in the Machiavellian ability and shrewdness (*abilità* and *furberia*) of the keen Piedmontese. Said Barzilai: "One of the defects he possesses in a notably greater proportion than all others is his tendency to rule and work upon the vices rather than upon the virtues of men." [31] Filippo Meda saw Giolitti as "the exponent of that political realism which may sometimes be offensive to moral idealism, but which is, nevertheless, a necessary product of the parliamentary regime." [32]

Essentially an honest and upright man to whose personal integrity even his bitterest enemies repeatedly paid homage, Giolitti came to be associated with the use of a system of electoral pressures, tamperings, even occasional violence (what Italians called *pressioni e brogli*) that had caused him to be characterized by Gaetano Salvemini, in an outburst of moral indignation, "Minister of the Underworld" (*Il Ministro della mala vita*).[33]

[29] Cf. Burzio, *op. cit.*, p. 74.

[30] For an early attempt to analyze *Giolittismo*, see N. M. Fovel, "*Il Giolittismo*," *Rassegna Contemporanea*, IV (1908), 106–24.

[31] *Atti Parlamentari*. "Discussioni della Camera dei Deputati. Tornata del 29 maggio 1909" (Session 1909–13), II, 1567.

[32] *Atti Parlamentari*. "Discussioni della Camera dei Deputati. Tornata del 7 aprile 1911" (Session 1909–13), XI, 13642. See also Burzio, *op. cit.*, p. 49, and F. Ciccotti, *L'Italia in rissa*, pp. 71–72.

[33] Salvemini, *Il Ministro della mala vita*. On Giolitti and Salvemini there is an enlightening contrast in P. Gobetti, *La Rivoluzione Liberale*, p. 72: "Being conditioned by the fixed principles in which he is rooted, he [Salvemini] does not free himself from the schematic in his appraisal of individuals. For twenty years he made himself wage a crusade against Giolitti who, albeit as a statesman, possessed his selfsame ideas and prejudices but presented them with the cynicism of the subduer rather than with the enthusiasm of the crusader."

The epithet stuck and was sometimes used and twisted out of all meaning by people who liked to heap all the sins, real and imagined, of Italian public life upon Giolitti's shoulders. Electoral corruption, decried in their day by such critics of the parliamentary system as Mosca, Turiello, and Pareto, was obviously neither an Italian invention nor a Giolittian monopoly. What was perhaps essentially Italian was the condition of the amorphous, passive, and, until 1912, disfranchised masses of the agricultural proletariat in the South who for centuries had suffered every form of injustice and oppression at the hands of the local oligarchies—wrongs not yet righted even after fifty years of political unity.[34] In his highly moral and ethical crusade for the economic, social, and civic betterment and enlightenment of the South already studied in connection with his Socialist activities, Gaetano Salvemini found in a man like Vito De Bellis, the ministerial candidate of the Apulian district of Gioia del Colle in the elections of 1904 and 1909, the symbol of an evil all could understand. Salvemini said in 1910: "Vito De Bellis is not a man: he is a symbol, a representative individual, an institution. He is *Giolittismo*." [35] The historian described minutely the preparations for the elections, the use of coercion (the *mazzieri* were electoral hooligans who used *mazze* or clubs to intimidate voters), bribery, fraud, even the show of public force, in order to insure the victory of the ministerial candidate. By his moral campaign Salvemini himself assumed the force of a symbol, that of the anti-Giolittian par excellence, and it was natural that in the general elections of 1913, when he offered his own candidacy in the district of Molfetta, he should have been fought tooth and nail by the ministerial henchmen whose idol was, on this occasion, an antimonarchist, Pietro Pansini a Republican.[36] This election of Molfetta gained the widest notoriety through its having been covered by one of Italy's greatest newspapermen, Ugo Ojetti, of the Milan *Corriere della Sera*.[37]

Vito De Bellis and Pietro Pansini, however, were by no means the only ministerial protégés, nor were Gioia del Colle and Molfetta or Bitonto, in Apulia, the only southern districts where electoral *Giolittismo* was practised.[38] The Italian parliamentary debates after the three Giolittian

[34] Cf. L. Franchetti, "Mezzo secolo di unità nell'Italia meridionale," *Nuova Antologia*, XLVI (1911), No. 945, 83–97, *passim*.

[35] Salvemini, *op. cit.*, p. 10.

[36] The results of the election at Molfetta were close, despite ministerial pressure in favor of Pansini, who received 5,008 votes, while Salvemini received 3,601 votes. See *Statistica delle Elezioni Generali Politiche alla XXIV Legislatura, 26 ottobre e 2 novembre 1913*, p. 10.

[37] See Salvemini, *op. cit.*, pp. 63–80, for Ojetti's article; also the memoranda *La Elezione di Molfetta per la Giunta delle Elezioni, La Elezione di Bitonto;* Salvemini, *Le memorie di un candidato,* for the author's experiences in the district of Albano in 1911. For an attempt to clarify Pansini's position in the election of 1913, see the article by a fellow Republican, N. Colajanni, "Strascichi elettorali. Da Molfetta a Cuneo," in *La Rivista Popolare*, XIX (1913), No. 22, 596–603.

[38] The description of Giolittian methods and of the elections of 1913 in J. Alazard, *L'Italie et le conflit européen*, pp. 7–30, may be read with some profit, but the author's biases and general motivation should be kept carefully in mind.

elections of 1904, 1909, and 1913 are replete with the most varied charges of ministerial abuses and interference in electoral contests. In April 1907, for example, the Syndicalist newspaper *Propaganda* (Naples) featured the underground acts of one "Peppuccio" Romano, reputed to be a Government protégé whom the paper accused of being the chief of the Camorra in the city of Aversa, the head of the *mala vita* of the entire Terra di Lavoro, a buyer of votes, a seller of communal council and parliamentary seats.[39] On May 26, 1907 Luigi Federzoni, the Nationalist journalist, writing under the pseudonym of "Giulio De Frenzi" in the *Giornale d'Italia*, Sonnino's organ, attempted to expose what he called the feudal methods and the electoral oppression of the Government's policy in the same Neapolitan region.[40] These articles were naturally greedily seized upon by the whole anti-Giolittian press and were noised about the country and in the Chamber of Deputies.

On May 25, 1909 the old leader of the *Fasci siciliani*, the Sicilian Socialist deputy De Felice-Giuffrida, gave the Chamber a minute exposé of Giolittian methods on his own island. De Felice divided electoral Giolittianism into two periods: that of preparation, during which prefects were given their instructions, communal councils were dissolved, local chieftains rallied; then came the period of action, when the *ministeriali* were assured of their victory through the application of all available methods of coercing voters.[41] Citing examples from the Sicilian districts of Paternó, Licodia, Licata, Castelvetrano, De Felice remarked: "Thus you, Honorable Giolitti, a fellow citizen of Massimo D'Azeglio who made Italians in Piedmont, come to make Italians in Sicily!" [42] The Republican Colajanni, also a Sicilian, half-seriously complained that it was unjust for Giolitti to show such partiality by applying his electoral methods only to the south of Italy, and he reproached the Prime Minister for his failure to foster the true principles of *italianità* where they were most needed.[43] Salvatore Barzilai, in turn, stressed the point that Giolitti took his good wherever he found it; in the North he depended upon the support of the democratic forces, won over by favoritism of all kinds; in the South he depended upon the local oligarchies.[44] The lack of political principles to animate his legislative programs made such ambiguity necessary for Giolitti, according to Barzilai.[45] As a result, Giolittian majorities in the Chamber were personal followings rallied around a man rather than true political groupings held together by common beliefs and ideas. The result of this system had been an estrangement, a widening of the gulf between Parliament and the life of the country:

[39] Cf. Cilibrizzi, *op. cit.*, III, 359.

[40] See G. De Frenzi, "Potestà feudale e metodi moderni—L'opressione politica elettorale governativa in Terra di Lavoro," *Giornale d'Italia*, May 26, 1907.

[41] *Atti Parlamentari*. "Discussioni della Camera dei Deputati. Tornata del 25 maggio 1909" (Session 1909–13), II, 1329–30, *passim*.

[42] *Ibid.*, p. 1331.

[43] *Ibid.*, "Tornata del 28 maggio 1909," II, 1503–04, *passim*.

[44] *Ibid.*, "Tornata del 29 maggio 1909," II, 1567–69, *passim*.

[45] *Ibid.*, p. 1569.

Either Parliament or the [workers'] Council, either Parliament or revolt! We, however, who have faith in Parliament, hope that by our solidarity we may bring about its regeneration and a return to the gallant battles for ideas that are capable of finding resonance in the country.[46]

On November 22, 1909, the independent Socialist deputy Ettore Ciccotti, having described the alleged intrigues between the Government (Giolitti) and the Neapolitan local boss Romano, cried out in the Chamber, in an outburst of rhetoric: "If not for the good fortune of Italy, at least for her honor, let someone capable of restoring it come—someone, if possible, who can make us forget all this! (*Great approval on the Extreme Left*)." [47]

Giolitti always listened to the charges brought against him in the Chamber by the members of the *Estrema* with great serenity and on occasion took the deputies to task with ironical remarks about the lack of proof for their allegations.[48] On May 28, 1909, he pointed out that the 189 electoral districts in the South had not brought any greater number of contested cases before the parliamentary electoral committee (*Giunta delle Elezioni*) than the remaining districts throughout the country. He ascribed the furore in that part of Italy to "the more noisy, violent, and vulgar" character of the electoral struggles there.[49] Such an answer, however, was no more than the completion of a vicious circle of charges and counter-charges since his adversaries maintained that it was precisely Giolitti's henchmen who caused the noise and violence.

The first general elections after the passage of the Electoral Law of June 30, 1912, were held on October 26 and November 2, 1913. The law had increased the electorate by 5,353,204 to a total of 8,672,249.[50] Salvemini's dream of universal suffrage for the poor peasants of the South seemed to have been realized through the will of Giolitti. Feeling and expectations ran high. The *Avanti!*, on October 1, 1913, stating that the Socialist program could be condensed in the small formula "Indict the [Libyan] War!" added in the characteristic style of its editor, Benito Mussolini:

Let us all get to work, whether we are illustrious or obscure. Let those who cannot make speeches spread newspapers, pamphlets, and circulars. It is necessary to stir, to agitate, to awaken the great masses of the people who, for the first time in history, have been called to pass judgment upon the rule of the governing classes.[51]

The *Avanti!* seemed to have forgotten that universal suffrage had been sponsored by Giolitti and that he was still the Premier of Italy. The results

[46] *Ibid.*, p. 1572.
[47] *Ibid.*, "Tornata del 22 novembre 1909," IV, 4345.
[48] See especially Giolitti's interruptions of De Felice's speech, in *Atti Parlamentari.* "Discussioni della Camera dei Deputati. Tornata del 25 maggio 1909" (Session 1909–13), II, 1330–31.
[49] *Ibid.*, pp. 1512–24, *passim.*
[50] See *Statistica delle Elezioni* . . . , p. xii.
[51] Quoted by Cilibrizzi, *op. cit.*, IV, 289.

of the elections, described elsewhere in the present work, proved the importance of that fact. From one end of Italy to the other, and especially in Socialist quarters, post-election disillusion was great. The *Civiltà Cattolica,* despite the Gentiloni Pact, wrote:

> History has recorded in its volume for this year of grace 1913 a juicy sentence: Liberalism is slowly dying in Italy because, while allowing the Socialists to drain too much of its blood, it has not, to date, permitted Catholics to revitalize it with healthful and vigorous blood.[52]

The Republican *Rivista Popolare* pointed out that the *mala vita* had spread from Gioia del Colle and Castelvetrano to half of Italy.[53] In Parliament the deputies of the *Estrema Sinistra* subjected Giolitti to the most formidable attack he had ever sustained. His secret understanding with Count Gentiloni, as has already been seen, was one of the most popular subjects of the anti-Giolittian harangues *(requisitoria).* As in 1909, the Chamber of Deputies became a kind of courtroom, pulpit, and forum at the same time. On December 5, 1913, Filippo Turati, having reasserted the Socialists' faith in parliamentary institutions, reproached the Government for furnishing arms to the enemies of the democratic system by its scandalous conduct and its lack of a majority based upon party lines.[54] The Neapolitan Socialist Carlo Altobelli launched on a review of the Giolittian method and lashed the Gentiloni Pact as a "deceitful and monstrous alliance between the *mala vita* and the sacristy." [55] On December 9, Arturo Labriola concluded his maiden speech in the Chamber with:

> There is a Catholic Italy, there is a Socialist Italy, there is an imperialist Italy, but there is no real Giolittian Italy. Giolittian Italy is a mediocre parliamentary expediency which has risen in the corridors and in the Chamber of Deputies: it is only good to impede, incapable of creating. This kind of an Italy must disappear.[56]

On December 17, the Republican Innocenzo Cappa, after having made an enthusiastic contribution to the condemnation of *Giolittismo,* said that it was a rebellious restlessness, a sorrow that made his voice cry out to Giolitti: "Allow me to say it: you are only a man, but, for the renovation of Italy, you must go!" [57] Those who are inclined to doubt the extent of freedom of speech and parliamentary immunity during the so-called dictatorship of Giolitti should ponder Cappa's words.

It was, however, the Socialist deputy from Genoa, Orazio Raimondo who made the classic indictment and gave the classic description of Giolittianism as a method of government. Delivered in the Chamber of

[52] "Gli insegnamenti delle elezioni generali a suffragio allargato," *La Civiltà Cattolica,* IV (1913), 524.

[53] "La grande requisitoria antigiolittiana," *Rivista Popolare,* XIX (1913), 623.

[54] *Atti Parlamentari.* "Discussioni della Camera dei Deputati. Tornata del 5 dicembre 1913" (Session 1913–14), I, 138.

[55] *Ibid.,* p. 158.

[56] *Ibid.,* "Tornata del 9 dicembre 1913," I, 271.

[57] *Ibid.,* "Tornata del 17 dicembre," I, 547.

Deputies on December 6, 1913, his speech deserves extended quotation.[58]
Said Raimondo:

The parties which fight one another in the country at large once again embrace
each other in the Chamber. To what do we owe this miracle? We owe it, like all
other miracles, to the policy of the Honorable Giolitti. He has had and still has
an overwhelming personal majority. The Democrats are with him for the laws
he grants them, the Conservatives are with him for the application they hope to
see of those same laws (*Bravo! on the Extreme Left*). The truth is, honorable
colleagues, that under a democratic banner we have imperceptibly arrived at
a dictatorial regime. The Honorable Giolitti has four times conducted the elections: in 1892, in 1904, in 1909, and in 1913. In his long parliamentary career
he has, moreover, nominated practically all the senators (*Laughter*), all the prefects, and all the other high officials in the administrative, judiciary, political,
and military hierarchy of our country (*Comments*). With this formidable power
of his—let us all recite our *mea culpas*—he has done the work of drawing parties
together by means of reforms and of drawing individuals together by means of
personal attention (*Comments*). Now, Honorable Giolitti, when parties forget
their programs, when those who come here leave at the doors the rags of their
political convictions, it means that a majority must be achieved by other means,
as all personal powers are forced to do: with trickery and corruption (*Approval
on the Extreme Left*). In this way, parliamentary institutions are annulled, party-
lines annihilated, and transformism, which has no justification whatsoever, is
achieved. . . . Honorable Giolitti, the country is not elevated above personal
ambitions by the subordination of the work of government to the exigencies of
a long and absolute parliamentary rule. (*Benissimo!*) . . . I hope, Honorable
Giolitti, that when you abandon power once again, you will not leave behind you
in the country a more profound and irreparable moral disorder. (*Great approval.
Long, repeated applause on the Extreme Left. Prolonged comments. Many deputies go to congratulate the speaker.*) [59]

Orazio Raimondo's speech was perhaps the most cogent analysis made
by any contemporary of Giolitti's system of government. Upon closer
examination, however, and considered in the light of all that has been
described in the preceding chapters of the present work, it will appear
more as the statement of a noble and rebellious faith on the part of an
independent spirit than as a deep probing of reasons. As such it is also
more of a lucid and eloquent report of symptoms than a profound diagnosis of causes.

No attempt can obviously be made to offer extenuating circumstances
to the most flagrant political and electoral immoralities with which
Giolittismo as a method came to be associated. All the Vito De Bellises
and "Peppuccio" Romanos in the world cannot be worth an ounce of the
moral and intellectual integrity of their adversaries who, like Gaetano
Salvemini, consecrated their entire life to the work of betterment and enlightenment of their more unfortunate and voiceless fellow Italians. And

[58] Margot Hentze, *op. cit.*, pp. 297–98, quotes parts of Raimondo's speech, but unfortunately cuts it at some very significant points.
[59] *Atti Parlamentari.* "Discussioni della Camera dei Deputati. Tornata del 6 dicembre 1913" (Session 1913–14), I. 184–95, *passim.*

yet, what has been said earlier in the present chapter of the existence of a psychological incompatibility between the idealistic Italian inspired by highly moral purposes and selfless ideals, and the realistic type best represented by Giolitti, moved by essentially political motives, must be also taken into consideration for a final appraisal. Salvemini—Giolitti—D'Annunzio: are they perhaps three eternal, contrasting aspects of the complex Italian character?

Giovanni Giolitti, with an apparently pedestrian, unheroic Machiavellian sense, worked with an Italy he inherited (some still say "usurped"!) from his Piedmontese predecessors and, despite all assertions to the contrary, he seemed to have both a policy and a goal. He found a country gathered under a monarchical flag and ruled by a Piedmontese dynasty. He accordingly governed as a faithful servant of his master and King. He found political parties and programmatic alignments among the old ruling classes in a weak and amorphous state, and, perhaps despairing in his own conservative heart of ever infusing a new life into them (as Sonnino and Salandra dreamed), he placed them in the limbo of useless survivors of another age. He found the framework of the state exposed to dangers, or at least to corroding influences, through the non-participation in its life by powerful forces old and new: the so-called Extreme Right, with its large masses of conscientious Catholic Italians, and the Extreme Left, especially the Socialists with their millennial dreams and their potentially constructive power when dreams were made the stuff of daily work. His policy of freedom for all within the limits of the law worked wonders where violence and coercion had been of little use. He found a nation of hard-working, aspiring, and intelligent people, whose exuberance he perhaps regarded as a defect. He nevertheless made possible an adventure in which their enthusiasm, their messianism, and their self-torturing national soul found a source of hope and their national dignity a source of strength. If he did not feed their ardor, he did not nurse their tragic inclination to self-abasement and self-vilification.

Giolitti's methods were in most cases questionable and of doubtful educational value. His real motives remain obscure despite the apparent simplicity of their unfolding. Few still question his real achievements. Had Giolitti merely worked for himself, as his enemies old and new assert? He was certainly ambitious, yet he died quietly at the serene age of eighty-six. For the bourgeoisie and the conservative classes? He had not harmed them in his policies, but he was not loved by them. Had he worked only for his master the King, for the House of Savoy, perhaps for the creation of that Socialist monarchy which tortured the dreams of the Missirolian theocrats? He could not have failed to serve faithfully and manfully the dynasty that had risen to rule the country from his own Piedmont. But it is more probable that had Giolitti been able to do the impossible by breaking through his exasperatingly anti-rhetorical shell, had he really possessed the genius of the true political artist who can mold a legend and a myth about himself, perhaps he would have answered that he had worked for his nation and his people—for Italy.

February 1906: The Sonnino Ministry in parliamentary session

The assassination of Umberto I (*drawing by Gennaro Amato*)

Francesco Saverio Nitti

Ernesto Nathan

Giuseppe Zanardelli

Luigi Pelloux

Giolitti as Deputy

Antonio Salandra

Gaetano Mosca

Sidney Sonnino

Tommaso Tittoni

Giolitti and Di San Giuliano

Visconti Venosta leaves for
the Algeciras Conference

Giolitti, Calvi, and Senator Roux

Enrico Ferri

Arturo Labriola

Giacomo Prampolini

Orazio Raimondi

Ettore Ciccotti

Luzzati, Schanzer, and Sonnino

Giolitti and his wife at Valdieri (1903)

Turati and Anna
Kuliscioff (1901)

Errico Malatesta

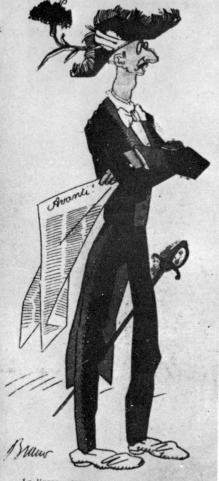

- La livrea e troppo grande per me, o io sono troppo grande per la livrea!

Leonida Bissolati

Benito Mussolini

Filippo Turati

Claudio Treves

Gaetano Salvemini

Rinaldo Rigola

SECTION TWO
GIOLITTIAN ITALY REVISITED

I

POLITICAL SOURCES
OF AN HISTORICAL CONTROVERSY

I, for my part, declare that my mind is carpeted with biases—religious, philosophical, scientific, social, political, national, and even personal—and that I constantly make use of my biases in my studies. I am not ashamed of this fact, because biases are not irreconcilable with scientific research. *

SALVEMINI

T HE rise, rule and ruin of Italian Fascism have left a profound impact on interpretations of the whole of post-Risorgimento history and particularly on that phase of it which is now rightly known as the Giolittian era (1900-1914). The revisions and reconstructions of this period of modern Italian history may technically be seen as a function of the vast and in many ways unique fruition of the Italian historiographical renaissance during the post-War period.[1] Those efforts may also be seen as a parallel development and part of an analogous attempt to

---

* Gaetano Salvemini, *Historian and Scientist* (Cambridge, Mass., Harvard University Press, 1939) , p. 75.

[1]The most exhaustive and useful bibliographical introduction to the vast new materials is through systematic consultation of the *Bibliografia Storica Nazionale,* Vols. V-XVII (1943-1955) (Rome, 1949-51; Bari, 1952-57) . For historiographical interpretation of some of the major new materials, see the excellent essays by Federico Chabod, "Gli studi di storia del Rinascimento" and Walter Maturi, "Gli studi di storia moderna e contemporanea" in Carlo Antoni and Raffaele Mattioli, eds., *Cinquant'anni di vita intellettuale italiana, 1896-1946. Scritti in onore di Benedetto Croce,* 2 vols. (Naples, 1950) , I, 127-207, 212-85. See also the articles by Cinzio Violante, Luigi Bulferetti, Giuseppe Giarrizzo, Guido Verucci, and Ugo Azzoni in Francesco C. Rossi, ed., "Prospettive storiografiche in Italia: Omaggio a Gaetano Salvemini," *Itinerari, rivista bimestrale di storia, letteratura e società* (Genoa) , IV (December 1956) , 441-570. Cf. Charles F. Delzell, "Italian Historical Scholarship: A Decade of Recovery and Development, 1945-1955," *The Journal of Modern History,* XXVIII (1956) , 374-88. Worthy of special notice are two outstanding bibliographical essays dealing respectively with the Italian Catholic and Socialist movements: Guido Verucci, "Recenti studi sul movimento cattolico in Italia," *Rivista Storica Italiana,* LXVII (1955) , 425-48, 529-54; and Leo Valiani, "La storia del movimento socialista in Italia dalle origini al 1921: Studi e ricerche nel decennio 1945-1955." *Rivista Storica Italiana,* LXVIII (1956), 447-510. 620-69.

assess the immediate Fascist past.[2]. But they contain on both an ideal and a practical level elements which differentiate them from these other developments. The very obscurity of the Giolittian era as well as the treatment accorded it in both Fascist and Liberal historiography has made it almost inevitably the testing-ground of a multitude of approaches, the polemical field par excellence of a persisting historiographical debate.[3]

Less than academic already during the period of consolidation of the Fascist dictatorship, as the antithetical positions taken by Volpe and Croce in the interpretations of the Giolittian era revealed,[4] the debate was reopened in the fervid Italian atmosphere of the post-War years and raged furiously for at least a decade. Thus it happened, at the start of a phase of historiographical development which reflected the larger problems of the post-Fascist reconstruction of Italy,[5] that a modest

[2]An exhaustive review of materials is in Emiliana P. Noether, "Italy Reviews Its Fascist Past: A Bibliographical Essay," *American Historical Review*, LXI (1956), 877-99. Cf. Nino Valeri, "Il fascismo interpretato," *Il Mondo*, July 5, 26, and August 16, 1952.

[3]Cf. Ugo Azzoni, "L'Italia dopo l'Unità," *Itinerari, cit.*, pp. 553-56; Walter Maturi, "Storia d'Italia dal 1870 al 1915," *Cinquant'anni, cit.*, I, 279-85; Nino Valeri, "Premesse ad una storia d'Italia nel Postrisorgimento," in Gabriele Pepe *et al.*, *Orientamenti per la storia d'Italia nel Postrisorgimento* (Bari, 1952), pp. 53-85.

[4]In an introduction entitled "A proposito di storia d'Italia," Gioacchino Volpe, *L'Italia in cammino*, 3rd ed. (Milan, 1931), pp. ix-xxviii, had plunged headlong into a polemical attack against Benedetto Croce's interpretation, in the *Storia d'Italia* (Bari, 1928), of the post-Risorgimento in general and of the Giolittian period in particular as a "eulogy of the past" done in the accents of a partisan *laudator temporis acti;* thus, Volpe insisted, Croce had presented an idyll of which Giolitti was the "hero" and Croce himself the "philosopher." On the "fortune" of Volpe's interpretation of Italian history during the Fascist regime, see Gaetano Salvemini, "I millenni di Gioacchino Volpe: Da Romolo a Mussolini," *Il Mondo*, February 16, 1954, pp. 13-14. On the problem of the Crocean interpretation, see Valeri in *Orientamenti, cit.*, pp. 60-2; Federico Chabod, "Croce storico," *Rivista Storica Italiana*, LXIV (1952), 515-25; Vittorio de Caprariis, "La storia d'Italia nello svolgimento del pensiero di B. Croce," in Francesco Flora, ed., *Benedetto Croce* (Milan, 1953), pp. 291-301; Domenico Petrini, "Benedetto Croce nella storiografia italiana," in Petrini and G. Calogero, *Studi crociani* (Rieti, 1930), pp. 100-05; Eugenio Garin, *Cronache della filosofia italiana, 1900-1943* (Bari, 1955), pp. 304-08; Michele Abbate, *La filosofia di B. Croce e la crisi della società italiana* (Turin, 1955), pp. 57-90; A. Robert Caponigri, *History and Liberty. The Historical Writings of Benedetto Croce* (London, 1955), pp. 238-47; Lelio Basso, "Petite histoire d'une démocratie manquée," *Esprit*, XXII (1955), 1483.

[5]On this larger problem of reconstruction after 1945, see M. H. H. Macartney, *The Rebuilding of Italy* (Cambridge, England, 1945); Muriel Grindrod, *The Rebuilding of Italy. Politics and Economics, 1945-1955* (London and New York, 1955); H. Stuart Hughes, *The United States and Italy* (Cambridge, Mass., 1953), particularly pp. 143-212; and statistical materials in *Ten Years of Italian Democracy, 1945-1955* (Rome, 1956), an official summary issued under the auspices of the Italian Presidency of the Council of Ministers. On a more critical level, and especially concerned with political,

monograph on the Giolittian period by this writer and the *Introduction* written for it by Gaetano Salvemini came to have a sort of unexpected primacy, at least at the time of publication.[6] Soon, however, they became almost automatically assumed as new points of reference by a somewhat promiscuous army of Italian reviewers and interpreters.[7] Most of these judged both the book and Salvemini's *Introduction* as parts of a common approach, which they were not; some viewed them as independent and differently conceived treatments of the same subject, which they indeed were; still others, among them Croce,[8] saw an actual antithesis between the study and the *Introduction*.

Be that as it may, by late 1945 and 1946 and then again in 1949-52, Giovanni Giolitti—his life, times and work—became once again a controversial figure of Italian history or perhaps more accurately of Italian historiography. The practical Giolittian polemics of 1914-15 and 1920-22 had now been converted into the ideal terms of an historiographical controversy.[9] In learned periodicals[10] as well as on the third pages of

social, and ideological problems, the articles by Leo Valiani, Gabriele de Rosa, Piero Calamandrei, Emilio Lussu, Achille Battaglia, Epicarmo Corbino and Mario Sansone in *Dieci anni dopo, 1945-1955. Saggi sulla vita democratica italiana* (Bari, 1955) .

[6] A. William Salomone, *Italian Democracy in the Making. The Political Scene in the Giolittian Era, 1900-1914*. Introductory Essay by Gaetano Salvemini (Philadelphia, 1945) ; the Italian translation (by Maria Teresa Galante Garrone) was titled *L'età giolittiana*. Introduzione di Gaetano Salvemini (Turin, 1949) . Salvemini's Introductory Essay will be cited hereafter as *Introduction* or *Introduzione* both in the text and in the notes.

[7] Only those will be referred to here who in their reviews or articles devoted their main attention to the larger historical and historiographical problems under discussion or who wrote, essentially, review articles. Two such articles, both by the eminent historian Nino Valeri, deserve special mention: "Giovanni Giolitti nella storiografia del secondo dopoguerra," in Ettore Rota, ed., *Questioni di storia del Risorgimento e dell'Unità d'Italia* (Milan, 1951) , pp. 1009-22; and the Introduction to Giovanni Giolitti, *Discorsi extraparlamentari* (Turin, 1952) , pp. 11-87.

[8] Benedetto Croce, "Una prefazione sbagliata," *Quaderni della "Critica,"* No. 16 (March 1950) , pp. 122-24.

[9] Three contrasting authoritative views of these historical polemics in Giovanni Giolitti, *Memorie della mia vita*, 2 vols. (Milan, 1922) , I, 509-51, 553-615; Antonio Salandra, *L'Intervento* (Milan, 1930) , pp. 211-88, and *Memorie politiche, 1916-1925* (Milan, 1951) , pp. 1-29; Luigi Albertini, *Vent'anni di vita politica*, 5 vols. (Bologna, 1950-53) , III, 157-96, 323-567. On Giolitti on the eve of the War of 1914 and the post-War period, see Vincenzo Galizzi, *Giolitti e Salandra* (Bari, 1949) ; Corrado De Biase, *L'incolumità di Giolitti e l'assalto a Montecitorio nel maggio 1915* (Rome, 1957) ; Nino Valeri, *Da Giolitti a Mussolini* (Florence, 1956) ; Gabriele De Rosa, *Giolitti e il Fascismo* (Rome, 1957) . All four of these studies are monographic, documentary, indispensable for a new appraisal of Giolittian politics during two of the three turning-points characterized by Luigi Salvatorelli as "Tre colpi di stato," *Il Ponte*, VI (1950) , 340-50.

Italian newspapers,[11] in reviews dedicated to politics and culture[12] no less than in partisan journals,[13] in articles and "discourses" on Giolitti,[14] in re-examinations of post-Risorgimento history from all angles,[15] in valuable memoirs[16] and in at least one popularized hagiographical biography,[17] the name Giolitti became strangely again almost an Italian

[10]Luigi Salvatorelli, "Giolitti," *Rivista Storica Italiana,* LXII (1950), 497-532; Elio Apih, "A proposito di Giolitti," *Nuova Rivista Storica,* XXXVII (1953), 500-06.

[11]See, for instance, from among a great variety and number, *La Nuova Stampa* (Turin), March 11, 1952; *Il Messaggero* (Rome), August 2, 1949; and the now defunct *Il Nuovo Corriere* (Florence), July 31, 1949.

[12]See Arrigo Cajumi, "Giolitti," in the special issue dedicated to "Piemonte" by *Il Ponte,* V (1949), 1001-08; Fausto Vignetti, "Giolitti e i socialisti," *Lo Spettatore Italiano,* II (1949), 4-7; and from among numerous articles which appeared on its pages after 1949, the following from the Roman weekly, *Il Mondo*: Nino Valeri, "Resurrezione di Giolitti," August 12, 1950, and "Giolitti scrittore," January 5, 1952; Fausto Nicolini, "Incontro con Giolitti: Benedetto Croce ministro," November 17, 1953; and by Paolo Serini, "La semplicità di Giolitti," May 3, 1952, "Il primo Giolitti," October 6, 1953, and "Da Giolitti a Mussolini," July 24, 1956.

[13]Giorgio Candeloro, "Giolitti e l'età giolittiana," *Società,* VI (1950), 129-44; Antonio Papa, "Orientamenti per uno studio su Giovanni Giolitti," *Belfagor,* V (1950), 687-704.

[14]Among the most significant was that by Palmiro Togliatti, *Discorso su Giolitti* (Rome, 1950).

[15]At least by implication in the outstanding piece of post-war Italian historical writing, Federico Chabod, *Storia della politica estera italiana dal 1870 al 1896.* Vol. I: *Le premesse* (Bari, 1951). See also Arturo Carlo Jemolo, *Chiesa e Stato in Italia negli ultimi cento anni* (Turin, 1948), pp. 501-08, and *Chiesa e Stato dal Risorgimento ad oggi* (Turin, 1955), pp. 194-203; Ivanoe Bonomi, *La politica italiana da Porta Pia a Vittorio Veneto, 1870-1918* (Turin, 1946), pp. 231-309; Gioacchino Volpe, *Italia Moderna,* 3 vols. (1946-52), II, 384 ff. In a serried analysis of Mosca's thought, Mario Delle Piane, *Gaetano Mosca. Classe politica e liberalismo* (Naples, 1952), offers new, unique insights into the political realities of Giolittian Italy. New, if contrasting, approaches to political and social Catholicism during the Liberal period in Giovanni Spadolini, *L'opposizione cattolica da Porta Pia al 1898* (Florence, 1954); Gabriele De Rosa, *La crisi dello Stato liberale* (Rome, 1955), pp. 9-67, and *L'Azione Cattolica,* 2 vols, (Bari, 1955-54), I, 303-21, 11, 57-78, 320-63; Fausto Fonzi, *I Cattolici e la società italiana dopo l'Unità* (Rome, 1953). The latest works by a fine French connoisseur of modern Italian political and religious history are worthy of consultation for their own excellence and as indirect reflections of some of the newer Italian approaches: Maurice Vaussard, *Histoire de l'Italie contemporaine, 1870-1946* (Paris, 1950), particularly pp. 61-100, and *Histoire de la Démocratie Chrétienne. France—Belgique—Italie* (Paris, 1956), pp. 219-37. In English, for a clear and sharp description of Giolittian liberal politics within the framework of pre-Fascist history, see now Denis Mack Smith, *Italy. A Modern History* (Ann Arbor, 1959), pp. 211-62, 281-88.

[16]Particularly two of dissimilar but real value by men who were close to Giolitti: Marcello Soleri, *Memorie.* Preface by Luigi Einaudi (Turin, 1949); Gaetano Natale, *Giolitti e gli Italiani.* Preface by B. Croce (Milan, 1949).

[17]Giovanni Ansaldo, *Il Ministro della buona vita. Giolitti e i suoi tempi* (Milan, 1949). The title of Ansaldo's book is, of course, a conversion of that in Salvemini's

household word. The Giolittian revival soon led to the unofficial publication by Nino Valeri of Giolitti's non-parliamentary speeches[18] and culminated in the official publication, at long last, by the Italian Government of a four-volume collection of Giolitti's parliamentary speeches.[19] Archival research in Giolitti's official and unofficial correspondence and on his family and personal papers is at present beyond the preliminary stages.[20] Together with these, the pertinent volumes in the long-awaited and precious publication of the Italian diplomatic documents[21] now so well advanced will within a relatively short time make of Giolitti, so long neglected, the most "documented" Italian Liberal statesman after Cavour.[22] Whether this immense *Giolittiana* will likewise succeed in revealing the "Man of Dronero" as historically significant as his great compatriot[23] and, perhaps more important, as beyond the realm of controversy as Cavour has, on the whole, been[24] until recently is a question which only time will properly answer. It is this writer's conviction that it will do both, but that time is not yet ripe. While awaiting that proverbial "verdict of history," however, it may not be altogether vain to help clear the dark forest of Giolittian controversy by removing some of the obstacles accumulated at its entrance. Preliminary and episodic as this work must necessarily be here, it may also prove fertile in its fashion or at any rate not without some profit as a review of the present status of the problem, if not as a tentative suggestion for possible solution.

The name of Giolitti has, since the first decade of this century, seldom been encountered on both the polemical and the historiographical levels without some reference to that of Gaetano Salvemini.[25] It was

---

notorious pamphlet—and epithet—*Il Ministro della mala vita* [1910], 2nd ed. (Rome, 1919). On Ansaldo and his new Giolittian "look" after Fascism, see Nino Valeri, "Due biografi di Giolitti," *Nuova Rivista Storica*, XXXIV (1950), 136-39, *passim;* Salvatorelli, "Giolitti,' *Rivista Storica Italiana*, cit., p. 499.

[18]Giovanni Giolitti, *Discorsi extraparlamentari*, cit. This collection replaces that pioneering and rare little volume by Luigi Salvatorelli, *Giolitti* (Milan, 1920) which until now has been indispensable for Giolitti's non-parliamentary speeches. On Valeri's edition, see Antonio Papa's long review in *Belfagor*, VII (1952), 595-600; and Aldo Garosci, *Pensiero politico e storiografia moderna* (Pisa, 1954), pp. 101-04.

[19]*Discorsi Parlamentari di Giovanni Giolitti. Pubblicati per Deliberazione della Camera dei Deputati.* 4 vols. (Rome, 1953-56). This huge collection was a belated but truly precious homage tendered by the Italian Chamber of Deputies to a former "great master." The good editorial labor has been done by Dr. Silvio Furlani. For appraisals of the first two volumes, see Paolo Serini, "Il primo Giolitti," *Il Mondo*, October 6, 1953, p. 7; Elio Apih, "Giolitti in Parlamento, "*Nuova Rivista Storica*, XXXVIII (1954), 419-23.

[20]Cf. Valeri's bibliographical notes in Giolitti, *Discorsi extraparlamentari*, pp. 83-7, and in *Questioni di storia*, cit., p. 1021. See Giolitti's letters to Camillo Corradini in

almost inevitable that the new Giolittian controversy after 1945 should somehow re-bind their names. This in fact happened, however, as a direct result of the circumstance which had led Salvemini to reassess Giolitti and his era on the basis of this writer's historical essay on Giolittian Italy.[26] There is no intention whatever here to speak of that essay except in so far as it constituted the occasion and vehicle of Salvemini's first revisionist re-evaluation of Giolitti. Neither is it intended or possible here to bring that essay "up to date" nor to modify and enlarge its scope and least of all, narcistically, to appraise it. This is not, properly speaking, a new analysis of Giolitti and his significance but rather a preliminary to a reappraisal. It seeks to be, above all, a contribution, based upon long historical reflection and study of an era this writer considers truly crucial in the history of modern Italy as well as upon personal recollections of Salvemini, toward shedding some light on the problem of the historian—Salvemini—and his reactions to an era of which he had been both "actor" and "judge."

This writer's historical essay on Giolittian Italy had included a brief treatment of Salvemini's socialist and anti-Giolittian activity.[27] But that essay was essentially devoted to an analysis of Giolitti's political pre-

---

De Rosa, *Giolitti e il Fascismo*, pp. 16-37.

[21]So far in none of the ten volumes of the series of *I Documenti Diplomatici Italiani* now being issued is there any official correspondence by Giolitti himself.

[22]On the present status of Giolittian documentation, see Valeri's notes cited above.

[23]See the illuminating contrast between Giolitti and Cavour as statesmen in Luigi Einaudi, *Il Buongoverno* (Bari, 1954), pp. 285-87; and in B. Croce and Einaudi, *Liberismo e Liberalismo*, ed. by Paolo Solari (Milan-Naples, 1957), pp. 182-84.

[24]The excellent study by Denis Mack Smith, *Cavour and Garibaldi 1860. A Study in Political Conflict* (Cambridge, Eng., 1954) has tended to reopen some Risorgimento problems in Italian historiography; see, for instance, Ettore Passerin d'Entrèves, *L'ultima battaglia politica di Cavour. I problemi dell'Unificazione italiana* (Turin, 1956), pp. 81-83, and notes, pp. 95-98, *passim*. See, on the other hand, the concise reconstruction of Cavourian politics in 1860 by Cesare Spellanzon in his introduction to Alberto Mario, *La camicia rossa* (Milan, 1954), pp. v-xxxviii.

[25]The publication of Salvemini's pamphlets on Giolitti's electoral methods in Southern Italy before 1914 insured an immediate linking of his name with that of Giolitti; cf. *Italian Democracy in the Making*, pp. 67, 70. On the "early" Salvemini, see Ettore Rota, *Una pagina di storia contemporanea: Gaetano Salvemini* (Milan, 1919); Enzo Tagliacozzo, "Gaetano Salvemini nei primi anni del secolo," *Nuova Rivista Storica*, XXXIV (1950), 265-86; Ernesto Ragionieri, "Gaetano Salvemini storico e politico," *Belfagor*, V (1950), 514-36, *passim*.

[26]Needless to say, Salvemini's *Introduction* proved to be, in Italian intellectual, historiographical, and even political quarters, one of the most interesting and "original documents" in the book; it aroused a mixture of genuine curiosity, wonderment, skepticism, and, in some—particularly the Croceans—expressions of self-vindication.

[27]*Italian Democracy in the Making*, pp. 55-57.

dominance, its sources and character, within the larger framework of an "Italian democracy in the making." The conclusion had been implicitly suggested that, whatever the defects and limitations of his methods, Giolitti had represented a constructive moment in the development of pre-1914 Italy toward a genuine liberalization of the Italian national structure and conscience. Salvemini had basically agreed with this conclusion despite the violence it appeared to do to his not unknown previous views.[28]

In the *Introduction* to the historical essay in which he figured so briefly, and his *"bête noire"* Giolitti so dominantly, Salvemini, with that mixture of fairness and objectivity which could so often characterize him, applauded the method and accepted the fundamental approach and intrinsic conclusion. The monographic study had presented Giolittian Italy—following the tumultuous decade (1890-1900) of social and national dissension[29]—as having been well on the road toward a sturdy and promising reconstruction of Italian political life. Salvemini's former castigation of Giolitti as *"Il Ministro della mala vita"* [1910] did not reappear. Giolitti was now characterized by him as "a corrupter" of "Italian democracy in the making," but as one who had not been worse and who had been definitely "better" than many of his contemporaries and successors in Italy, indeed in Europe itself.[30]

This obvious reversal of opinion was impressive, almost dramatic, for anyone who had the least acquaintance with Italian political literature, and in some quarters it was turned into a sort of historiographical *cause célèbre*.[31] The sources of this almost sensational reversal of opinion were variously ascribed, depending, in most cases, on the personal, political, professional and even sentimental reactions it elicited in those for whom both Giolitti and Salvemini were more than just vague names, not mere ghosts of Italian things and battles long since past. Few critics correctly isolated and emphasized the more genuine sources of Salvemini's shift

---

28 *Ibid.*, p. 114.

29 *Ibid.*, pp. 44-46. On the pre-Giolittian period, see Napoleone Colajanni, *L'Italia nel 1898. Tumulti e reazioni* (Milan, 1899); Filippo Turati—Anna Kuliscioff, *Carteggio.* I. *Maggio 1898-Giugno 1899.* ed. by Alessandro Schiavi (Turin, 1949), pp. xix-xxxiii. See also the analysis of the problems of the aftermath of the tumultuous decade in Gabriele De Rosa, *La crisi dello Stato liberale,* pp. 126-52, *passim.*

30 *Introduction,* p. xv.

31 Most of the Italian reviewers of the English edition and practically all writers on the Italian translation gave some prominence to Salvemini's new position as revealed in the *Introduction;* for illustrations of contrasting views, see Valeri, "Giovanni Giolitti nella storiografia del secondo dopoguerra," *Questioni di storia, cit.,* pp. 1018-19; Salvatorelli, "Giolitti," *Rivista Storica Italiana, cit.,* pp. 497-98; Candeloro, "Giolitti e l'età giolittiana," *Società, cit.,* pp. 139-40; Togliatti, *Discorso su Giolitti,* pp. 14-15.

of judgment.[32] Given the climate of post-War Italian opinion with its tendency toward the conscious or unwitting "empiricization" of many areas of theoretical thought, there appeared an element of simplification which unduly stressed only one aspect of Salvemini's mind.

Thus the impact of Salvemini's shift of emphasis on Giolitti's place in Italian history led in some cases to an almost unavoidable search for the single explanation. His contribution to the so-called "rehabilitation" of Giolitti came to be ascribed most frequently to Italy's "experience with Fascism," that is, to a purely practical source on the national and, for Salvemini, personal level. The bulk of the new Giolittian commentaries seemed to succeed in creating the image of a single-dimensional Salvemini, of Salvemini as a function, so to speak, of *giolittismo* and nothing else. In this confusing and perhaps largely unconscious new Italian portrait, the old historian first "came back" to Italy after many years of exile in part as a refugee from Fascism and even more as Giolitti's converted ancient foe. The candidate from Molfetta, defeated in the elections of 1913 by a Giolittian henchman and the *mazzieri*,[33] now a whole generation later was practically seen as returning to do a strange ideal homage to his arch-antagonist Giovanni Giolitti! Needless to say, such a portrait of Salvemini was sketchy and unfinished: it lacked those very elements which made it worthy of attention.

When the monograph on *Italian Democracy in the Making* was written and Salvemini's *Introduction* penned, Europe was still under the receding wave of the Nazi-Fascist deluge and the future of Italy was barely emerging from the dark shadows of political collapse, of the institutional uncertainty and of physical and moral ruin. Had the essay itself and the *Introduction* been affected by the European catastrophe and by the Italian tragedy within it? Undoubtedly, but also unconsciously. An historical work dealing with the recent past whose impact upon the present is still live and powerful can hardly escape the pressure of the combination of circumstance and events upon the historian's psychological needs subtly astir. From these sometimes spring the historical reason's urgency to search for answers to the mind's demand and right to understand and reappraise on the risky, that is, on the human side of eternity. Absolute commitment to "presentism" and relativism need hardly be posited on the threshold of such undertakings. Integrity and intelligence, a solid faith in truth and some capacity to seek it are indispensable requisites. Friedrich Meinecke came close to an apparent repudiation

[32] See Valeri's penetrating comments in the Introduction to Giovanni Giolitti, *Discorsi extraparlamentari*, pp. 65-69.

[33] *Italian Democracy in the Making*, p. 109.

of the conclusions issuing from long work and considered judgment on the character and spiritual sources of German history when, first after 1918 and more dramatically after 1945, some such pressure and needs conspired in him toward a reassessment of the origins of the European and German catastrophes in our time.[34] Benedetto Croce, too, particularly in his histories of Europe and of Italy written during the floodtide of Fascism, took the admirably calculated risk involved in sailing his historical craft between the Scylla of absolute, and potentially meaningless, objectivity and the Charybdis of the contingent reassertion of freedom's congenital bonds with nineteenth-century history.[35] It is, obviously, only when schematic ideology and empiric interest, political or otherwise, are superimposed upon the genuine, vital requirements of the historical intelligence that truth suffers a real danger. If the further conversion, no matter how ably masked, is made of those impulses into driving forces of practical political passions, interpretation almost immediately becomes prejudice and historical judgment the pawn of some dogma. All veils then become transparent and partisan opinion stands exposed as the shield of self-interested political action.

Salvemini's judgment on Giolitti and on Giolittian Italy as formulated in his *Introduction* clearly belonged to the first category, that of the personal historical intelligence grappling with new understanding of an era in which he had been an "actor," and not to the second category, that of interested and practical political passion. In the *Introduction* he wrote:

While during those years I practised, as well as I could, my profession of historian (which has always been my true profession), I devoted my spare time to a political crusade. The reader will find in this book the crusader and not the historian.[36]

To the author he had written:

[34] Cf. Friedrich Meinecke, *Die Idee der Staatsräson in der neueren Geschichte,* ed. by Walther Hofer (Munich, 1957), particularly pp. 481-510, *passim.,* and *The German Catastrophe. Reflections and Recollections,* translated by Sidney B. Fay (Cambridge, Mass., 1950), pp. xi-xiii, 7-24. On Meinecke's and other German historians' revisionism, cf. Hans Kohn, ed., *German History: Some New German Views* (London, 1954), particularly W. Hofer's essay "Toward a Revision of the German Concept of History," pp. 187-205; and Pietro Rossi, *Lo storicismo tedesco contemporaneo* (Turin, 1956), pp. 473-501, *passim.*

[35] For Croce's interpretation of the nineteenth century, see especially Chabod, "Croce storico," *Rivista Storica Italiana,* cit., pp. 491-525; Caponigri, *History and Liberty,* Part Three, p. 169ff.

[36] *Introduction,* p. xv.

I have learned from your book a great deal of information which had escaped me at the time when history was being made.[37]

In order properly to reconstruct and clarify Salvemini's reappraisal of the Giolittian era a more direct personal note is here absolutely necessary on the circumstances of his writing the *Introduction*. The little work on *Italian Democracy in the Making* [*L'età giolittiana*] was conceived and written before the author knew or met Salvemini. In the spring of 1943 Salvemini was personally shown the final draft of the work on which he expressed general approval, generous encouragement, with disagreement only on the characterization of two minor personages in the Republican and Socialist parties: "No other remarks!"[38] The War then took its toll, among much more terrible things, upon the publication schedule of the manuscript essay until 1945 when, at the publishers' suggestion, Salvemini was asked to write a presentation. In the spring of that year the lengthy *Introduction* arrived. Such, in brief, are the facts on Salvemini's writing of what no one at all then even remotely imagined would prove to be an opening salvo in the Giolittian battle of the books. The important point in an otherwise almost purely private matter lay, as it turned out, not merely in this unexpected "primacy." No less noteworthy, perhaps, is the fact that Salvemini had had, between his readings of the manuscript, two years during which, had he seen fit, he could have changed his first reactions to it. Like most other men, of course, he had many other things to do during those two years—and what years!—than to think of the book or of Giolitti, but again the fact was that in 1945 he not only had the same opinion of the character of the work but also and definitely more important he accepted the new Giolitti who appeared therein with only the moderate qualifications he stated in the *Introduction*.

When the work, with Salvemini's *Introduction*, reached Italy late in 1945 and 1946 it precipitated something more than an academic "sensation." Most Italian critics, commentators, and historians, perhaps too precipitously but with a large measure of justification, pounced upon and emphasized, among other things, Salvemini's "final" acceptance of Giolitti. His qualifications were on the whole lost sight of in the flood of the exegetical literature.[39] Penitential acknowledgment or anything

37 From a letter to the writer dated July 11, 1943.

38 The men were Giuseppe Gaudenzi and Francesco Ciccotti; cf. *Italian Democracy in the Making*, pp. 31, 60, 74, 76.   .

39 Some Giolittian exegesis reached "popularizing" dimensions through broadcasts of a "course" on Giolitti by Radio Italiana; cf. the remarks on the Giolittian "radio course" in Salvatorelli, "Giolitti," *Rivista Storica, cit.*, pp. 498-99.

resembling it made by public figures almost automatically stimulates genuine intellectual curiosity. At times it seems to act as a channel of vicarious catharsis. Be that as it may, what seemed important in this matter at the moment and for many years to come was the apparent fact that at long last Gaetano Salvemini had gone to his Giolittian Canossa.

The writer saw Salvemini many times from the first meeting in Cambridge in the spring of 1943 to the old historian's last summer in Sorrento in 1957. No matter what else was the subject of many long conversations—books, men, ideas, politics, history, friends, work-in-progress, Europe, Italy—two topics inevitably arose: Giolitti and the "Questione del Mezzogiorno."[40] Not always necessarily connected, often separately, but Giolitti and that "Problem" were invariably discussed. On the Mezzogiorno, the impression persisted, during those years, that Salvemini was growing more and more disillusioned, sometimes expressing himself with an almost cruel bitterness which in others would have been cynicism. This culminated, it seemed, in his "confessing," in the course of the last conversation, in July 1957, that he no longer felt that the Mezzogiorno had the "capacity" or "desire" for its own "redemption."[41] When, on the other hand, Giolitti was the subject of conversation, one could trace with the passing of those years a growing indulgence, a tendency to attenuate the means and to accentuate the ends of his political action.[42] Frequently Salvemini would launch upon an outright

[40] Salvemini's writings on the "Problem of the South" are now collected in the volume *Scritti sulla questione meridionale (1896-1955)* (Turin, 1955). See also his Preface to Bruno Caizzi, ed., *Antologia della questione meridionale* (Milan, 1950), pp. 9-13. The best historical-analytical treatment of the Problem is the almost classic work by Friedrich Vöchting, *Die italienische Südfrage* (Berlin, 1951), now available in an excellent Italian translation done under the auspices of the Cassa per il Mezzogiorno, *La questione meridionale* (Naples, 1955), in which see particularly pp. 154-55.

[41] At the two Italian Socialist Party Congresses which he attended—Florence, 1908, and Milan, 1910—Salvemini had become a thorn in the side of the North-Italian leadership of the Party through his reiteration of the double theme of "autonomy" and "solidarity" to be given the South in its efforts at "self-liberation"; cf. *Italian Democracy in the Making*, pp. 56-57. Vöchting, *La questione meridionale*, pp. 353-62, discusses "the problem of the possibility" of resolving the Southern Problem through the *meridionalista* alternatives, of one of which Salvemini had been the most fervent and eloquent spokesman.

[42] How radical a change Salvemini's distinction of Giolittian "ends and means" really was may be best illustrated by recalling Turati's revealing taunt at the Milan Congress of the Socialist Party in 1910: "When Salvemini, with his love for paradox, declares that he would renounce universal suffrage should it be offered by a Giolitti ministry, I can only answer him that we, after having prepared it with our strength and our sacrifices, have already accepted the freedom of association and the freedom of strike from Giolitti. As far as I am concerned, being convinced of the utility of universal

defense of the statesman Giolitti and of some of his pre-1914 political work, though never of his system. One could not help espying a sort of correlation between his mellowing judgment on Giolitti and the evidently increasing despair over the fate of the South whose moral paladin Salvemini had for so long passionately been.[43] To the very last conversation, as he lay on his death-bed, when Salvemini spoke of Giolitti in those tones, it was hard to restrain the words of one of the historian's best disciples from coming to mind:

Conditioned by the fixed principles in which he is rooted, he [Salvemini] does not free himself from the schematic in his appraisal of individuals. For twenty years he made himself wage a crusade against Giolitti, who, albeit as a statesman, possessed his selfsame ideas and prejudices but presented them with the cynicism of the subduer rather than with the enthusiasm of the crusader.[44]

Now, in the light of Salvemini's last writings and articles on Giolittii and particularly of that which appeared in the Florentine review, *Il Ponte,* in 1952, under the title of "Fu l'Italia prefascista una democrazia?"[45] some of the personal impressions and reflections registered here may appear more paradoxical than ever. For especially in this latter article Salvemini seemed to be repudiating in approach and in treatment the evaluation he had made and the judgment he had passed on Giolitti and Giolittian Italy in his *Introduction* of 1945. A careful analysis and

suffrage for the proletariat, I would accept it not only from Giolitti but, if necessary, from the Pope himself." See *Resoconto stenografico dello XI Congresso Nazionale del Partito Socialista Italiano. Milano, 21-22-23-24-25 ottobre 1910* (Rome, 1911), p. 270. Cf. *L'età giolittiana*, pp. 121-24.

43 Salvemini's *meridionalista* crusade during the Giolittian period, within and outside the ranks of the Italian Socialist Party, is now fully documented in his *Scritti sulla questione meridionale,* Part II, "L'età giolittiana," pp. 147-508. For appraisals of Salvemini's activity and influence within other currents of *meridionalismo,* see Caizzi, ed., *Antologia della questione meridionale,* pp. 40-42; S. F. Romano, *Storia della questione meridionale* (Palermo, 1945), pp. 57-65; Guido Dorso, *La rivoluzione meridionale,* new enlarged edition (Rome, 1945), pp. 124-25; Gabriele Pepe, *Pane e terra nel Sud* (Florence, 1954), pp. 62-63; Manlio Rossi-Doria, *Riforma agraria e azione meridionalista* (Bologna, 1948), p. 1; Francesco Compagna, *Labirinto meridionale. Cultura e politica nel Mezzogiorno* (Venice, 1955), p. 136; Gaetano Cingari, *Giustino Fortunato e il Mezzogiorno d'Italia* (Florence, 1954), p. 206. Cf. the revealing episode recounted by Antonio Gramsci, *La questione meridionale* (1927) (Rome, 1951), pp. 14-16, and the interpretative rectification by Salvemini in *Scritti, supra,* Preface, pp. xxiii-xxvi.

44 Piero Gobetti, *La rivoluzione liberale. Saggio sulla lotta politica in Italia* (Bologna, 1924), p. 72, quoted in *Italian Democracy in the Making,* p. 108, note 33.

45 In *Il Ponte,* VIII (1952), 11-23, 166-81, 281-97. Salvemini's article will hereafter be cited as "L'Italia prefascista," *Il Ponte,* with page references.

collation of the two pieces reveal at some points almost contradictory, if not mutually exclusive, phrases. In his 1952 article the emphasis on negative elements is more accentuated; the documentary references and the evidence as well as the statistical materials are obviously pejorative; the mode of attack and the presentation are more argumentative; the tone has become openly polemical. Though the Salveminian style, which was always the man, is unmistakable in both pieces, noticeable differences in phraseology and, more significantly, thematic divergencies and contrasting tonalities can be easily observed between the two articles. Nevertheless, the two articles are in essence and in spirit not contradictory; the conclusions are basically the same; the final assessment of Giolittian Italy as a "democracy in the making" results fundamentally unchanged.[46]

Both external and internal evidence point to this essential concordance of the article with the *Introduction* on the basic historical conclusion. Paradoxically, this is emphasized by an otherwise unexplainable methodological anomaly. In the article Salvemini uses verbatim some of the key phrases of the *Introduction* acknowledging the "making" of an Italian democracy during the pre-1914 period. But against his usual procedure and method, even in those of the article, Salvemini makes no reference to the source, his own or otherwise, of these key phrases from either the English of the Italian edition of the work whence the question has ensued. Since neither carelessness nor lapse of memory can really account in Salvemini for this anomaly the paradox becomes intelligible first of all on a psychological level. As will be further pointed out below, the 1952 article is at once as the very title implies, an elaboration of a query and an argument against a multiplicity of contrasting opinions. It is not a calm exposition of historical matter, as the frequently violent tone suggests. Salvemini is here debating, promiscuously, often furiously, with Croce, Ansaldo, Natale, and especially with Togliatti.[47] He therefore assumes that his stand on the Giolittian era has once and for all been made clear: an Italian democracy had been in the making by 1914.

If one compares Italy as it was in 1860 with that of 1914 it is not possible to deny the immense progress, not only economic but also political and moral, made in that half-century. In 1914 Northern and Central Italy was still far from that level of democracy which had been reached by Switzerland, the Scandinavian countries, England, the United States, and even France. But Italy was on the way. It had not a "perfect" democracy but a democracy "in the making."[48]

[46] Cf. *Introduction*, pp. viii, xiv-xv; *Introduzione*, pp. ix-x, xxvi-xxviii; "L'Italia prefascista," *Il Ponte*, pp. 295-97.

[47] "L'Italia prefascista," *Il Ponte*, pp. 174, 175-76, 177, 286-89, 295-96.

[48] *Ibid.*, p. 297.

Thus he wrote in 1952. In the *Introduction,* seven years earlier, he had said:

Italian democracy would have needed still another generation of trial and error before becoming not a "perfect" democracy but a less "imperfect democracy."[49]

At the close of the article of 1952 he reiterated:

If Italy had had another thirty years of that economic, intellectual, and political progress, even the South would have become included in what was then the zone of "civilization." Those thirty years were not given. The First World War came. But this is another story.[50]

It is clear that Salvemini's historical "stream of consciousness" on the problem of Italian democracy had remained continuous, in need of no further points of reference beyond those intrinsic to the documentation with which he assumes everyone is by now acquainted. When, however, the flow of that historical consciousness encounters the more direct Giolittian obstacle, that is, the problem of Giolitti as distinguished from that of his era, Salvemini veers, cries out in protestation, or even becomes exacerbated and turns about to smash those obstacles the more violently. It is, therefore, in this special problem within the larger historical problem that a real change in Salvemini's view most glaringly appears. There is here an impressive and genuine "reversion."

Salvemini's "reversion" in 1952 to something even more extreme than his pre-1914 position in his judgment of Giolitti does appear to make shambles of his 1945 characterization. Giolitti now returns no longer as a mere "corrupter," not even as the old *ministro della mala vita,* but as the "forerunner" of a true destroyer of that promising if "imperfect democracy" of the Giolittian and pre-Fascist era. In the *Introduction* Salvemini had placidly written:

Looking back at the work of the crusader after thirty years, I find that I have nothing to regret. I must acknowledge, however, that I would have been wiser had I been more moderate in my criticism of the Giolittian system. My knowledge of the men who came after Giolitti in Italy as well as of other countries in which I have lived during the last twenty years has convinced me that if Giolitti was not better neither was he worse than many non-Italian politicians, and he was certainly less reprehensible than the Italian politicians who followed him. For while we Italian crusaders attacked him from the Left accusing him of being—and he was—a corrupter of Italian democracy in the making, others assailed him from the Right because he was even too democratic for their taste.

49 *Introduction,* p. xiv; *Introduzione,* pp. xvi-xvii.
50 "L'Italia prefascista," *Il Ponte,* p. 297.

Our criticism thus did not help to direct the evolution of Italian public life toward less imperfect forms of democracy, but rather toward the victory of those militarist, nationalist, and reactionary groups who had found even Giolitti's democracy too perfect. . . . If it were possible for me to live again in Italy between 1900 and 1914 with that modicum of experience which I have gained during these successive thirty years, I would not omit any of my censures of the Giolittian system, but I would be more indulgent and I would regard with greater suspicion those who found pleasure in my criticism because they wanted to lead Italy in the opposite direction from that which I envisaged for her.[51]

Thus spoke the historian in 1945 about Giolitti and about the "crusader" Salvemini's anti-Giolittian "censures" during the pre-1914 period. In this judgment Giolitti appeared ambivalently as a "corrupter," when seen from the democratic Left, and as an artificer, when seen from the conservative Right, of "Italian democracy in the making." But it is patently Salvemini's sense that the Right had had a more correct view of Giolitti's function and goals than the Left.

In the 1952 article, however, the judgment shifts onto a different level, a dramatic cleavage is reintroduced between Giolitti and a sort of anti-Giolittian "self-making" of Italian democracy. Now Giolitti's work becomes completely submerged again, in Salvemini's revision, within the persisting resistance of the Italian "parliamentary oligarchy" which acted only under pressure from "outside" forces and under the duress of political expediency:

If "to concede" means to cease a resistance which has become very dangerous, we may rightly say that Giolitti "conceded" the freedom to organize and to strike to the workers. . . . Giolitti had the good sense to understand that it was necessary to change route and not to continue the policy of the "blindered mule" in the new social and psychological conditions of the Italian people. It would be foolish to deny him that good sense. But it should be clearly kept in mind that when Giolitti decided to make that "concession" the Italian workers had already, thanks to their own sacrifices and determination, taken that concession by themselves [da sé].[52]

But soon, even beyond that cleavage emphasized by Salvemini between the statesman Giolitti and the democratic forces of his times, a more drastic historical and moral judgment replaces that of a Giolitti seen as a "corrupter." Now Giolitti appears as the "precursor" of Mussolini and his "system" becomes the antecedent of that of Fascism:

The difference between Mussolini and Giolitti was one of degree and not of

51 *Introduction*, p. xv; *Introduzione*, pp. xxviii-xxix.
52 "L'Italia prefascista," *Il Ponte*, p. 175.

kind. Giolitti was for Mussolini what John the Baptist was for Christ: he paved his way.[53]

Here indeed more than a complete "reversion" has occurred. The calm historical judgment on Giolitti as a "corrupter" has been transformed into a passional value-judgment on Giolitti as a "forerunner." The two judgments stem from different, almost irreconcilable, sources. They belong to contrasting spheres of thought and sentiment. Salvemini seemed more than ever divided against himself and as if held in intellectual and psychological suspense between politics and history.

[53] *Ibid.*, p. 285. As Nino Valeri has in part pointed out, in the Introduction to Giolitti, *Discorsi extraparlamentari*, p. 52, Salvemini in his characterization of Giolitti retained the idea but changed both the context and the phraseology of its first suggestions in Don Luigi Sturzo, *Italy and Fascismo*, tr. by B. B. Barclay (London, 1926) and of its specific use in Angelo Tasca, *Nascita e avvento del fascismo* (Florence, 1950), p. 188, where Giolitti is styled "the John the Baptist of Fascism."

II

THE GREAT DEBATE
ON THE GIOLITTIAN ERA

The masks of Giolitti are as manifold as the political parties and inclinations of the Italians, who, divided as they may be by the smoke of their hatreds and loves, are similarly bound to the image of a Giolitti now transfigured into a tutelary deity of the motherland. *

NINO VALERI

Why had the new dramatic shift of emphasis and judgment occurred between 1945 and 1952 and how can it be reconciled with the growingly less severe, personal mellowing in Salvemini's opinion of Giolitti? The answer to this question is not simple and it must be sought on a number of levels in connection with Salvemini's far from simple personality and mode of thought. One of those levels reveals an interesting combination of methodological and psychological factors which apparently led Salvemini, in his vision of Giolittian Italy, to an oscillation between the point of view of the reformer, the "crusader," as he styled himself, and the historian, to the unresolved contrast within him between the actor and the critic of that historical era. This antinomy in Salvemini was part of his intellectual and spiritual complexity.[1] It lay beyond the schematisms which have too frequently been utilized to characterize his mind and personality, his historiographical work and his political activity.

Piero Gobetti had perhaps seen right, at least in part: Salvemini, the self-conscious anti-Giolittian, was after all a "Giolittian" by nature but not by temperament.[2] The "apostle" Salvemini castigated the "dom-

---

* Nino Valeri, "Giovanni Giolitti nella storiografia del secondo Dopoguerra," Ettore Rota, ed., *Questioni di storia del Risorgimento e dell'Unità d'Italia* (Milan, Dott. Carlo Marzorati, 1951), p. 1020.

[1] See Ernesto Rossi, "Il nonconformista," *Il Mondo,* September 17, 1957, pp. 1-2.

[2] The oscillation between a "temperamental" and a "rational" approach to Giolitti was in some respects still apparent in 1945-52. Both in the *Introduction,* p. xiv, and in the article, "L'Italia prefascista," *Il Ponte,* p. 297, he implied agreement with Giolitti's view—later summarized in *Memorie,* II, 522-23—that in 1914-15 Italy needed peace for the preservation and consolidation of her material and political life. On the other hand, in a review—"Albertini 1914-15," *Il Mondo,* February 9, 1952—of the published volumes of Albertini, *Venti anni di vita politica, cit.,* Salvemini reiterated his own democratic-interventionist and anti-Giolittian views; see also Salvemini, "I manutengoli del

inator" Giolitti because he saw in him a protagonist of the same historical action, of the making of Italian democracy, but also an antagonist in whose character, political nature, and *modus operandi* Salvemini felt his own democratic afflatus, his undaunted "enthusiasm," perversely reflected as the cold calculation of the politico, the "cynicism" of the Piedmontese Liberal statesman. Cavour had perhaps not troubled Mazzini's pursuit of his ideals as Giolitti hounded Salvemini's political conscience. Let his historical rationality play without trappings or potential entrapments upon the purer level of historical reality and Salvemini would almost automatically assign it its proper function as an instrument of objective analysis and dispassionate judgment. This he had done admirably, inspiringly, particularly in those pioneering monographs on early Florentine history, on the French Revolution, and on the nineteenth century.[3] This he had sought to do, more briefly but almost as serenely, in the re-vision of Liberal Italy sketched in the *Introduction*. Let, on the other hand, anyone drive him to see a Giolittian reflection in his own political personality and Salvemini would as mathematically rouse himself to reject that reflection as spurious and to castigate it with violent retort. This occurred repeatedly in the late 1940's and culminated in his article of 1952.

The great Giolittian polemic in which Salvemini found himself involved during these latter years unleashed in him again the old political passions. This time, however, these had no immediate practical object but rather what he felt to be the necessity for reasserting the truth on an otherwise academic question: Had pre-Fascist Italy been a democracy? But this question was not only "academic" in the loose sense of the word,

---

fascismo," *Il Ponte*, VIII (1952), 419-28, *passim*. On the complex diplomatic and political problems posed for and in Italy by the outbreak of the First World War, see now *I Documenti Diplomatici Italiani. Quinta serie: 1914-1918*. Vol. I. August 2-October 16, 1914 (Rome, 1954); Luigi Albertini, *The Origins of the War of 1914*, tr. and ed. by Isabella M. Massey. 3 vols. (London, 1952-57), III, 296-363. Cf. Alberto Caracciolo, "L'intervento italiano in guerra e la crisi politica del 1914-15," *Società*, X (1954), 809-26, 986-1012; Paolo Alatri, "Luigi Albertini," *Belfagor*, VIII (1953), 51-74, and "Interventismo, Fascismo, Resistenza nella recente storiografia," *Belfagor*, IX (1954), 61-86.

[3] Preeminently the following: *La dignità cavalleresca nel Comune di Firenze* (Florence, 1896); *Magnati e Popolani in Firenze dal 1280 al 1295* (Florence, 1899); *La Rivoluzione francese, 1788-1792* (Milan, 1905; new ed., Bari, 1954); *Mazzini* [1905], 4th ed. (Florence, 1925); *I partiti milanesi nel secolo XIX* (Milan, 1899); "Carlo Cattaneo," Preface to *Le più belle pagine di Carlo Cattaneo* (Florence, 1922); *Appunti di storia del Risorgimento italiano: 1815-1918* (Trent, 1920); "L'Italia politica nel secolo XIX," in *L'Europa nel secolo XIX* (Padua, 1925); *La politica estera dell'Italia dal 1871 al 1915*, 2nd ed. (Florence, 1949). The publication of Salvemini's *opera omnia* is now being planned in Italy.

it was also unnecessary now since he was in basic agreement on it with all but one—Ferruccio Parri[4]—of his actual or putative major disputants. But perhaps, it turned out, that was not the real question, though it was obviously of the very essence. For Salvemini, as always, the true problem was Giolitti. Once again, as so often before and after 1914, Giolitti came to plague his vision of an Italian democracy in the making and played havoc with his historical judgment on it. The blurring of that vision and the pressure on that judgment were almost solely due to the Italian flood of Giolittian exegetical literature[5] which willy-nilly and for contrasting motives equated Giolitti with his Italy and made of Italian democracy, imperfect though Salvemini judged it to have been, a function of Giolittian democratic initiative.

This, for Salvemini, was the question: Whatever democratic progress— material, political, moral—he was willing to concede had been made before the First World War, he insisted to the very end that it had been made "from below," and not "from above," against Italy's political class and not by it or through its leadership. By dint of resistance against "reactionary policies," of immense "sacrifices," of a collective "determination," the Italian "working-class movement," organized or not, succeeded in "bending" Giolitti, this twentieth-century "exponent of enlightened despotism," to the liberal cause. When, as quite clearly in 1901, Salvemini maintained, "the coincidence between the pressure of the workers' movement and [Giolitti's] personal predispositions and political interests" occurred, for that moment at least, Giolitti was "turned into a statesman."[6] This coincidence between the real needs and strong wishes of the people and the political interests of Giolittian statecraft was a happy constructive accident. But it was neither perpetuated automatically nor freely extended to other areas of national life except for a price or under

4 For the background and context of Parri's idea on pre-Fascist Italy, see Bruno Widmar, "Ferruccio Parri," *Belfagor*, XIII (1958), 177-88. Parri's denial of any reality to a pre-Fascist Italian democracy had occurred, symptomatically, in the course of a "debate" with Benedetto Croce in September 1945. In one of the few *addenda* to the *Introduzione*, p. xxvii, as well as in "L'Italia prefascista," *Il Ponte*, pp. 295-96, Salvemini ascribed Parri's denial of a pre-Fascist Italian democratic development to the Resistance leader's being a *"credente nell'ideale della perfetta democrazia."* See Parri's homage to his staunch friend, "Preghiera per Salvemini," *Il Ponte*, XIII (1957), 1159-61.

5 The most significant contributions to the new Giolittian literature are reviewed in Valeri's essays and in those by Salvatorelli, Candeloro, and Papa.

6 "L'Italia prefascista," *Il Ponte*, pp. 175-76, *passim*. On these beginnings of Giolittian policy, see Giacomo Perticone, *Gruppi e partiti politici nella vita pubblica italiana*, 2nd ed. (Modena-Rome, 1946), pp. 126-34; Carlo Morandi, *I partiti politici nella storia d'Italia*, 2nd ed. (Florence, 1948), pp. 51-53; De Rosa, *La crisi dello Stato liberale*, pp. 128-35.

other circumstances and contingencies of popular pressure and political interest, as those surrounding that other great Giolittian "concession," universal suffrage, revealed in 1911-12.[7]

Strangely enough, Luigi Albertini, an anti-Giolittian from the advanced Northern Liberal Right, had castigated Giolitti on the pages of the Milanese *Corriere della Sera* before 1914 and then again in his monumental memoirs, exactly for those moments of "coincidence" between Giolittian political requirements and democratic and "socialist" pressure. These same moments which Salvemini judged to have been too rare and prophylactic Albertini saw as milestones toward that "most torbid of reactions" which "eleven years" later, *particularly through universal suffrage,* came to Italy as Fascism.[8] Evidently, whether viewed from Salvemini's Democratic Left or from Albertini's Liberal Right but for diametrically opposed reasons, Giolitti seemed to have been cast for the role of "forerunner" of Mussolini. Irony dogged again Salvemini's revised *antigiolittismo* and a real nemesis loomed from other quarters. Albertini's posthumously published memoirs constituted the only "concordant-discordant" "Salveminian" voice in the strong Giolittian chorus which was rising as if by spontaneous generation on the Italian historiographical and literary scene during that almost incredible neo-Giolittian *biennium mirabile* of 1949-50.

Those two years saw issuing from the Italian presses, one after another, the writer's *L'età giolittiana,* with Salvemini's "pro-Giolittian" *Introduction,* Natale's *Giolitti e gli Italiani* and Galizzi's *Giolitti e Salandra,* both with Prefaces by Croce, Soleri's *Memorie,* Ansaldo's *Il Ministro della buona vita,* and Togliatti's *Discorso su Giolitti.*[9] The massive figure of Giovanni Giolitti walked abroad again in Italy. Through the accident of the translation of the book with Salvemini's *Introduction at this time,*

---

[7] "L'Italia prefascista," *Il Ponte,* p. 290. Cf. the account, simple in form, extremely subtle in fact, which Giolitti gave of his initiative in the great electoral reform of 1911-12, in *Memorie,* II, 306-10.

[8] Albertini, *Venti anni di vita politica,* II, 66: "Here was the heart of the matter and I persist to this day in believing—I can never repeat it enough—that the evils with which we have always been afflicted, which periodically came to the surface of our existence, and which have brought us eleven years later [1911-1922] at the mercy of the most torbid reaction, have issued and have been fed by the conception prevalent after 1900: that the country could not be governed with the resources and ideas of the Constitutional Party but must live at the pleasure and tolerance of the Socialists by seeking a continual adjustment to their will." On Giolitti and the Socialists during the early phase of the new liberal period, see Giolitti, *Memorie,* I, 173-82; and the interpretations in *Italian Democracy in the Making,* pp. 46-48, 51, 58-59, 72-74, 111, 112-13; Salvatorelli "Giolitti," *Rivista Storica Italiana, cit.,* pp. 519-23, 527-29; De Rosa, *La crisi dello Stato liberale,* pp. 126-52; Valeri, *Da Giolitti a Mussolini,* pp. 15-16.

[9] *Supra,* ch. I notes 6, 9, 14, 16, 17.

Giolitti seemed to cast a strange new anti-Salveminian shadow on the land as if, at least in part, under Salvemini's own auspices.

The real wonder would have been if Salvemini had not reacted to this unexpected turn in Giolitti's historical fortune. The fundamentally anti-Salveminian inspiration of most of those new Italian works—intrinsic in Natale, Soleri, and Galizzi,[10] direct in Togliatti,[11] obviously sardonic in Ansaldo's very title—was patent. But there was, strangely, even more. With most of these works, with the all-too-obvious but not complete exception of Togliatti's *Discorso,* another shadow, that of a thorough-going Giolittian par excellence still alive during those years, unwittingly reinforced Salvemini's Giolittian nemesis: Benedetto Croce. Towering behind the works of Natale, Galizzi, and Soleri[12] was Croce's historical reconstruction of post-Risorgimento Italy and of Giolitti's liberal function in its program. If Croce's *History of Italy* was an "historical idyll"[13] possessed of a "Panglossian" character,[14] as Salvemini had at times referred to it, the new "evidence" brought by Natale, Soleri, and Galizzi tended to testify either to a reality which Salvemini had never seen or to a documentation whose validity he was unwilling to acknowledge. Croce's "optimistic" and "historicistic" reconstruction of a lost Giolittian world almost without shadows and of an era which the philosopher had seen as one of those rare but "certain definite times of refreshment and peace, cheerfulness and prosperity"[15] was now being documented by men of true Liberal faith and of unquestioned integrity. The problem was genuine and unavoidable.

Yet one might venture that if the new *Giolittiana* had stopped with the works of Natale, Soleri, and Galizzi, Salvemini would *not* have roused himself again in anti-Giolittian fury. For on the whole those works con-

[10] Gaetano Natale was the sole living member of this "Giolittian" group, Vincenzo Galizzi having died in 1930 and Marcello Soleri in 1945; the posthumous publications, however, were no less effective, if more generic, than Natale's book toward the Giolittian revival. See Natale, *op. cit.,* pp. 507-48, on Giolitti's "conflict with the Utopians"; Soleri, *op. cit.,* pp. 31-33, for direct criticism of those who qualified Giolitti as a "corrupter" and a "dictator"; Galizzi, *op. cit.,* pp. 12-32, for a fine defense of Giolitti as true liberal statesman *vis-à-vis* the Liberals of the Right among whom Salandra had been an outstanding spokesman.

[11] Togliatti, *Discorso su Giolitti,* pp. 11, 14-16, 29.

[12] Cf. Croce's Preface to Natale, *op. cit.,* no page reference, but i-iii; Croce's presentation of Galizzi, *op. cit.,* pp. vii-xxiv; and Soleri, *op. cit.,* pp. 171, 206, 251.

[13] See the beautiful but critical analysis of this or similar characterizations of Croce's *History* in Chabod, "Croce storico," *Rivista Storica Italiana, cit.,* pp. 516-18, 525-30.

[14] *Introduction,* p. viii; *Introduzione,* p. ix; "L'Italia prefascista," *Il Ponte,* pp. 174, 295-96, *passim.*

[15] B. Croce, *A History of Italy, 1871-1915,* translated by Cecilia M. Ady (Oxford, 1929), p. 214.

tained little with which he could really seek quarrel and quite a bit with which he could not but agree. At any rate, in dealing with these men, particularly with Albertini, Salvemini was certain he could "converse." Even if he decided to continue to disagree with them, he could do so upon the tacit assumption that they did not "cheat at the game," as he was wont to say. They had breathed the same historical air and spoke the same political and moral language as he.

Despite appearances this found some confirmation in Salvemini's very significant if merely implicit "rapprochement" with Croce. Below the surface of their perennial ideal and political quarrel Salvemini and Croce were bound by the invisible threads of a common historical and moral milieu if not by *forma mentis*. As always, practically to the very end, Salvemini claimed at best that he sometimes "manage[d] to understand" Croce's philosophy[16] and at worst that he was "born blind" to it.[17] This was far from true of Salvemini's understanding of Croce's historical works. Though a very wide gulf of a multiform character obviously separated them in their interpretation of Italian history, as witness their official Giolittian exegesis, fundamentally, but particularly toward the end of their lives, they appeared in greater agreement than they perhaps suspected. They had been born and had matured, albeit so differently, into the same Italian and European historical milieu. Their long lives had been spent in seeking "to carry on their trades," each in his fashion, in the midst of great changes and wars and catastrophes, for their country and their ideal European worlds. Equally fearful of the new "iron age," toward the end they became almost equally nostalgic for a world they had differently helped to make and which now could be no more: their vanished nineteenth century, their promising Liberal Italy, their fertile "Giolittian era."

We in our heart of hearts [wrote Croce in his war-time diary on March 1, 1944] live as yet in the expectation that a world might be born again similar to and a continuation of that in which we lived before the War of 1914: a world of peace, work, and national and international cooperation. And in this lies the source of our profound anguish: that that hope vanishes ever more and, worse still, that it grows dimmer and darkens. We must foresee not the resurgence of that world, its continuation and betterment, but an infinite succession of shocks and revulsions and ruins through revolutions and wars which will last

16 G. Salvemini, *Historian and Scientist. An Essay on the Nature of History and the Social Sciences* (Cambridge, Mass., 1939), p. 87.

17 The expression *"nato cieco"* to Croce's philosophy occurs in Salvemini's review of Aldo Mautino, *La formazione della filosofia politica di Benedetto Croce*, 3rd ed., (Bari, 1953) in *Il Ponte*, X (1954), 811.

through a half century if not longer and which may never achieve anything
positive but lead to the *finis Europae*.[18]

As if to echo Croce's fearful reflections, in 1953 Salvemini wrote:

We, that is to say a half dozen melancholy and harmless survivors, are the last
heirs of an illustrious race which is rapidly vanishing, erratic blocks abandoned
in the plains by a glacier that has sought refuge on the mountain top. And
that glacier was called "liberalism," "democracy," "socialism," during the century which the witless wretch, Léon Daudet, called "the stupid nineteenth
century" while we insist in considering it the most intelligent, the most human
and humane of centuries. *Morituri te salutant!*[19]

There was even more than this common nostalgic remembrance of
things past in Croce's and Salvemini's personal afflatus during their last
years. In long conversations held with each of them during their last
months of life—in April 1952 with Croce and in July 1957 with Salvemini
—the writer spoke with them at great length about Giolitti.[20] Almost
incredibly, each expatiated with evident pleasure on Giolitti in almost
similar accents of admiration, mixed with some pride in Croce, with
respect in Salvemini. Both accentuated the positive in Giolitti—Croce
with persistent understatement, Salvemini with subtle jocular emphasis.
There was again in both their tones the suggestion of a self-conscious
nostalgia for an era and a man, Giolitti, whom Croce had later had as a
faithful friend and Salvemini as a not unworthy "enemy." Remarkable,
indeed, was the unconscious tendency toward a final agreement on Giolittian ground by these two antithetical representatives of a vanishing generation of Italian intellectual "giants."[21]

Patently it was neither Croce nor the new "Crocean documentation"
on Giolitti that led Salvemini to espouse the polemical counteroffensive
of the 1952 article. Whatever part may be assigned to his psychological
reaction against the exaggerated penitential garb in which he was made
to appear by those who pounced upon his Giolittian qualifications in
the *Introduction*, it proved secondary to a more decisive factor. The more
than implicit attacks from certain quarters on his old and new Giolittian
views, the ironic and worldly-wise commentaries by the sophisticates of

18 B. Croce, *Quando l'Italia era tagliata in due. Estratto di un diario: Luglio 1943-
Giugno 1944* (Bari, 1948), pp. 87-88.

19 G. Salvemini, "La pelle di zigrino," *Il Mondo*, February 21, 1953, p. 3.

20 The conversations were held respectively at Croce's house in Via Trinità Maggiore,
Naples, and at Villa la Rufola in Capo di Sorrento.

21 On the tendency toward such a "reconciliation" even on historical grounds, see the
suggestive remarks by Walter Maturi, "Gli studi di storia moderna e contemporanea,"
Cinquant'anni, cit., I, 280-81; and the more extensive and direct discussion of the
problem by Ugo Azzoni, "L'Italia dopo l'Unità," *Itinerari, cit.*, pp. 553-56.

politics, the pseudohistorical and pseudomoralistic "drawing of lessons" from his allegedly ineffectual and unrealistic anti-Giolittian crusade,[22] now evidently interpreted as "sound and fury signifying nothing," spurred Salvemini to descend into battle again. This was to be waged bifrontally, against the two extremes of neo-Giolittian Right and Left whose chief spokesmen were Giovanni Ansaldo and Palmiro Togliatti.[23]

In his 1952 article Salvemini repudiated both extremes. Understandably, however, there was less direct Salveminian fury against Ansaldo than against Togliatti. The ironical conversion of the notorious epithet for Giolitti [Il Ministro della mala vita], first coined in his 1910 exposé of the far-from-exemplary Giolittian electoral methods in the South, into Ansaldo's dulcet title [Il Ministro della buona vita] for an appealing hagiographical portrait left Salvemini no choice but to judge it for what it was: a clever anti-Salveminian shaft from the disillusioned extreme Right—political and intellectual. Salvemini would not be drawn to expend too much energy upon such a benign biohistorical exaggeration which seemed almost a "caricature" of Croce's "idyll."[24] He might even agree that the Giolittian ancien régime had guaranteed an intimate dolcezza di vivere to some Italians. Certainly he would not dispute the right of any neo-Giolittian convert to fondle, after the deluge, sweet remembrances of things past through nostalgic half-fantasies of sojourns in Arcadia. But if not on bread alone neither solely on myth can historians live. At any rate, he had always Albertini, also from the Right, to match against Croce and perhaps ultimately both to pit against Ansaldo. But that battle to the Right had already been fought in fact long ago—and then in part again in the Introduction. Ansaldo, therefore, for all his undeniable literary ability and biographical cleverness, could be safely left to the sensation-mongers and the dilettanti of history. Palmiro Togliatti, however, had presented a different kind of neo-Giolittian exegesis. This deserved more careful attention.

Togliatti's Discorso su Giolitti had been first delivered before a large and somewhat sophisticated audience in Turin early in 1950. The position and political authoritativeness of the speaker, his official leadership

22 See especially Ansaldo, Il Ministro della buona vita, pp. 280, 354, 407, 471; Togliatti, Discorso su Giolitti, pp. 15-16, 29.

23 "L'Italia prefascista," Il Ponte, cit., pp. 175, 176, 177, 286-89.

24 Ansaldo, op. cit., p. 354: "Of all of Giolitti's opponents Salvemini was the most serious. . . . It was precisely Salvemini who in 1912, having lost the light of reason as a result of the unlucky election of Molfetta, hurled against Giolitti the charge of being 'ministro della mala vita.' And it was just then (the irony of it!) that the only period of 'good life' (buona vita) which, under the guidance of Giolitti, modern Italy has had, was coming to an end."

and widespread reputation as theoretician of the Italian Communist Party, and his early association with Antonio Gramsci, the unique Italian Marxist activist-philosopher, founder, and revered martyr of the Party, gave Togliatti's speech something more than academic significance.[25] The Italian Communist leader's "Discourse" may superficially have appeared to be a purely historical and personal commentary by a sympathetic Piedmontese politician, Togliatti, on the old Piedmontese Liberal statesman, Giolitti. It was, of course, more than that. While, on the one hand, it brought into sharper focus some of the annotations on Giolitti contained in Gramsci's prison-notebooks, it served notice, on the other, of a quasi-official Italian Marxist recognition of the Giolittian problem so far visibly monopolized by the "bourgeois camp."[26] In a way

[25] That the political, intellectual, and moral mantle of Antonio Gramsci was Togliatti's by the fullest rights of inheritance is, of course, almost unquestioned in official Italian Communist quarters; it has been held to be open to some fundamental doubts in former or non-Communist Italian quarters. For the official interpretation see the implicit kinship predicated in the reprint of three "discourses" on Gramsci by P. Togliatti, *Gramsci* (Rome, 1949), pp. 9-71, 73-91, 92-128, respectively dealing with Gramsci as "Leader of the Italian Working Class" (1937), "Gramsci, Sardinia, Italy" (1947), and "Thinker and Man of Action" (1949); P. Togliatti, ed., *Trenta anni di vita e lotte del Partito Comunista Italiano. Quaderni di "Rinascita,"* no. 2 (Rome, 1951), an anthology, apparently designed as official Italian Communist Party history, assumes throughout the continuity of leadership from Gramsci to Togliatti; L. Lombardo Radice and G. Carbone, *Vita di Antonio Gramsci* (Rome, 1951), particularly pp. 105-06, 177-78; and Marcella and Maurizio Ferrara, *Conversando con Togliatti* (Rome, 1954), a sort of official biography. For altogether different treatment and emphasis, see Fulvio Bellini and Giorgio Galli, *Storia del Partito Comunista Italiano* (Milan, 1953), pp. 131-202, 203-72, which constitute the two central chapters on Gramsci and Togliatti respectively, and pp. 50 ff., 96-104, 398-401; Angelo Tasca, *Nascita e avvento del fascismo*. Preface to the Italian edition, pp. xxxi-xxxii, 1, lxv-lxvi; Ignazio Silone, *Uscita di sicurezza* (Florence, n. d.), pp. 43-71.

[26] Gramsci, who had been condemned by Mussolini's Special Tribunal for the Defense of the State, was imprisoned in 1926 and was released, practically on the point of death, in 1937. While in prison Gramsci had written, despite the strict surveillance, a voluminous set of notebooks containing, in some parts, materials for a sketch of a unique critique of Italian history and culture from a Marxist point of view—the *Quaderni dal Carcere*. The posthumous publication of the *Quaderni* under various rubrics collectively known as *Opere di Antonio Gramsci*, 7 vols. (Turin, 1947-51) constituted one of the major "cultural"—and, of course, potentially political and ideological—events of the post-war period. The periodic release of the Gramsci volumes coincided, crucially in many respects, with the height of the new "Giolittian debate" and affected it among most sectors of the Italian intelligentsia. From a vast and growing literature on Gramsci and the impact of his thought, see Guido Morpurgo-Tagliabue, "Gramsci tra Croce e Marx," *Il Ponte*, IV (1948), 429-38; "More about Gramsci," *The Times Literary Supplement*, December 5, 1952, p. 796; Aldo Garosci, "Totalitarismo e storicismo nel pensiero di Gramsci" in his *Pensiero politico e storiografia moderna, cit.*, pp. 193-257; Mario Sansone, "La cultura," in *Dieci anni dopo, cit.*, pp. 533-36. The

it also revealed, among other things, that that interpretation of the problem had by now become a matter of some consequence in the Italian and perhaps even European ideological struggle.[27]

Apparently paying homage to a statesman whom Togliatti, by the very local origins they had in common, could lay a claim to appreciating and understanding in the nuances of his personal and local character,[28] and after denying that "Marxists, Communists" by reason of their alleged "Manichean" vision "of history and the world"[29] are incapable of historical objectivity, the Communist leader proceeded to analyze Giolitti as a "progressive," positive liberal-democratic Italian and European force in the period of transition from "the old conservative Italy" to the "new imperialist Italy."[30] Togliatti's Giolitti seemed cleverly, almost successfully, rescued from the historic clutches of Croce's "idyllic" high personage of a quasi-utopian epoch and Salvemini's "corrupter" of an autonomous Italian democracy in the making. In Togliatti's thesis Giolitti became the wise, if historically "conditioned" guide, the most advanced but necessarily limited member of Italy's older political class. Giolitti appeared almost in the guise of a bold rider of a recalcitrant Italian democratic steed, a steed, however, which for Togliatti never reached the "true" destination, if for no other reasons, because that destination lay beyond its resources and beyond the rider's "historic mission." By

---

Quaderni, together with Gramsci's political articles of 1919-22 later reissued in the volume L'Ordine Nuovo, 1919-1922 (Turin, 1955), contained a wealth of direct or suggestive references to the liberal era and to Giolitti, whom Gramsci, in La questione meridionale, p. 22, had characterized as "the personification of the bourgeois dominance in Italy." Gramsci's analysis of Giolitti's "dilemma" in 1911-13, in Il Risorgimento (1949), pp. 97-99, as well as in his other writings, apparently required some "officious" coordination in the light both of the almost ubiquitous impact of Gramsci's ideas and of the Giolittian vogue of 1949-52. Togliatti's Discorso at Turin in 1950 acted as an "authoritative" and "organic" sketch for a Marxist reinterpretation of Giolitti and his era.

[27] In Italian Marxist periodicals, Salvemini and this writer—who had written on Giolitti before 1945—were both categorized as exponents of the so-called "Third Force" movement; see Candeloro, "Giolitti e l'età giolittiana," Società, cit., p. 140, and the reference to such descriptions in Valeri, "G. Giolitti e la storiografia del secondo dopoguerra," in Questioni di storia, cit., p. 1022. More significantly, careful analysis of Togliatti's extremely compact and, in parts, very subtle, Discorso su Giolitti, reveals that it is in fact an effort to translate into the terms of Marxist-Communist dialectics a specific historical problem and a great political personality. For Togliatti's direct or tendentious utilization of official doctrine in the "narration," see Discorso, pp. 27-28, 37-44, 57-59, 62-64, 66-67, 75, 78-79, 85-94, 95-96.

[28] Togliatti, Discorso su Giolitti, pp. 95, 108, contain direct references to Piedmontese affection for Giolitti.

[29] Ibid., p. 41.

[30] Ibid., p. 64.

1914, with Giolitti—Togliatti concluded—Italian democracy was no longer "in the making," because it was, so to speak, already made to the limit of its possibilities: " . . . That democracy, we know it now, could not progress, and when one cannot progress one turns back and is swept away."[31]

This was indeed a turning upside down of Salvemini's vision of Giolittian Italy. Certainly more than by any neo-Crocean defense or hagiographical homily he became incensed by what he regarded a form of ideological scholasticism which did violence to his own and others' less self-assured quest for historical truth. To what he considered polemical violence Salvemini reacted now with equal, if not greater, polemical violence. Almost furiously he let his own sweep over not only the "immediate opposition" to the Right and to the Left but also over the more remote, even to his recent revision on Giolitti contained in the *Introduction*. Now, at last, Salvemini re-enveloped them all in his criticism and condemnation: Croce's "idyll" and its most recent illustrators; Ansaldo's rose-tinted ancestral portrait from the Italian family-album; Togliatti's Piedmontese-Marxist "realism" and "structural contradictions" and, inevitably, Salvemini's own "new" Giolitti. Suddenly, unexpectedly, in the new polemical atmosphere, Salvemini reopened the whole question.

In all this strange mixture of sweetness and light and iron dialectical laws, Salvemini protested, whence then had Fascism come to Italy? It was thus, almost in desperation, that he had recourse to a sort of *deus ex machina*: Giolitti had "paved the way" for Mussolini. That the two, personally and historically, belonged to different species of Italian and European humanity, that they had sought, with different means, diametrically opposed ends, Salvemini but briefly considered.[32] In desperate situations desperate measures. Salvemini's "third" Giolitti—after the *ministro della mala vita* and the "corrupter" of "Italian democracy in

---

31 *Ibid.*, p. 95.

32 "L'Italia prefascista," *Il Ponte*, pp. 178-81, 286-94, *passim*. For Salvemini's fuller and calmer reconstruction of the nature of Fascism and its leader, see his volume on *The Fascist Dictatorship in Italy* (New York, 1927), particularly chapters I-II, pp. 3-120. For a review of the newer literature on Mussolini and Fascism, see Noether, "Italy Reviews Its Fascist Past: A Bibliographical Essay," *American Historical Review*, *cit*. Particularly illuminating insights and documentary evidence on the character of the Liberal and Socialist crisis of which Mussolini was the beneficiary are to be found in Valeri, *Da Giolitti a Mussolini, cit.*, chapters iii-v and the archival documents appended to them; Pietro Nenni, *Storia di quattro anni,* 2nd ed. (Rome, 1946), especially valuable on the Socialist disintegration after 1919; Tommaso Fiore, *Un popolo di formiche* (Bari, 1951), six uniquely acute "political letters," written from January 1925 to August 1926, on the Fascist conquest of a Southern agrarian region, Apulia; and the revealing correspondence in Filippo Turati-Anna Kuliscioff, *Carteggio. V. Dopoguerra e fascismo, 1919-1922*, ed. by Allessandro Schiavi (Turin, 1953).

the making"—would now slay the old and new Giolittian mythologies in one fell swoop. His *furor polemicus* now broke the dikes of his own purely historical "flow of consciousness." Perhaps against his real wish, certainly against his recent expectation, Salvemini was once again forced to abandon the serene company of Clio and seek refuge in the realm of his old political and polemical Furies.[33] A Salveminian cycle was definitely ended.

Less evident, below the surface of Salvemini's new passional mood, there stirred, at its worst, a resurgent schematic approach to civil life seen as a process of perpetual warfare between the governed and the rulers—a warfare marked only by temporary truces and contingent accords of the kind he had espied and pointed to in connection with Giolittian politics in 1901 and 1911-12. But there was also here, at its best, the rebursting forth of his fundamentally dualistic conception of politics. Whatever else might differentiate the Croceans, Ansaldo, and Togliatti in their interpretations of Giolitti and Liberal Italy, they appeared to have in common mere varieties of what Salvemini considered a monistic conception of the historical process.

Salvemini, who on the whole recoiled from formal philosophizing on history,[34] in his last Giolittian essay implicitly reasserted his almost hypostatic belief in the necessity of safeguarding the idea of the essential duality constituted by the imprescriptible freedom of the individual and the tendentious voracity of the State in whomsoever incarnated. That belief in turn, demanded vigilance for the prevention of the dangerous identification, which not only politicos but even historians are subject to and often find expedient, of national societies with their multiform expressions. In our time, he felt, this had led in theory and in fact, particularly in Europe, to the sterile equation between nations and peoples and the grim Leviathans which had often sought to devour them. In these fears and beliefs perhaps lay the true bedrock of Salvemini's persistent nonconformism, the sources of the essential antinomy which characterized his approach to politics. The main stages of his larger political and historiographical activity appeared to have been stamped with those fears and beliefs. They had deeply affected his challenging attitudes toward the Italian Socialist Party before 1914,[35] toward

33 Cf. "L'Italia prefascista," *Il Ponte, loc. cit.,* supra.

34 In his *Historian and Scientist, cit.,* Salvemini has perhaps unconsciously written on the "philosophy of history" while consciously pursuing investigation of "historical methodology." The entire series of essays in the book is deserving of systematic analysis in the light of Salvemini's own historiographical production.

35 *Italian Democracy in the Making,* pp. 57-58. For a full documentation of Salvemini's Socialist period and for his attitudes toward the Italian Socialist Party both

Giolitti before and after 1914, toward Italian intervention in 1915, toward "renunciation" and Wilsonianism in 1918-19, toward Fascism, and toward Communism. The often over-decried Salveminian "sectarianism" was basically a function of the man's anti-authoritarian intellectual and temperamental bent. He undoubtedly sometimes allowed his psychological tendencies to lead him to magnify his suspicions as to the nature of all politics and the function of most ideologies but he never allowed them to betray his consistent democratic and libertarian passions.

By practical self-acknowledgment Salvemini had only two intellectual masters: Carlo Cattaneo[36] and Gaetano Mosca.[37] The study of Cattaneo had left upon him the imprint of a solid "Lombard realism," an abiding lesson on the real and potential evils of all massive organizations, be they of power or of culture. In Cattaneo's teaching he had found at the same time a confirmation of an almost ancestral distrust of the State and an inspiration for a persistent federalist belief in minimal but realistic institutional and political groupings.[38] Cattaneo's historical-humanistic

---

before and after his "disenchantment," see the articles and speeches collected in his *Tendenze vecchie e necessità nuove del movimento operaio italiano. Saggi critici* (Bologna, 1922), from which Caizzi, ed., *Antologia della questione meridionale*, pp. 327-36, has reprinted the Preface under the title "La deviazione oligarchica del movimento socialista." Salvemini's writings and speeches on Socialism and the Question of the South are now available in his *Scritti sulla questione meridionale*, in which see especially pp. 138-40, 147-58, 219-25, 309-36, 379-92, 435-40.

36 On Salvemini's "discovery" of Cattaneo in the winter of 1898-99, see *Scritti sulla questione meridionale, Preface* (May 1955), p. xvi: "Anche oggi, mezzo secolo e più dopo di allora, ritorno con gioia e nostalgia a quel tempo come al più bello della mia vita. Con quanta intensità il mio cervello lavorava allora! 'Aqua, nix, grando, spiritus procellarum'. Oh, la gioia e l'ebrezza di quella gioventù!" Perhaps Salvemini's most beautiful essay is that with which he prefaced the precious selection from Cattaneo's works: *Le più belle pagine di Carlo Cattaneo, cit.*, pp. i-xxxi. From a vast literature, see now the critical essay on Cattaneo by one of Salvemini's most eminent former "pupils," Ernesto Sestan, ed., *Opere di G. D. Romagnosi, Carlo Cattaneo, Giuseppe Ferrari* (Milan-Naples, 1957), pp. xxi-xxxix, xlix-lv; and the collection of non-historical writings edited by Alberto Bertolino: Carlo Cattaneo, *Scritti economici*, 3 vols. (Florence, 1956).

37 Salvemini, *Historian and Scientist*, pp. 138-41; *Introduction*, pp. xv-xvi. See also *Italian Democracy in the Making*, pp. 18-21, for a brief analysis of Mosca's *Teorica dei governi e governo parlamentare* (1884), 2nd ed. (Milan, 1925); and the systematic and brilliant study by Mario Delle Piane, *Gaetano Mosca. Classe politica e liberalismo, cit.*, particularly pp. 297-375, *passim*. Delle Piane's *Bibliografia di Gaetano Mosca* (Florence, 1949) is an indispensable tool for Moscan research.

38 *Le più belle pagine di Carlo Cattaneo*, pp. xvii-xxxiii, 87-98; *Scritti sulla questione meridionale*, pp. xvi-xix, xxxvi-xxxix, and the following articles: "La questione meridionale e il federalismo" [1900], pp. 67-107; "L'autonomia comunale e il Congresso di Parma" [1901], pp. 125-35; "Federalismo, regionalismo e autonomismo" [1945],

positivism,[39] the essentially empirical method, supported as it came to be in Salvemini by a mixture of illuministic faith in rationality and an unromantic "populist" inclination, had succeeded in creating that typical Salveminian attitude characterized as *"problemismo."*[40] Reality, historical or actual, came to be seen by him as reducible to the problems it posed whether for understanding or for action. Political, economic, and social problems were not amenable to organic attack but were rather divisible into areas of possible resolution on a *"caso per caso"* basis.[41]

Mosca, on the other hand, had supplied a hard-headed Southern "nominalism" which, through the analysis of the interaction of power, interests, and ideology in the dynamics of politics, reinforced in Salvemini the tendency to dissect political reality into the categories of the pragmatic ends toward which it appeared to be directed. Salvemini came to regard Mosca's distinctions between ruling and political classes and of these from the masses of the people as a kind of hypostatic "Mosca's Law" for historians.[42] The functional uses of ideology, achieved through the varying "political formulas," did not automatically minimize its

---

pp. 592-99; "Federalismo e regionalismo" [1949], pp. 600-15; "Che cosa è lo Stato" [1951], pp. 616-17. On Cattaneo's activity and thought, with particular reference to his federalist ideas, see Alberto Mario, *Teste e figure* (Padua, 1877), pp. 375-485, *passim,* and Appendix, pp. 486-558; Alessandro Levi, *Il positivismo politico di Carlo Cattaneo* (Bari, 1928), pp. 108-37; Mario Borsa, *Carlo Cattaneo* (Milan, 1945), pp. 45-54, 59-66; Luigi Salvatorelli, *Il pensiero politico italiano dal 1700 al 1870,* 4th ed. (Turin, 1943), pp. 335-65, *passim;* Kent Roberts Greenfield, *Economics and Liberalism in the Risorgimento. A Study of Nationalism in Lombardy, 1814-1848* (Baltimore, 1934), pp. 197-99, 203-08.

39 *Le più belle pagine di Carlo Cattaneo,* pp. iii-vi; Levi, *Il positivismo politico,* pp. 20-50; Salvatorelli, *Il pensiero politico italiano,* pp. 341-46; Sestan in *Opere,* pp. xxvi-xxx, xxxviii-xxxix.

40 One of Salvemini's acutest "'disciples," Piero Gobetti, *La rivoluzione liberale,* new ed. (Turin, 1948), pp. 98-99, thus characterized *"problemismo"*: "Infatti, uscito dal socialismo senza critica e senza crisi, egli [Salvemini] chiarí il suo illuminismo come problemismo; più che una fede un canone descrittivo, un mezzo di capire."

41 The connection between Salvemini's *problemista* empiricism and his federalist political philosophy was cryptically synthesized in his "Federalismo, regionalismo e autonomismo," *Scritti sulla questione meridionale,* p. 598: "Quando si sostituisca il metodo federalista o autonomista al metodo centralista o burocratico, ogni problema deve essere risoluto caso per caso." A relatively long list of references to Salvemini's use of the phrase *"caso per caso"* could be culled from his writings after his "discovery" of Cattaneo.

42 Salvemini, *Historian and Scientist,* p. 139. See the elaboration of Mosca's theories, particularly in reference to the Southern Question, by another of Salvemini's "disciples," Guido Dorso, *Dittatura, classe politica e classe dirigente* (Turin, 1949), pp. 121-84. Cf. Salvemini's letter to Dorso, dated August 15, 1945, in *Scritti sulla questione meridionale,* pp. 589-91.

intrinsic value, but again only *"caso per caso,"* that is, depending on the real character of political regimes.[43]

Thus Cattaneo's method and Mosca's "laws" helped to spell a concept of political realism for Salvemini. The "realists" in politics, he had written,[44] could be divided into those of "good sense" and the "inept" ones. The "sensible" realist "does not take any ideology seriously, but keeps himself in readiness to utilize them all on a *caso per caso* basis— since even other people's illusions are useful real forces." The "inept" realist unilaterally holds fast to "all the cynical and immoral ideologies" and comes to regard as unworthy of a statesman every initiative which might be ascribed to the inspiration of a moral element. The "inept" realist, therefore, precludes his own exploitation of all the "instruments of action which might be available to him in this field of reality." The "inept" realist may thus find himself recoiling in terror equally from the "politics of the clean hands" and from that of "the soiled hands" and "nine times out of ten" is left with "empty hands."[45]

When faced with the problem of such a statesman as Giolitti, Salvemini seemed to be torn by the very antinomies he espied at the heart of politics. Giolitti apparently exemplified most of the principles which post-Machiavellian politics had elaborately illustrated and yet he tended to elude them all. A proper Salveminian *"caso per caso"* approach to the problem of Giolitti could not but lead, as indeed it did, to a set of contradictory estimates. Salvemini had basically adopted this procedure by *distinguos* particularly in the *Introduction*. But now the new Giolittian deluge of over-sympathetic reappraisals descended upon him. He found no alternative, at least for the moment, but to reiterate and elaborate upon a still somewhat generic distinction between Giolitti and his era, between the statesman and the Italian "workers and peasants." He judged this sufficient now unto his larger purpose of re-severing the idol from the idyll in Ansaldo's book and of rescuing Giolitti from the grip of Togliatti's dialectic—the better to demolish or convert Giolitti into a forerunner of Mussolini. In the process he assuaged his new and not unfounded fears, as he later openly confessed,[46] that the moderate historical

[43] *Historian and Scientist*, pp. 139-40.

[44] In contrasting the "imperialist interventionism" of Di San Giuliano with the "democratic interventionism" of Bissolati in 1914; see G. Salvemini, *Dal Patto di Londra alla Pace di Roma* (Turin, 1925), pp. xxxvi-xxxvii.

[45] *Ibid.*, p. xxxvii.

[46] In the Preface to his *Scritti sulla questione meridionale*, p. xx, written in May 1955, Salvemini announced the imminent publication of a new work to be called *Le elezioni giolittiane nell'Italia meridionale*. The reason for his concern that it come out "without great delay" offers a key—on the psychological level perhaps the crucial one—toward an understanding of his post-1945, "second," Giolittian revisionism as

revision in the *Introduction* could be further exploited by the political and ideological Right and Left as his organic and definitive "recantation" on Giolitti.

Thus Salvemini's deeply felt, almost personal, "Giolittian" dilemma was resolved. He now found himself again equidistant from the principal wings of those whom he called the *"nostalgici della politica giolittiana."* If possible, he would perhaps have liked to stand with the old representatives of his own vanishing "illustrious race"—Croce and Albertini. But he knew only too well that not only they, too, were hopelessly divided on Giolitti but also that he could never accept either Croce's optimistic "pro-Giolittian" reconstruction nor Albertini's pessimistic interpretation of the Giolittian era. For Croce's and Albertini's approaches to the problem were both essentially "anti-Salveminian." Both were rooted in the old fears of the Liberal "Notables" that a quasi-anarchic revolt of the Italian masses had been of the essence of the Giolittian period. But while Croce had hailed Giolitti as a *tamer,* Albertini had castigated him as an *instigator* of that revolt. If, therefore, Fascism had come to Italy, for Croce *despite* Giolitti and for Albertini *because* of Giolitti, Salvemini could not accept the basic rationale of either assertion. He was forced to reject them both and the premises of their appraisals and thus ended, as always, by constituting an historiographical "party unto himself." This reassertion of the validity of his own vision of the Giolittian era was ultimately made the more impelling as a direct result of the pressure he felt upon him through the works of

---

expressed in his 1952 article "Fu l'Italia prefascista una democrazia," *Il Ponte.* The explanation was given in the course of an interview with and thus reported by Domenico Zucàro, "La stanza di Salvemini," *Il Mondo,* May 29, 1936, p. 7: ". . . The idea of his collecting his writings on this argument (a volume entitled *Le elezioni giolittiane nell'Italia meridionale*) in an organic manner [*in modo organico*] goes back some ten years. The idea originated, Salvemini explains to me, from the Introduction he wrote for Salomone's *L'età giolittiana* [*Italian Democracy in the Making*]. He had written on that occasion that, with the experience he had gained during the years since 1913 and in the light of the political action of Mussolini and Hitler, if he could have lived again in that period, while he would not have changed the essence [*i fatti*] of his denunciations, he would have been less harsh in his criticism of Giolitti's policy in Southern Italy. This statement of his was taken by the 'nostalgics' of Giolittian politics [*i nostalgici della politica giolittiana*] particularly in the South, as a recantation of what he had written during the period 1902-13 on that policy. Even Croce participated in expressions of such opinions on his position. But Salvemini had found it easy to retort that to prefer Giolitti to Mussolini and Hitler did not mean that Giolitti thereby becomes the ideal statesman. Thus he vowed to return on the subject. . . . For the purpose of placing Giolitti objectively within the framework of the whole of Italian history, Salvemini has compiled a history of electoral methods used in Italy since 1848."

those pseudodemocratic worshippers of the State who had lately come to light sentimental and ideological candles before their newly-discovered Giolittian idol. Salvemini, the perennial iconoclast, had roused himself to smash that idol even if it had involved a sort of cruel self-laceration. Only thus, as he had once said in different circumstances, could a man "keep his soul."

Salvemini had found himself torn again in an old intimate war—a war between the practical, in his case, the "political," reason and the theoretical, that is, his "historical," reason. This apparent disharmony, this battle for unity constituted his essential personality;[47] it was thus his "fate." From beginning to end, as teacher and scholar, as democratic "activist" and historiographical master, as apostle of freedom and defender of the mind's duty to seek and speak the truth, Salvemini devoted his tireless intellectual energies to a quest for balance between thought and action. While, in his time, many merely preached it and remained fairly unscathed by the brutality and cruelty all active participation is heir to, Salvemini never shirked the responsibility of asserting and exemplifying that fundamental unity. In the "Machiavellian" world into which he was born and acted, his "fate" was fraught with dangers and self-exposed to error. Yet he always felt and acted upon the assumption that those risks must be taken. The different spheres—that of thought and that of action—must not lead to distraction, he believed, in the necessary dedication to the pursuit not only of freedom and justice but also of truth. The method of Cattaneo, whom he so consistently admired, and the spirit of Mazzini,[48] whom he unconsciously emulated, perhaps contributed toward a polarization in his character but also toward a vigilant straining for conciliation in his life and mind between the necessities of politics and the requirements of morality. Here, too, lay the

[47] Two Italian literati, themselves closely associated in their careers and stemming from a common cultural ground in pre-1914 Italy, emphasized—in widely separated moments—the "disharmony" rather than the search for "unity" in Salvemini's personality; Renato Serra, *Epistolario*, ed. by L. Ambrosini, G. De Robertis, and A. Grilli, 2nd ed. (Florence, 1953), p. 407, wrote to Ambrosini on October 11, 1911: "Gli è che tu hai una grande superiorità su Salvemini e tutta la sua compagnia che non nomino; essi scrivono di politica e di economia con fervore e con astio, col desiderio di corregere di rifare di mescolarsi alla pratica e pur con la boria di chi alla pratica è superiore; e allora, con tali pretese, questa gente che non dispone nè di un voto nè di un uomo nè di un soldo, fa ridere insieme e fa rabbia. Essi non sanno essere nè contemplativi nè attivi; e poi fanno i moralisti. . . ."; Giuseppe Prezzolini, *L'Italiano inutile* (Milan, 1953), p. 264: "C'è nella vita politica di Salvemini un elemento permanente, ed è la *scissione*. Quello che per altri è una decisione difficile e talora tragica della vita, per Salvemini è un'abitudine. Ci ha fatto il callo. Non ha fatto che separarsi dai gruppi, dai partiti, dai fogli ai quali s'era unito. . . .". Italics in text.

[48] See the beautiful close of his *Mazzini, cit.*, pp. 187-88.

sources of the ideal conflict in him between the "passion" demanded by
constructive political action and the "science" necessary for genuine
historical thought. Those who have assisted at or read of his almost
Socratic last hours[49] can have little doubt that at the end Salvemini's
efforts in this sense had been crowned by fulfillment.

The road toward that fulfillment had not, however, been without
struggle, difficulties, uncertainties. But it had been marked, no matter
how one may choose to assess it, by an essential consistency. Had he been
only an incorrigible "Jacobin," an inveterate "anticlerical," and unbend-
ing "doctrinaire," a moralistic "pedagogue"?[50] The phrase-mongering
involved in such characterizations can be no substitute for thoughtful
analysis and dispassionate understanding of the man. Whatever element
of truth about Salvemini they may contain, singly or together, these
judgments are far from exhausting it. Certainly none of them nor all of
them together could have sufficed to give him the stature and significance
he assuredly had in contemporary Italian culture and politics.

Salvemini was one of Italy's most celebrated historians. With whatever
ultimate limitations even in this his "true profession," that position of
eminence had been acknowledged to him from the most authoritative
and unprejudiced quarters.[51] Historian: that had been his true profes-

[49] See "Parole di commiato," *Il Ponte,* XIII (1957), 1158; Ernesto Rossi, "Il nonconformista," *Il Mondo, cit.,* p. 2.

[50] No great difficulty would be encountered for the isolation and documentation of
any or all of these appellations since Salvemini has left a rather overabundant supply of
occasional pieces which might tend to justify them; see for instance some of the articles
and speeches collected in his *Il programma scolastico dei clericali* (Florence, 1951) and
Clericali e laici (Florence, 1957). On the other hand it is worthy of note that the
death of Salvemini on September 6, 1957, elicited in Italy a collective reaction to an
event of national significance; none of these characterizations was contained in the
Italian Radio reports and commentaries, while only in extreme partisan cases did some
variations of them occur in journalistic and editorial comments; see the editorial
resumé of the more negative among such comments as reported in "La morte di un
laico," *Il Mondo,* September 17, 1957, p. 2. The following Italian newspapers, consulted
in Italy on September 7, 8, 9, 1957, offered a revealing cross-section of political and
ideological opinion through their commentaries on Salvemini: *Il Messaggero,* Christian-
Democratic, Rome; *Il Tempo,* "National-Liberal," Rome; *Il Corriere della Sera,*
Conservative-Liberal, Milan; *La Stampa,* Liberal-Democratic, Turin; *Avanti!,* Socialist,
Rome; *L'Unità,* Communist, Rome.

[51] Among others by Benedetto Croce, *Storia della storiografia italiana nel secolo
decimonono,* 3rd ed. rev., 2 vols. (Bari, 1947), II, 143-47, *passim.* See also the com-
memorative essays by two outstanding members of the younger Italian generation of
historians: Franco Venturi, "Salvemini storico," *Il Ponte,* XIII (1957), 1794-1801;
Rosario Romeo, "Salvemini storico," *Il Mondo,* September 24, 1957, p. 9. From a
growing number of articles and books on Salvemini written within two years of his

sion. But that was not to be his sole dedication. He never conceived—long before special names were invented for the horns of the modern intellectual's dilemma—that "engagement" or "isolation" represented real choices. Involvement in his fellowmen's—particularly in his poorer Southern *contadini's*—struggle for dignified existence was also a mission, a spontaneous "crusade" for him. Unlike the bulk of the so-called "humanistic bourgeoisie" of the South-Italian rural milieus,[52] his first "emigration" was to the North but his spirit never abandoned the numerous Molfettas of the South. *Trasformismo*, the hydra-headed, voracious, self-renewing monster of all modern Italian politics, could never touch him nor cast its spell upon him. Never did even the faintest shadow of participation in any *trahison des clercs* darken his way in the service of his chosen causes. He may, it is true, have unduly divided his intellectual and moral energies and sometimes expended them too generously in almost hopeless endeavors. But in this too was the man, this too was his "fate." Disenchantment born of close familiarity with and awareness of the positive responses to Giolittian wooings by his first great political love, socialism, led him quickly and without regrets to the bold decision to "go it alone" in the ceaseless fight for his political ideas and social ideals. Armed with his new political lance, the review *Unità* (1911-1920), Salvemini broke it again and again not quixotically, for magnificent causes, during one of modern Italy's most tortuous periods.

Thus Salvemini had devoted his "spare time" to fight with word and

---

death, the following may be singled out as most rewarding: the entire issue of *Rassegna Storica Toscana*, IV (1958), dedicated to Salvemini; Ernesto Sestan, "Salvemini storico e maestro," *Rivista Storica Italiana*, LXX (1958), 5-43; Enzo Tagliacozzo, *Gaetano Salvemini nel cinquantennio liberale*. Quaderni del *Ponte*, No. 8, (Florence, 1959); Lelio Basso, *Gaetano Salvemini socialista e meridionalista* (Manduria, 1959); Cesare Vasoli, "L' 'Unita' di Salvemini," *Il Ponte*, XIV (1958), 1382-1406; Gianni Sofri, "Salvemini e la storia del Risorgimento (Considerazioni a proposito di un libro recente," *Rassegna Storica del Risorgimento*, XLVI (1959), 61-72; Dante A. Puzzo, "Gaetano Salvemini: An Historiographical Essay," *Journal of the History of Ideas*, XX (1959), 217-35; and the collection of lecture-essays by E. Sestan, E. Garin, R. Villari, A. Saitta, and E. Tagliacozzo in the volume edited by them: *Gaetano Salvemini* (Bari, 1959).

52 On the "humanistic bourgeoisie," see Salvemini, "La piccola borghesia intellettuale nel Mezzogiorno d'Italia," first published in Prezzolini's *La Voce*, May 16, 1911, now reprinted in Salvemini, *Scritti sulla questione meridionale*, pp. 412-26, and in Caizzi, ed., *Antologia della questione meridionale*, pp. 353-74. See the elaboration of Salvemini's concept of the Southern Italian intellectual bourgeoisie by Dorso, *Dittatura, classe politica e classe dirigente*, pp. 150-53, and by Gramsci, *La questione meridionale*, pp. 30-34.

deed for the making of an Italian democracy in which, he hoped, the "privileged" workers of the North and the disinherited peasants of his South might equally participate—against Giolitti.[53] Against Giolitti, too, he found himself in strange promiscuous company when Italy's decision for war was being made in 1914-15—with men who were his antitheses in ends and means: Salandra, Sonnino, D'Annunzio, Mussolini.[54] If there was in this, as afterthoughts in some quarters later suggested, a sort of "guilt" by unconscious association,[55] Salvemini was willing to accept it—and to distinguish proudly that on his "defendant's bench" were also the great ghosts of Luigi Albertini and Leonida Bissolati.[56] At any rate, he never dreamed of joining the old and new ranks of Italy's "Antirisorgimento" whose exponents might among, other things, find it logical to evoke the political beauties of "old Vienna" and then invoke the Hapsburg bastion of a Europe they had always considered a mere "geographic expression." Salvemini never unleashed his nostalgia that

53 Luigi Einaudi, *Il Buongoverno*, p. 286, in an article on "Liberismo e comunismo" [1940-41], was in agreement with Salvemini on two essential points: that Giolitti had been essentially a "sceptic" and that he had not realized his "one great idea," that is, to make it possible for the workers and the peasant classes "to participate in the political and economic life of the country." Salvemini, however, had believed that Giolitti had been *unwilling* to bring this about completely and had done so partially only under pressure "from below," while Einaudi thought that in reality Giolitti had been *incapable* of doing it because of a lack of the necessary qualities, both practical and ideal.

54 On these personages, in connection with their interventionism of 1914-15, see Albertini, *Venti anni*, III, chaps. i-v, vii-ix; Galizzi, *op. cit.*, pp. 46-57, 109-11; Valeri, *Da Giolitti a Mussolini*, pp. 20-25. See also the following: Salvemini, *La politica estera dell' Italia*, pp. 263-77, and *Dal Patto di Londra alla Pace di Roma*, pp. ix-xix; G. A. Borgese, *Goliath, The March of Fascism* (New York, 1938), pp. 86-110; René Albrecht-Carrié, *Italy at the Paris Peace Conference* (New York, 1938), pp. 3-34, *passim;* and, to be read with the greatest caution, G. Pini and D. Susmel, *Mussolini. L'Uomo e l'opera*, 4 vols. (Florence, 1953-55), I, 230-93.

55 Something even more serious than such suggestion is made in Prezzolini, *L'Italiano inutile*, p. 273: "La sua politica non lascia traccia, perchè anche quando riuscí non fu compiuta da lui, ma da altri per motivi differenti e per scopi lontani dai suoi; come il suffragio universale che fu *attuato* da Giolitti, ed usato dai clericali per creare il partito popolare, e come l'intervento nella guerra del 1915, che produsse il fascismo, anzi fu il primo vero atto di imposizione fascista, il vero inizio del fascismo. Al quale Salvemini (cieco come sempre) collaborò." Italics in text.

56 On Albertini, see the description of his policy on the *Corriere della Sera* in his *Vent'anni di vita politica*, III, 269-82, 511-32; Salvemini, "Albertini 1914-15," *Il Mondo*, February 9, 1952; Alatri, "Interventismo, Fascismo, Resistenza nella recente storiografia," *Belfagor, cit.*, pp. 61-72. For Bissolati, see Ivanoe Bonomi, *Leonida Bissolati e il movimento socialista italiano* (Rome, 1929), pp. 143-70; L. Bissolati, *Diario di guerra* (Turin, 1935), pp. 15-23; Salvemini, *Dal Patto di Londra alla Pace di Roma*, pp. xxxv-xxxviii; Borgese, *Goliath*, pp. 140-43.

far, exactly because he believed in Europe as much as in Italy and thus gave the great spirits of Cattaneo and Mazzini, perhaps even Cavour, no reason to stir.[57]

[57] Salvemini, *Dal Patto di Londra alla Pace di Roma,* p. xxxviii: "Per noi, democratici italiani, il programma, su cui non era lecito transigere, era quello dello smembramento austriaco e del compromesso adriatico: necessario alla vittoria e necessario alla pace. E su questi due punti, solamente su questi due punti, non transigemmo mai." For a relatively brief, lucid summation of the almost irrepressible conflict between Austria and Italy during the Giolittian era, see William C. Askew, "The Austro-Italian Antagonism, 1896-1914" in L. P. Wallace and W. C. Askew, eds., *Power, Public Opinion, and Diplomacy.* Essays in Honor of Eber Malcolm Carroll by His Former Students (Durham, North Carolina, 1959), pp. 172-221.

III

GIOLITTI AND SALVEMINI
BETWEEN POLITICS AND HISTORY

*Historical knowledge springs from action, that is, from the need to make
clear and identify again those ideals of action which had become dimmed
and confused: the re-thinking of the past thus makes possible again the
identification of those ideals and serves as preparation for new action.**

CROCE

The great crisis following the First World War and exasperated nationalism found Salvemini and Giolitti momentarily arriving, from
opposite directions, at the same crossroads of Italian and international
politics. Unwittingly, they found themselves in agreement, both in fact
and in spirit, perhaps for the first time since their uneven duel had begun.[1] This happened fleetingly but significantly before Giolitti, once
again at the helm, revealed that turn[2] in his political stewardship which
insured disaster for the recovery, let alone the renovation, of Italian

---

* Benedetto Croce, *La storia come pensiero e come azione*, second ed. rev. (Bari,
Gius. Laterza & Figli, 1938) , p. 174.

[1] The writer has heard from Croce's own lips, with slightly more details, the revealing episode he recounted in "Una prefazione sbagliata," *Quaderni della "Critica,"*
cit., p. 123. Though Croce makes no reference to the date, the Giolittian expression
of agreement with, and the encomium of Salvemini probably occurred at the November 24, 1920, sitting of the Italian Chamber of Deputies, at which Salvemini delivered
his speech in defense of the Treaty of Rapallo between Italy and Yugoslavia; see
Dal Patto di Londra alla Pace di Roma, pp. 323-52, for Salvemini's speech. For verbal
exchanges between Salvemini and Giolitti, see 'Il ritorno di Giolitti," in Salvemini,
Scritti sulla questione meridionale, pp. 527-29, reprinted from the *Atti Parlamentari*,
Chamber of Deputies, sitting of July 2, 1920; and *Discorsi Parlamentari di Giovanni
Giolitti*, III [sitting of December 21, 1919], 1701-02, and IV [sitting of December 3,
1920], 1810-13.

[2] Cf. the lively exchange between Giolitti and the Socialists, in *Discorsi Parlamentari*,
IV [sitting of November 17, 1920], 1797-1800. On the larger character and motivating
forces of this new turn in Giolittian politics and in post-War Italian fortunes, see the
sensitive and sensible insight in Federico Chabod, *L'Italie contemporaine. Conférences
données a l'Institut d'Études Politiques de l'Université de Paris* (Paris, 1950) , pp. 39-40.
For a systematic analysis of the political involution and of the parliamentary sterility
of Italian socialism during the so-called "Red biennium" the bulk of which corresponded to the last Giolittian ministry, see Spartaco Cannarsa, *Il biennio rosso, 1919-
1921: Il socialismo in Parlamento, XXVa Legislatura* (Naples, 1958) , especially pp.
20-42.

democracy. This proved the more ironical because it was now Giolitti himself who first rose to call attention dramatically, indeed demagogically for the first time in his long career, to the necessity for an organic renovation—structural as well as political—of Italian life. For a brief illusive moment in post-War Italian history Salvemini appeared almost a pacific conservative in contrast to the roused Piedmontese statesman who cried that it was time for a great change in Italy—and did so in such quasi-revolutionary language as to earn, with the compliments of the Notables of the Right, a new epithet: "Bolshevik of the Annunziata."[3]

Giolitti had issued from his almost enforced retirement only late in 1919. With his justly famous Dronero speech of October 12 of that year he had broken his sullen four-year "national silence" and disengagement from the conduct of the war.[4] In quasi-Salveminian style, he compounded logic and righteousness to lash at all those who had brought the war's "misfortune" on Italy through "sentimentalism" when "national honor and great interests" had not been at stake.[5] Giolitti had then proceeded to formulate and detail an organic program of reform which contained enough conservative material to assuage the fears of the liberal Right and enough revolutionary phraseology to win the adherence of the liberal Left. The War, said Giolitti,

has transformed Europe both from the geographic point of view—by creating upon the ruins of great Empires many small nations in conflict with one another —and from that of political institutions—by reducing to a minority the peoples governed by monarchy. It has changed all values, political, social, economic, and financial. It has therefore marked the beginning of an absolutely new

[3] Valeri, *Da Giolitti a Mussolini*, p. 30. On Giolitti's post-War Ministry, see his *Memorie*, II, 553-87, 589-615; Tasca, *Nascita e avvento*, pp. 87-101, 109-24; Luigi Salvatorelli and Giovanni Mira, *Storia del Fascismo. L'Italia dal 1919 al 1945* (Rome, 1952), pp. 80-87, 103-08; Gabriele De Rosa, *Storia del partito popolare* (Bari, 1958), pp. 158-84.

[4] Giolitti's Dronero speech is reprinted in its entirety both in *Discorsi Parlamentari*, III, 1726-45, and in *Discorsi extraparlamentari*, pp. 294-327, and is extensively commented upon in his *Memorie*, II, 555-63. Between his last speech in Parliament, as Prime Minister on March 4, 1914, and the Dronero speech of October 12, 1919, Giolitti spoke very briefly on only four occasions in the Chamber of Deputies: December 5, 1914, in support of Italian neutrality; November 14, 1917, in favor of an *union sacrée* after Caporetto; December 20, 1917, disclaiming support for a separate peace by Italy; November 23, 1918, to demand that a special Parliamentary Committee be set up to report on the charge of treason levelled against him by a member; see *Discorsi Parlamentari*, III, 1696-97, 1698, 1699, 1700. During much the same period Giolitti spoke five times before the Cuneo Provincial Council; see *Discorsi extraparlamentari*, pp. 276, 285-86, 287-88, 288-91, 292-93.

[5] *Discorsi Parlamentari*, III, 1730.

historical period. Woe to us if we should not take full cognizance of these transformations—if we should want to start again on the path of the past.[6]

The "old fox" had come out of his lair apparently to administer a stunning lesson in realism to the political lions on the Right and to the ideological lambs on the Left who together had perhaps thought him forever banished from the central arena.

Giolitti's Dronero speech must without doubt rank as one of the truly Mephistophelian documents in the whole political literature of a waning Liberal Italy.[7] It helped bring Giolitti back to power for the last time but it brought neither a social revolution nor a true Giolittian restoration to a distraught Italy. More than most of his opponents and despite his verbal repudiation, he proved to be a prisoner of the past.[8] For Giolitti experience did not become on this tragic occasion the much-vaunted wise teacher but a rather dubious counsellor. With his eyes fixed backwards upon the pre-1914 methods of his apparent success in dealing with social and political unrest, he was to misjudge the genuinely revolutionary temper of post-War Italy.[9] No fit of absentmindedness on his part could have proved more calamitous than the tragic trick which his diffracted historic vision played upon him and on the Italian social and psychological situation during his last crucial tenure of power. When Giolitti relinquished that power, Fascism had been emboldened to knock much harder at the gates and, what was worse, to have greater confidence that those gates could be opened from within rather than come crashing down upon it from without.[10]

Before that last Giolittian rôle had been played out in the murky Italian atmosphere of 1921, there occurred that brief, strange moment when Giolitti and Salvemini seemed to change, indeed to exchange, their traditional postures. The Italian tragedy of errors of which this was a

6 *Ibid.*, III, 1735.

7 Cf. Valeri's comments on the Dronero speech in his Introduction to Giolitti, *Discorsi extraparlamentari*, pp. 49-51.

8 See De Rosa, *Giolitti e il Fascismo*, p. 77; Nenni, *Storia di quattro anni*, p. 93; Salvatorelli and Mira, *Storia del Fascismo*, p. 104.

9 See the direct references to his conscious application in 1920 of the methods of 1904 in Giolitti, *Memorie*, II, 598.; *Discorsi Parlamentari*, IV [sitting of September 26, 1920], 1784-91, for his defense of the "neutralist policy" adopted by the Government during the "occupation of the factories" by North Italian workers. For an authoritative assessment of Giolitti's economic and social policies in 1920-21, see Luigi Einaudi, *Il Piemonte e gli effetti della guerra sulla vita economica e sociale* (Bari, 1925), pp. 147-60, and *La condotta economica e gli effetti sociali della guerra italiana* (Bari and New Haven, 1933), pp. 318, 329-33, 359, 366-70, 380-81, 401-02.

10 Cf. Tasca, *Nascita e avvento*, pp. 186-88; Valeri, *Da Giolitti a Mussolini*, pp. 60-61, 99-103, 183-91.

mere episode was rooted in many factors, internal and international. A comparison between Giolitti's Dronero program and Salvemini's writings in his *Unità* during 1919-20 seems to reveal not only their agreement on many general points but also that the one had adopted a more extremist position and a more positive tone on certain social and institutional problems—among them the Monarchy—than the other.[11] It was, however, in foreign policy that their basic accord was clearest. Sonnino and D'Annunzio, in unwitting collaboration with Wilson and Trumbic, had tended to insure that momentary reconciliation between the stolid neutralist and the democratic interventionist of 1914-15. By pinning the European and Italian hopes of peace on "the rocks of Dalmatia"[12] and Fiume, those men not only accentuated the Italian elements of frustration and disillusionment but also the tenuousness of the new international order. While Salvemini and Bissolati, together with other *rinunciatari*, were seeing their liberal-internationalist cause turn to bitter dust,[13] at home and abroad, exponents of a different "renunciation" from theirs were seizing their chance to put on trial before an already embittered international and a miasmic Italian public opinion the entire structure upon which both the diplomacy and the mystique of interventionism had rested.

In his Dronero speech Giolitti voiced authoritatively, for the first time since the equivocal *union sacrée* following Caporetto, the resentful bitterness of repressed partisan opinion and of the amorphous masses which had borne burdens and privations of the War. Cannily taking the pulse of the situation, Giolitti prescribed strong medicine not only for the "great patient," the Nation, but also for the political and ideological doctors who, he insisted, had aggravated her condition.[14] The Giolittian

---

[11] See the analysis in Enzo Tagliacozzo, "Salvemini e il 1919," *Il Mondo,* December 21, 1951, pp. 9-10. While Giolitti was generically intimating that the Monarchy might be "expendable," Salvemini had written in his *Unità,* May 10, 1919: "With the Monarchy, if possible, with the republic, if necessary." Salvemini's post-1918 positions on the basic problems of Italian internal politics in the widest sense may now almost systematically be traced through the articles collected in B. Finocchiaro, *"L'Unità" di Gaetano Salvemini* (Venice, 1958) , pp. 583-786, *passim.*

[12] Salvemini, *Dal Patto di Londra alla Pace di Roma,* p. 311.

[13] For Salvemini as a Wilsonian and a *rinunciatario,* see his articles and speeches in *Dal Patto di Londra alla Pace di Roma,* pp. 246-305; his article of May 3, 1919, in the *Unità,* on Wilson's defection from Wilsonianism on the Adriatic peace, pp. 270-74. Cf. the translation and comments in Albrecht-Carrié, *Italy at the Paris Peace Conference,* pp. 146-47.

[14] *Discorsi Parlamentari,* IV [sitting of November 17, 1920], 1800: ". . . Non dobbiamo dimenticare che l'Italia dopo la guerra è un paese in condizione di grave malattia, ha necessità di una cura radicale, profonda, e che solamente la concordia tra tutti i cittadini onesti e amanti del paese può raggiungere questo fine. (*Applausi*

prescription, however, contained enough liberal-internationalist ingredients to give Salvemini and his friends some hope that it might serve to cure the "great patient" of most of her ills. Desperately, Salvemini continued to fight to rescue at least what he regarded as the ideal meaning of Italy's war and of the victory which he insisted on reading in terms of a fruition of the Risorgimento within a possible Wilsonian Europe.[15] It was thus that hopefully he found himself grasping at that minimum of the Bissolatian dream and of the Wilsonian program, which, with the Treaty of Rapallo of November 1920, Giolitti and Sforza were able to salvage.[16] Unfortunately, however, at the very moment when, as Giolitti had reiterated upon reassuming power five months earlier, further pursuit of the approach which had led to Rapallo in other, wider spheres of an embattled nationalistic Europe might have contributed toward a larger and sturdier pacification,[17] Giolitti himself consciously helped to put out the lamps in Liberal Italy. His misjudgment of the character of nascent Fascism ironically cooperated toward the resurgence "at home" of the ultranationalistic creature he had curbed "abroad" in Fiume.[18]

---

vivissimi e prolungati—Rumori all'estrema sinistra)." See, on the other hand, Salvemini's reiterated later contention that in 1919-22 Italy was a "malade imaginaire," in his "Economic Conditions in Italy, 1919-1922," Journal of Modern History, XXII (1951), 29-36; Mussolini diplomatico (Bari, 1952), pp. 17-33; and Prelude to World War II (Garden City, N.Y., 1954), pp. 17-120, passim.

15 Dal Patto di Londra alla Pace di Roma, pp. 333-38, for direct references to Tommaseo, Mazzini, and Cattaneo on the Slavic question.

16 Ibid., p. 324, for the phrase "the compromise of Rapallo." See Giolitti's defense of the Treaty of Rapallo in Discorsi Parlamentari, IV [sitting of November 27, 1920], 1803-04. Cf. Count Carlo Sforza, Contemporary Italy: Its Intellectual and Moral Origins, translated by D. and D. De Kay (New York, 1944), pp. 266-85, passim.

17 Discorsi Parlamentari, IV [sitting of June 24, 1920], 1749: "Il fine principale al quale deve oggi tendere la nostra politica estera è quella di assicurare la pace più completa e definitiva al nostro Paese e a tutta l'Europa, condizione questa indispensabile per poter iniziare sicuramente l'opera di ricostruzione." On the unrealized promise of Rapallo after 1922, see H. Stuart Hughes, "The Early Diplomacy of Italian Fascism" in Gordon A. Craig and Felix Gilbert, eds., The Diplomats, 1919-1939 (Princeton, 1953), p. 213.

18 On the sources of Fascism's ultranationalist external activism, see Luigi Salvatorelli, Irrealtà nazionalista (Milan, 1925), pp. 179-90, and "Lineamenti del nazional-fascismo" [May 1, 1923], reprinted in Nino Valeri, ed., Antologia della "Rivoluzione Liberale," (Milan, 1948), pp. 376-85. On the fruition of ultranationalism and its attempted translation into early Fascist foreign policy, see Salvemini, Mussolini diplomatico, pp. 41-42; Mario Donosti (pseud.), Mussolini e l'Europa. La politica estera fascista (Rome, 1945), pp. 9-10; Raffaele Guariglia, Ricordi, 1922-1946 (Naples, 1949), pp. 12-14; Piero Quaroni, Valigia diplomatica (Milan, 1956), pp. 20-22. I Documenti Diplomatici Italiani. Settima serie: 1922-1935. Vols I-II, October 31, 1922—February 22, 1924 (Rome, 1953, 1955) now permit a systematic study of the transition.

After September 1920, Giolitti's negative, officially non-interventionist, policy vis-à-vis the Italian political and social struggle found itself running parallel with the positive official approach to the grave problem posed by the year-long burning of D'Annunzio's "national passion" in Fiume. Giolitti's "neutralist" internal policy, inspired as it was by an anachronistic and misplaced "liberal" philosophy, in reality tended to favor and abet the very forces which—once the inanity of the Maximalist uproar and the ineffectuality of the "Bolshevik" upsurge in the Northern industrial centers had become unequivocal[19]—were now most urgently in need of restraint if not of repression.[20] Those forces, old and new, were finding in *squadrismo* and Fascism their channel and banner. But rather than repressing or restraining them Giolitti chose to tame them in his "ancient" fashion. Less through active collaborationism than through a dangerous defection in his control of the growing cleavage between his correct official orders and their implementation in the actual field of the Italian social and political battle,[21] Giolitti mistook Fascist activism for mere youthful exuberance *("giovani ed animati di spiriti combattivi")* in search of an outlet *("sfogo")* and of legal representation in the Parliament.[22]

[19] Salvemini, *The Fascist Dictatorship in Italy*, p. 34: "The so-called Italian Bolshevism of 1919-20 was nothing but an exasperating outbreak of uncoordinated restlessness among large sections of the Italian people, to which the worst elements of the ruling class replied by an exhibition of cowardice out of all proportion to the actual danger." In July 1921, Lenin and Mussolini unknowingly crossed their interpretative swords on the question of Bolshevism in Italy. At the Third Congress of the Communist International, held in June-July 1921, Lenin reported: "Italian Communists have not always been sufficiently Communists. During the occupation of the factories has a single Communist appeared? No, at that moment Communism did not yet exist in Italy"; quoted by Edoardo D'Onofrio, "Lenin, la rivoluzione russa e l'Italia," in Togliatti, ed., *Trenta anni di vita e lotte del P. C. I., cit.,* p. 35. On July 2, 1921, Mussolini wrote: "To say that a Bolshevik danger still exists in Italy is to mistake certain oblique fears for realities. Bolshevism is beaten"; quoted in Tasca, *Nascita e avvento,* p. 521. On Italian working-class and Socialist reactions to the Russian Revolution, see the summary of the disenchanting impressions of Communist Russia by two members of an Italian Socialist Mission, Gregorio Nofri and Fernando Pozzani, *La Russia com'è.* Preface by Filippo Turati (Florence, 1921) which, on the eve of the Livorno Congress and the founding of the Italian Communist Party, concluded, pp. 153-57, that Russia was then "the country furthest removed from the realization of socialism." See now the study by Franco Ferri, "La Rivoluzione d'Ottobre e le sue ripercussioni nel movimento operaio italiano," *Società,* XIV (1958), 73-100.

[20] Cf. Valeri, *Da Giolitti a Mussolini,* pp. 100-01.

[21] De Rosa, *Giolitti e il Fascismo,* p. 76.

[22] Giolitti, *Memorie,* II, 610: "In quelle elezioni [May 1921] entrò pure nel parlamento, con un manipolo di una trentina di deputati, la piú parte giovani ed animati da spiriti combattivi, il partito fascista; ciò che io considerai cosa vantaggiosa, perchè il fascismo constituendo ormai una forza reale nel paese, era bene avesse la sua rap-

In fact, he merely succeeded in allowing the worst energies of the *squadristi* a free play which, against his hopes, far from exhausting them saw them grow sturdier, bolder, ever more eager and confident of total success. What was worse, in his irrepressible and blind optimism[23] Giolitti took little note that gradually some of the most precious resources of the Liberal State were either in incipient disintegration or actually functioning as a shield for *its and his* most lethal enemies. These he misjudged almost completely in what they were becoming and really wanted. True, the "handful" of "youthful" and "energetic" Fascist deputies who, in May 1921, were elected not without at least indirect Giolittian connivance and evident self-satisfaction, gave their movement a new look of legality and respectability. But throughout the country the agitation of their followers and sympathizers did not thereby cease. There was no real truce in the clamor stirring among the lower middle classes.[24] Disaffected intellectuals, misguided idealists, and frustrated D'Annunzian dreamers could no longer mask the brutal terror which, with practical impunity, the armed squads and counterrevolutionary activists were imposing upon crucial zones of Northern and Central Italy. Behind them, meanwhile, there began looming the giant shadows of massive agrarian and industrial interests and "militarist, nationalist and reactionary" elements perhaps in search of a "Bonapartist adventure."[25]

It has been magisterially pointed out by Federico Chabod that it was in the autumn of 1920, after the worst phase of the Italian political and economic crisis had passed, that a "great fear" retrospectively gripped "a large part of the Italian middle class."[26] That "fear of revolution"

---

presentanza parlamentare, secondo il mio antico concetto che tutte le forze del paese devono essere rappresentate nel Parlamento e trovarvi il loro sfogo."

23 Valeri, *Da Giolitti a Mussolini*, p. 101, characterizes Giolitti ". . . ottimista qual'era, come tutti gli uomini di forte volontà . . . ."

24 On the social and intellectual character of the younger Fascist activists, see the overtly sympathetic description in Pini and Susmel, *Mussolini*, II, 117, and the authoritative analysis in Tasca, *Nascita e avvento*, pp. 532-35. Cf. the journalistic debate of 1919-23 in which Adriano Tilgher, Giovanni Ansaldo, and Luigi Salvatorelli, among others participated, now under the rubric of "La polemica sui 'piccoli borghesi'" in Nino Valeri, ed., *La lotta politica in Italia dall'Unità al 1925. Idee e documenti*, 2nd ed. (Florence, 1958) , pp. 478-91.

25 De Rosa, *Giolitti e il Fascismo*, p. 77: "La borghesia capitalistica della città e della campagna aveva abbandonato il giolittismo, non credeva piú nella sua forza politica, e tentava la via dell'avventura bonapartista."

26 Chabod, *L'Italie contemporaine*, p. 39: ". . . C'est ainsi qu'au moment même ou le danger allait en décroissant, la peur, la crainte de la révolution devinrent de plus en plus grandes, dans une large partie de la bourgeoisie italienne. Il arrive, vous le savez,

when danger was really past, like most such collective psychological phenomena, was then still unfocused, without precise direction. By the spring of 1921, however, thanks in part to Giolitti's errors of omission and commission, that fear had not only taken positive shape and clear direction but had also already engaged in successful breaches within and against the Liberal State. When Giolitti relinquished power, strategic islands of legality—geographic and political—had been irreparably lost to the surging but organized violence of Fascism.[27] In 1920-21 Giolitti had, so to speak, given back with his left hand all that his right hand had deftly gained by default in Turin and Milan in September 1920 and by action at Rapallo and Fiume in November-December 1920. The real tragedy of Giolittian statecraft ultimately consisted in the fact that by April-May 1921 it had freely surrendered to Mussolini the finest and most promising fruits of its victory over D'Annunzio. Giolitti made that "free gift" when there was the least need to grant it and the best, if not quite the last, chance to restrain the more crafty exponent of a "national revolution." In this defection, it may be suggested, much more than in any he may have committed before 1914,[28] lay Giolitti's gravest political "sin" and for this he was "punished" not only by his resounding failure but also by the ingratitude of the Fascist beneficiaries.[29]

Giolittismo was dead. An unmourned casualty of the War, its funeral oration had been eloquently, if obliquely, read at Dronero on October 12, 1919, by no other than Giolitti himself. No one—not even Salvemini— has ever delivered a better indictment of *giolittismo* than its inventor in a speech which marked also his political resurrection. But the oration over, Giolitti refused to give it final burial. In its last ghostly reappear-

---

qu'après un danger physique la peur vous prenne parfois, lorqu'en se retournant en arrière, on se rend compte des difficultés que l'on vient de traverser. La peur peut être aussi rétrospective."

[27] There is almost general agreement among Italian authorities that the winter-spring 1921 marked a crucially favorable turn in Fascist fortune; cf. Salvemini, *The Fascist Dictatorship in Italy*, pp. 46-88; Salvatorelli and Mira, *Storia del Fascismo*, pp. 103-12; Chabod, *L'Italie contemporaine*, pp. 47-52; Tasca, *Nascita e avvento del Fascismo*, pp. 138-89; Nenni, *Storia di quattro anni*, pp. 129-44; Valeri, *Da Giolitti a Mussolini*, pp. 99-101; De Rosa, *Giolitti e il Fascismo*, pp. 72-80, and *Storia del partito popolare* (Bari, 1958), particularly pp. 159-84, *passim*.

[28] In "L'Italia prefascista," *Il Ponte*, p. 295, Salvemini had thus evaluated Giolitti's alleged "crime and punishment": "In May 1915 Giolitti was overwhelmed by a Parliament which he himself had reduced to a shadow without substance. Giolitti was punished where he had sinned."

[29] See in Pini and Susmel, *op. cit.*, II, 120, the report of Mussolini's self-satisfaction over Giolitti's failure to "tame" him. Cf. the brief summary of the results of the elections of May 1921 in Mario Vinciguerra, *I partiti politici italiani dal 1848 al 1955* (Rome, 1956), pp. 136-37

ance, therefore, *giolittismo* revealed itself as only Giolitti's sterile and "inept realism" wrapped in pseudo-Machiavellian garb. Seeking to bring it forth again through the spurious union of the quasi-revolutionary program contained in his Dronero speech and the crypto-transformistic policies adopted in the face of rising Fascism, Giolitti spelled disaster for both his program and his policies. *Giolittismo* had indeed become anachronistic and impotent. But *transformismo,* which was its enduring political soul, re-emerged from its Giolittian ashes and was to be reincarnated in Mussolinian politics before and after the seizure of power.[30] Giolitti's oracular liberal-democratic Dronero "manifesto" had perhaps come too early and brought too little before it gave way to Mussolini's Sibylline nihilistic-nationalist contradictions. There was little wrong with that "manifesto" which a consistent Giolittian effort really to act upon it might not have cured. But while it was reiterated in June 1920 it was half-forgotten in December.[31] Thereafter it stood only to bear witness to the truth of Giolitti's own Machiavellian but unconsciously self-condemning maxim: "Political history reveals no example that sermons have ever had great effect, since the statesman is expected not to preach but to act."[32] Perhaps no one instinctively knew this better in his fashion than the man who, in that same October 1919 which had heard the Dronero "sermon," had proclaimed to his followers: "We Fascists do not have any ready-made doctrines: our doctrine is *the deed.*"[33]

A new era was now breaking over Italy. Before 1914, under Giolittian auspices, Italian democracy had been strenuously but undeniably in the making. Even more promising had then been the perceptible fusion within the fabric of the Nation of some of its saner political and moral elements. A true representative figure and leader of the older Italian ruling class and of its liberal ethos, Giolitti had consistently if not always wisely steered his politics toward canalizing the democratizing process. His larger statecraft, meanwhile, revealed few prejudices against the free play of forces making for that fusion. The Great War and its immediate aftermath played havoc with both the democratic advance and the

---

[30] On the "self-reproducing" capacities of *trasformismo,* see Dorso, *La rivoluzione meridionale,* pp. 27, 251-52, and *Dittatura, classe politica e classe dirigente,* pp. 36-39.

[31] Cf. the prophetic enunciation of the sole Italian alternatives as ". . . l'inizio di un sicuro risorgimento o di una rapida decadenza," in Giolitti's programmatic speech before the Chamber of Deputies on June 24, 1920, *Discorsi Parlamentari,* IV, 1747-54.

[32] Giolitti, *Memorie,* II, 554: "Ma nella storia politica non c'è esempio che le prediche abbiano mai avuto grande effetto, richiedendosi dall'uomo di Stato non il sermoneggiare ma l'agire."

[33] Mussolini at the Florence Congress of the Fascist Party, quoted in Tasca, *Nascita e avvento,* pp. 54, 545: "Noi fascisti non abbiamo dottrine precostituite, la nostra dottrina è il *fatto.*" Italics in text.

"moral" direction of the Nation. With his final return to power in an historic situation which eluded both the grasp of his older liberal politics and the circle of its pre-War ethos, Giolitti's "defection" was almost guaranteed. He now found himself unknowingly contributing toward the unmaking of Italian democracy, just as his opponents accelerated its crisis, and his successors insured its waning. Whatever the combined force of politics, economics, a world war, social and moral dissension, and Fascism did to Italy after 1919, the tragic turn of events belonged to a history which Giolitti may have indirectly helped to prepare but did not make during his classic era before 1914. Only his successors—among whom, ironically, the "last" Giolitti of 1920-21—really made that history.

Salvemini's views of Giolitti's part in the final waning of Italian democracy were a function of his larger interpretation of Giolittian politics. But, as has been suggested, those views involved a more intimate contradiction than that which the post-1945 Giolittian battle of the books in Italy had forced him to reveal. The fact remains that, while the two were not ultimately unconnected, the Salveminian corpus of Giolittian writings seems to accord, relatively speaking, a greater "indulgence" to the "last" Giolitti than to the protagonist of the classic Giolittian era.[34] True that in an early work (1927) on the rise of Fascism in Italy Salvemini clearly pointed to Giolitti's "responsibility"—but "at the end of 1920."[35] Thus it was symptomatic of his final views that in his last Giolittian essay Salvemini had recourse to that extreme characterization of Giolitti as the "John the Baptist" of Mussolini not in reference to 1920-21 but rather to 1900-14. It is, of course, clear from the context of the 1952 article that Salvemini was adverting to a special question— electoral abuses and parliamentary control—but there is an obvious disproportion between the character of the question and the severity of the characterization. Moreover, Salvemini's judgment on Giolitti's "adventist" role is not only based on partial, indirect, and historically problematical grounds but it is also against his own previous assessment of Giolitti's "responsibility" "at the end of 1920" as well as against the

34 See Salvemini's exchange with Giolitti in the Chamber of Deputies on July 2, 1920, in *Scritti sulla questione meridionale*, pp. 528-29, in the course of which the independent deputy suggested both that Giolitti's "own" grant of universal suffrage could now, after the war, operate in a sense contrary to the Giolittian "methods of the past" and that, in case a choice should be imposed between a "return to that past" and "revolution," he would "without hesitation, through desperation, choose the latter." Cf. also Enzo Tagliacozzo, "Salvemini nel 1920," *Il Mondo*, December 29, p. 9, for references to Salvemini's cautious admiration for Giolitti's *"abilità."*

35 Salvemini, *The Fascist Dictatorship in Italy*, p. 56

original uses of the idea and phraseology—Giolitti as the "John the Baptist of Fascism" in 1920-21—by Angelo Tasca.[36]

This chronological displacement or transfer of Giolitti's political and historical responsibility might be understood, if not justified, had Salvemini been addicted to reducing the historical process to an unbroken chain of causality. In that case one would find him compulsively remounting, in writings on contemporary Italy, beyond Giolitti—through the alleged "series of dictatorships" by Crispi, Depretis, even Cavour, and the theory of the Risorgimento as a "missed revolution"—finally to return to the point of departure: the assumption, which practically always is merely a conclusion, that Fascism was a "logical culmination" of the whole long range of Italian history. But this was not the case for Salvemini. All that has been said here of Salvemini stands against such an assumption on his part—his entire *cursus historicus*, his *forma mentis*, his empiricism, his *problemismo*, and especially his reiterated conviction that "Italian democracy" had been "in the making" before 1914. The explanation for Salvemini's own "diffraction" is perhaps simpler, if far from too obvious.

Salvemini's 1952 article, which is formally historical-analytical, is unintentionally a rare autobiographical compendium. Like all such it is revealing both for what it says and for what it does not say. In writing on the question of whether and to what extent "pre-Fascist Italy" had been a "democracy," Salvemini singled out as connecting link between the defections of two contrasting historical periods Giolitti's function as "forerunner" of Mussolini. From a more purely historical point of view, this cannot but seem at once as too much and too little. But, as has already been pointed out, it apparently served his polemical and psychological purposes. Whatever practical reasons existed for that treatment and the resulting overemphasis of that link, perhaps a significant key lies more in Salvemini's political biography than in his historiographical approach.

The fact was that in 1919-20, through the ironic twist in the Italian and international situation, Salvemini had indeed become a "Giolittian" *malgré lui* in ways absolutely inconceivable for his pre-1914 career. If only briefly, now he had staunchly come to hope that Giolitti's "liberal" foreign policy might be turned into a function of democratic internal policy. Moreover, a new but enduring admiration for Giolitti's "political capacity," for that professional "ability" only whose negative manifestations he had previously known by indirect personal experience, now took

[36] Tasca, *Nascita e avvento*, p. 188; Valeri in the Introduction to Giolitti, *Discorsi extraparlamentari*, p. 52.

form in Salvemini—and it was genuine and based upon direct observation in the Parliament. During the last years of his life he consistently evinced that admiration in all his conversations on Giolitti. One almost suspected that in 1920 Salvemini had felt that in politics little could be denied Giolitti *per il bene come per il male*—if the "old Magician" only willed it. The hope, it is true, was blasted but the memory—personal and historical—lingered to preserve the image of a real time of promise. Unconsciously, perhaps, but visibly, that image tended to attenuate his judgment on that time and, if indirectly, on the "last" Giolitti. The polemical pressure of 1949-50, in turn, unquestionably helped Salvemini to re-sharpen his old anti-Giolittian animus but, at the same time, to concentrate it upon the Giolitti of the pre-1914 era. In this, too, Salvemini appeared as if torn between a secret memory of politics and the severer claims of history.

The victory of Fascism had led Giolitti to an obscure but dignified retirement and final disengagement;[37] it led Salvemini to a new effort to stand up against a repression which made that of the Giolittian *mazzieri* appear relatively mild—to stand pat, not to give in (*non mollare*), to resist the horror of the tyranny with the weapon of conspiracy.[38] Then came defeat at home and the long exile, but also a more coherent engagement in the apparently endless fight against the repressive regime—for an Italian "freedom and justice" which now transcended the *caso per caso* procedure of normal political activity.[39] This now demanded no longer mere bits of "spare-time," but persistent and continuous dedication. The days of the brief anti-Giolittian pamphlets were over forever now that all Italians, he felt, lived "under the axe of Fascism" and the dangerous shadow of upstart adventurism in foreign policy.[40] The immi-

[37] Cf. Giolitti's letters to his staunch political and personal friend, Camillo Corradini, in De Rosa, *Giolitti e il Fascismo,* pp. 15-37.

[38] Cf. *Non Mollare* [1925], the clandestine anti-Fascist organ, now reissued (Florence, 1955) in fine photostatic reproduction, preceded by rich documentary articles by Salvemini, Ernesto Rossi, and Piero Calamandrei.

[39] For Salvemini's work and activity as a political exile there is as yet no complete study; see, however, the data in Aldo Garosci, *Storia dei fuorusciti* (Bari, 1953) and *La vita di Carlo Rosselli,* 2 vols. (Rome-Florence-Milan, 1945) ; Luigi Salvatorelli, "L'opposizione democratica durante il fascismo" in *Il secondo Risorgimento. Nel decennale della Resistenza e del ritorno alla democrazia, 1945-1955* (Rome, 1955) , pp. 97-180, *passim.* See the reconstruction by Salvemini of the assassination of Carlo and Nello Rosselli, "L'assassinio dei Rosselli" in Ernesto Rossi, ed., *No al fascismo* (Turin, 1957) , pp. 257-304.

[40] Two major works by Salvemini dealing with Fascist internal and foreign policy were: *Under the Axe of Fascism* (New York, 1936) , now translated into Italian as *Sotto la scure del Fascismo* (Turin, 1948) and *Mussolini diplomate* (Paris, 1932) , later elaborated in the Italian edition, *Mussolini diplomatico, cit* His *Prelude to World War II, cit.,* is largely a study of the antecedents and repercussions of the Ethiopian War.

nent fall of Fascism and the Italian collapse of 1943-45 found Salvemini at his post as the perennial nonconformist and as a castigator of the "makers" of Italy's times of trouble. His version of what was to be done with Italy,[41] however, was much less a question in the empirical and humanistic-historical tradition of Cattaneo than a program, almost a manifesto, compounded of both reason and wrath in the organic manner of Mazzini.

It was in these circumstances, as has been seen, that he was asked to reappraise, as a historian, Giolitti's position and work in that mixture of realities and hopes which had been Giolittian Italy's "democracy in the making" before the era of "'states-ruin and world wars." On the basis of new evidence and new perspectives Salvemini assessed that era's larger work not negatively; he acknowledged its great promise even as he condemned its defections; he judged his own active part in it as not altogether without error. Giolitti now appeared to him as a sort of friendly enemy, a bifrontal realist whose methods he must still condemn but whose positive, if limited and short-lived, achievement he could not but recognize. Soon, however, in another kind of Italian historic circumstance and under renewed polemical pressure, Salvemini felt impelled to retrace some of his recent steps in the judgment on Giolitti but, as consistent as ever, he again acknowledged that if *not with* Giolitti— in fact, practically *against him*—an Italian democracy had nevertheless been "in the making" during the Giolittian era. Almost to the eve of his death Salvemini seemed uncertain and hesitant as to the proper relationship he as historian could establish between Giolitti and the character of his times. To the very end, he spoke wistfully of the necessity of "placing" Giolitti within the "real framework" of modern Italian history. Meanwhile, both protagonist and historian remain in the undefined zone which lies between politics and history.

41 Cf. G. Salvemini and Giorgio LaPiana, *What To Do With Italy* (New York, 1943) ; "Gli Italiani son fatti cosi," a short, lively article by Salvemini written during the immediate post-War period [1947] is now in Luisa Sturani, ed., *Antologia della Resistenza* (Turin, 1951), pp. 1-4. On the background, Italian and international, of Salvemini's assessment of the new Italian *Kriegschuldfrage*, see Aldo Garosci, "Salvemini radicale americano" in *Pensiero politico e storiografia moderna, cit.*, pp. 173-79; Franco Catalano, *Storia del C. L. N. A. I.* (Bari, 1956), pp. 24-26, *passim*, and the notes: Roberto Battaglia, *Storia della Resistenza italiana* (Turin, 1953), pp. 19-66, *passim*. Cf. the whole of the good study by Norman Kogan, *Italy and the Allies* (Cambridge, Mass., 1956).

EPILOGUE: SALVEMINI AND THE REVOLT
AGAINST *GIOLITTISMO*

Gaetano Salvemini rightly gauged and avowed that Italian "militarist, nationalist, and reactionary" elements had exploited for their own ends his criticism of Giolittian democracy. But he perhaps failed to take sufficient notice, historically, of the fact that these elements were not Italian inventions of the Giolittian era. Elsewhere they took different names and forms but acted in an analogous sense. They were often merely functions of even more demoniacal forces in modern Europe on the eve of its greatest historic crisis—the War of 1914. In the end, it was perhaps this crisis in the European organization of power as well as of culture which smashed the delicate balance, internal and international, within which the liberal, democratic, and socialist promise of the nineteenth century to which Salvemini paid the highest homage could have borne fruit.

On the eve of that war, Giolitti had rightly prophesied that Italy—her economy, resources, institutions, social structure—might not survive an international conflict of Giants into which she need not, if her political class so chose, immerse herself. The Bissolatian democratic interventionists, among whom Salvemini proudly counted himself as a spokesman, had countered that it was precisely as a necessity of physical survival in an otherwise potentially Germanic Europe, but also as an opportunity of political and moral liberation from all that had become stifling and sterile in Giolittian Italy, that the ordeal by war might not be shirked. Once the optimates in power—anti-Giolittian but also congenitally anti-Bissolatian—had made the preservation of Italian neutrality impossible, "Italy's War" was seen by the democrats as a possible channel for a liberal European revolution and as a definitive revolt against the evils of *giolittismo*.

The War of 1914 proved to be much less and yet much more. With the collapse of "historic Europe" within which an Italian democracy had been in the making all ideals were transfigured and many great hopes belied. It was now that the merely potential *"gran rifiuto"* by all the antiliberal and antidemocratic forces obscurely stirring during the Giolittian era burst forth as the true "precursor" of the emerging nihilistic-totalitarian revolution.[1]

The grim spectacles of the European catastrophes of 1914-18 and 1939-45 and their aftermaths thus became for Salvemini but functions

[1] Some of these conclusions are further elaborated in this writer's forthcoming study on the twentieth century's *Prelude to a Great Rebellion*.

of his fixity upon the sources of Italy's recurrent tragedy in the twentieth century. Giolitti was converted in his view into a "demiurge,"[2] almost a scapegoat of that tragedy, not because the "old fox" had not done enough but because he had not done more to "make" a democracy in Italy. This alone, Salvemini finally insisted, might have acted as a bulwark against the tenacious and powerful blows of the persisting oligarchical elements which, again and again—in 1914-15, in 1919-22, in 1943-45—decided Italy's political and moral destiny. One is almost tempted to imagine that if Giolitti had not existed Salvemini's fervid moral conscience might have led him to invent him. But his unique historical intelligence would undoubtedly just as promptly have led him to unmask that invention and pulverize it in the name of reason, the sole goddess who never failed him and to whom he was unfailingly faithful. However cruel the strain often imposed upon himself by his disingenuous sojourns in the realms between politics and history, he never strayed into mythology except to do homage to that goddess.

As for the man Salvemini, there were no grey zones of uncertainty in the inspiration of his personality, in the consistency of his devotion to the cause of human dignity during an age of violence and of unspeakable inhumanities perversely exalted as necessary transvaluation of values. He withstood without self-pity the most cruel blows of his personal fate; alone, he often fought fierce battles as the champion of the voiceless, the humble peasants of his South;[3] fearlessly, he contributed toward tearing again and again the mask of decency from the face of modern tyranny. Reality eluded him, say the false "realists" of politics and morality: Was he not the anachronistic, if selfless, Don Quixote of modern Italian culture? The irony of history has already offered some answer to that equivocal query. The disarmed prophet's name and vision have become flesh of an Italian reality which the "inept realists" can never grasp. Whatever the heights of moral indignation or the depths of despair his contemplation of men's errors and failures, not excluding his own, had sometimes involved, Gaetano Salvemini, this anti-Machiavelli stamped with deep

[2] One of the most penetrating and suggestive older essays is that by Filippo Burzio, "Giolitti" [first published in Bacchelli's *La Ronda* in 1921] in *Politica demiurgica* (Bari, 1923), pp. 41-79, in which Giolitti appears as a unique Italian "demiurge": "this division-chief, this notary, this provincial," "this incorruptible corrupter," the "Bolshevik of the Annunziata."

[3] Recalling his pre-1914 activity on behalf of the Southern peasantry, particularly of Apulia, in 1955 Salvemini wrote, *Scritti sulla questione meridionale*, Preface, p. xxviii: "Una sera, che in una campagna del mio migliore amico conversavamo in crocchio sotto il cielo stellato, nella dolce frescura succeduta a una giornata di estate, un contadino mi disse: 'Tu non ci hai mai ingannati.' Quelle parole, pronunciate nella oscurità, mi si infissero nell'anima, e non l'hanno abbandonata più."

Socratic features, had never despaired of human intelligence and of courage and integrity nor of their capacity to help in the ceaseless search for truth. In an era of self-torturing intellectualism, semantic scholasticism, and ideological Byzantinism, he exemplified the simplicity and dignity still attainable through the possession and assertion of those elementary values. These, too, were the man; these, too, were woven into the essence of his meaning.

"This man has not lived only for himself"—thus wrote Salvemini of Mazzini at the close of one of his most beautiful early works.[4] After more than half a century's journey of his own through "conflict and adversity," Salvemini earned that estimate also for himself. The ideal legacy of his life will long endure. The political and intellectual passions which almost continuously rose to stir him to thought and action now seem the "perishable elements" in the making of that life, in the molding of that legacy. They may at times have tended to disturb him profoundly and to mar the serene pursuit of his "real profession." But in the iron age through which he lived and worked he saw no other escape except into conformity and passive complicity with the rising tide of moral nihilism. Those passions had therefore been also the indispensable nourishment for his spirit's fruition and now, in retrospect, seem to offer keys to the core of his teaching. Like Mazzini's for him, his own life and legacy will always be there as "inspiration to the weary" and "comfort to the defeated" in the continuing battles for "freedom and justice." These, from mere philosophic abstractions, had been translated for him through strenuous struggles into elemental necessities of daily existence. For these—by whatever other names he had called them: "Risorgimento," "federalism," "Europe," "liberalism," "democracy," "socialism"—he had fought almost from the start. For these, too, some of his well-beloved spiritual children had not been afraid to suffer, even to die. He lived long enough to witness the tragic passing of worlds and values and men he truly loved. But he also saw the beginnings of historic changes whose leavening elements were the ideals he had cherished and the inspiration he had offered.

4 *Mazzini, cit.,* p. 188.

CHRONOLOGY

1900

July 29. Assassination of King Humbert. Beginning of reign of Victor Emmanuel III.

September. Rome Congress of the Italian Socialist party: maximum and minimum programs adopted.

December. Franco-Italian rapprochement and agreements over Morocco and Tripoli.

1901

February. Ministry of Giuseppe Zanardelli, with Giovanni Giolitti as Minister of the Interior.

Beginning of so-called "Liberal springtide" in Italian politics in contrast to reactionary policies of Crispi and Pelloux governments.

1902

January–February. Strike of railwaymen of Mediterranean Line. Threat of general strike.

Imola Congress of Socialist party: ascendancy of Filippo Turati's Liberal socialism.

November. Prinetti-Barrère exchange of notes strengthening Franco-Italian entente.

1903

July 20. Death of Pope Leo XIII.

August 4. Election of Pope Pius X.

October 29. Resignation of Zanardelli whose Government had put an end to political reaction at home; contributed to a reconciliation between the state and the working classes; recognized the Southern problem and made some provisions to relieve the South; initiated tax reform to relieve the poorer classes; strengthened Franco-Italian diplomatic entente.

November 3. Giovanni Giolitti's Ministry.

1904

April 8 to 11. Bologna Congress of the Socialist party: Enrico Ferri's Center group holds together Filippo Turati's Reformist wing and Arturo Labriola's Revolutionary wing and preserves formal unity of Socialist party.

April 24 to 29. Visit of French President Loubet and Foreign Minister Delcassé to Rome. Widespread international repercussions and acute diplomatic and political-religious crisis in Italy and in France.

May 30. Giolitti enunciates theory of the two parallels in relations between Church and state in Italy.

May. Popular outbreaks in the South at Cerignola (Apulia).

September. Outbreaks and bloody conflicts in Sardinia and in Sicily.

September 15 to 20. General strike throughout Italy.

November 6 and 13. General political elections: partial removal of *non expedit* and formal participation of Catholics in elections in North Italy.

1905

February–March. Presentation and debate of bill in Chamber of Deputies proposing State regulation of railways. Railwaymen's obstructionism.

March 4. Resignation of Giolitti and his cabinet.

March 16 to 27. Tommaso Tittoni's Ministry.

March 28. Ministry of Alessandro Fortis.

May. Railwaymen's strike. Chamber of Deputies approves bill for state regulation of railways.

August 16. Outbreaks and violent clashes in Grammichele in Catania province.

December 22. Fortis re-forms Ministry.

1906

January–April. Algeciras Conference on Moroccan Affairs: Visconti Venosta supports France.

February 2. Fall of Fortis Cabinet.

February 8 to May 27. Sidney Sonnino's Ministry: Sonnino's first "Hundred Days."

February 24. Catholic political congress held in Florence: formation of *Unione popolare cattolica italiana* and the *Unione elettorale.*

May 8–9. Strike over demand of ten-hour working day in Turin quickly spreads to Milan, Genoa, Bologna, Florence, Livorno, and Rome. Bloody clashes between police and strikers.

May 10. Turati motion in Chamber of Deputies designed "to prevent proletarian massacres by the public force" defeated by vote of 199 to 28.

May 12. Socialist deputies in the Chamber resign en masse.

May 14 to 21. Demonstrations and skirmishes between strikers and police continue in Italy and the Islands.

May 27. Fall of Sonnino.

May 29. Giolitti's "Long Ministry" begins.

June 29. Conversion of national debt and reduction of interest from 4% to 3½% amid national applause.

October 7 to 10. Rome congress of Socialist party: victory of Enrico Ferri's integralism, middle way between Turati's reformism and Labriola's syndicalism. Rise of Italian Confederation of Labor.

1907

June. Definite break between Socialists and Syndicalists.

June–October. Italian participation in Second Hague Peace Conference.

July 3. Papal Syllabus on Modernism.

July. Anticlerical agitation.

September 8. Encyclical *Pascendi Domini gregis* condemning Modernism.

1908

February 18 to 27. Great debate on school question and relations between Church and state in the Chamber of Deputies.

July. Young Turk Revolution.

September 19 to 22. Florence congress of Socialist party: overwhelming Reformist victory.

October. Annexation of Bosnia-Herzegovina by Austria: acute international crisis. In the Chamber of Deputies Salvatore Barzilai and Alessandro Fortis lead in expressions of Italian diffidence over Austrian moves in the Balkans.

December 28. Earthquake at Reggio di Calabria and Messina.

1909

March 7 and 14. General political elections. Practical removal of *non expedit* on participation of Catholics in political elections and enunciation of new formula: *cattolici deputati, non deputati cattolici* (Deputies who are Catholics, not Catholic deputies), of whom twenty-one were elected to Parliament.

October 23 to 25. Visit of Tsar Nicholas II and Izvolski to Italy. Racconigi Agreement (Izvolski-Tittoni) in which Italy engaged herself to regard with benevolence Russia's interests in the Straits and Russia, Italian interests in Tripoli and Cyrenaica.

December 2. Fall of Giolitti Cabinet.

December 10. Sonnino Ministry: beginning of Sonnino's second "Hundred Days."

1910

March 31. Fall of Sonnino. Ministry of Luigi Luzzatti.

May 28. Chamber of Deputies passes Law for Maritime Conventions.

July. Passage of Daneo-Credaro Law for Primary Education.

May–November. Senator Giorgio Arcoleo's proposal for reform of the Senate on Liberal lines stirs animated discussion in parliamentary circles and throughout the country.

October 21 to 25. Milan congress of Socialist party: debut of Benito Mussolini at a national congress of the Socialist party.

December 3 to 5. Florence Nationalist congress under leadership of Enrico Corradini, Scipio Sighele, Luigi Federzoni, Luigi Villari, Maurizio Maraviglia, and others.

December 21. Luzzatti sponsors "modest" electoral reform in the Chamber of Deputies.

1911

March 1. Launching of Nationalist party organ, *L'Idea Nazionale.*

March 18. Fall of Luzzatti on question of electoral reform.

March 29. Giolitti Ministry again.

March–June. Celebration of fiftieth anniversary of Italian unification.

May. Arcoleo's bill for the reform of the Senate rejected by that body.

June. Giolitti presents his own bill for more extensive electoral reform to the Chamber of Deputies.

Debate on bill for State Monopoly of Life Insurance.

June–November. Second Moroccan Crisis.

September. Tripolitan question agitated in Italian press.

September 23 to 27. Acute diplomatic crisis over Italian-Turkish relations.

September 28. Italian ultimatum delivered to Turkey.

September 29. Italian declaration of war on Turkey.

October 5. Italian forces land at Tripoli.

October 15 to 18. Modena Congress of Socialist party: case of Leonida Bissolati further exacerbated by outbreak of Libyan War. Ascendancy of Mussolini in Socialist ranks.

November 5. Proclamation of Italian annexation of Tripoli.

1912

January–April. Italian naval demonstrations and operations in the Aegean and in the eastern Mediterranean.
  Occupation of Dodecanese Islands.
February 23. Approval of Decree of Annexation of Libya by overwhelming vote in Chamber of Deputies.
March 14. D'Alba attempts to assassinate King Victor Emmanuel: deputies, including Reformist Socialists, go en masse to congratulate the King on his escape.
April 4. Passage of State Monopoly of Life Insurance Act.
April–May. Chamber debates Giolitti's electoral reform bill.
June 30. Passage of Electoral Reform Act granting practical universal suffrage by increasing the electorate from less than three and a half to over eight and a half million voters. Salaries for deputies approved.
July 7 to 10. Reggio Emilia Congress of Socialist party: trial and expulsion of right-wing Socialists (Bissolati, Ivanoe Bonomi, Angiolo Cabrini, Guido Podrecca) from the party. Victory of revolutionary Socialist faction under leadership of Mussolini who becomes editor-in-chief of official party organ, *Avanti!*
October 18. Treaty of Lausanne ends the war with Turkey.

1913

October 26 and November 2. General political elections, first since passage of Electoral Reform Act of 1912. Strengthening of Conservative bloc, increase of Socialist and Catholic deputies.
November 8. Giornale d'Italia publishes interview of Count Vincenzo Ottorino Gentiloni, president of the *Unione cattolica italiana,* revealing Catholic aid given in elections to Conservative and Giolittian candidates.
December. "Gentiloni Pact" arouses anti-Giolittian as well as anticlerical forces in Chamber of Deputies and throughout the country. Giolitti passively weathers the storm.

1914

March 10 to 31. Following bolt of Giolittian parliamentary majority by the Radical party, Giolitti resigns.
  Ministry of Antonio Salandra.
April 26 to 29. Ancona congress of Socialist party: complete triumph of Mussolinian forces. Expulsion of Freemasons.
June 7 to 11. Red Week. Insurrectionary movement led by Errico Malatesta and sponsored by Mussolini spreads throughout central Italy, particularly in the Marches and in Romagna.
June 28. Assassination of Franz Ferdinand at Sarajevo.
August 3. Proclamation of Italian neutrality in First World War.
November 29. Mussolini expelled from Italian Socialist party for war-mongering activities.

1915

May 23. Italy joins the Allies by declaring war on Austria.

BIBLIOGRAPHY

The following is intended principally, although not exclusively, as a bibliography on the period treated in the text. Just as in the text, there is here some extension both into earlier and later periods. The student of this period of Italian history soon discovers that his first and greatest difficulty is the lack, in Italian and in English, of even the most elementary bibliographical aids. Although the following bibliography makes no pretense to completeness, it covers the most important literature available outside of Italy. The semi-topical arrangement may, it is hoped, be found helpful and suggestive for the further study of a period of Italian history in its first stages of exploration both historically and bibliographically.

This arrangement is as follows:

PRIMARY SOURCES

SECONDARY WORKS

I. General, Political, Social, Economic, and Cultural
II. Parliamentary History, Political Parties, and Political Thought
III. The Church, Catholics in Politics, Christian Democracy
IV. Socialism
V. Nationalism, Nationalist Currents, The Libyan War
VI. Giolitti and *Giolittismo*
VII. Periodicals

PRIMARY SOURCES

Atti Parlamentari: Discussioni della Camera dei Deputati:
    Session of 1900–02, 7 vols.
    "   " 1902–04, 14 vols.
    "   " 1904–09, 21 vols.
    "   " 1909–13, 21 vols.
    "   " 1913–19, 19 vols.
The debates of the Chamber of Deputies are indispensable sources for the study of the period. A parliamentary history of Italy in the pre-Fascist period that avails itself of the full resources of the debates is still to be written.
——: *Discussioni della Camera dei Senatori:*
    Session of 1900–02, 4 vols.
    "   " 1902–04, 8 vols.
    "   " 1904–09, 14 vols.
    "   " 1909–13, 12 vols.
    "   " 1913–19, 5 vols.
The debates of the Italian Senate are not as important as those of the Chamber of Deputies; they are, however, most useful for a study of conservatism in Italy.
Bollettini.
    Issued by various ministries.

Bollettino Parlamentare.
    For summaries of parliamentary activity and occasional statutes.
Gazzetta ufficiale del Regno d'Italia.
    Daily; for text of laws, royal decrees, administrative regulations, etc.
Inchiesta parlamentare sulle condizioni nelle provincie meridionali e nella Sicilia.
    Rome: Tipografia nazionale di Giovanni Bertero & Co., 1910–11.
Indice sistematico cronologico della legislazione italiana: leggi, decreti e regola-
    menti dal 1861. Volume dal 1861 al 31 dicembre 1922. Belluno: Soc. Edit. bel-
    lunese, 1923.
La Libia negli Atti del Parlamento e nei provvedimenti del Governo. Ed. by
    Emilio Pagliano. 3 vols. Milan: Pirola, 1912.
Manuale ad uso dei Deputati al Parlamento nazionale. XXI Legislatura. Rome:
    Tipografia della Camera dei Deputati, 1904.
Ministero di Agricoltura, Industria e Commercio. Direzione Generale della Sta-
    tistica. *Statistica delle Elezioni Generali Politiche, 6 e 13 novembre 1904.*
    Rome: Bertero, 1904.
———. *Statistica delle Elezioni Generali Politiche alla XXIII Legislatura, 7 e 14*
    marzo 1909. Rome: Bertero, 1909.
———. *Statistica delle Elezioni Generali Politiche alla XXIV Legislatura, 26*
    ottobre e 2 novembre 1913. Rome: Bertero, 1914.
———. Ufficio del Lavoro. *Le organizzazioni operaie cattoliche in Italia.* Pub-
    blicazioni dell'Ufficio del Lavoro. Serie B,No. 35. Rome: Off. Poligrafica
    Italiana, 1911.
Parlamento. *Il monopolio delle assicurazioni sulla vita.* Rome: Bertero, 1913.
    This work is in two parts: the first being the debates in the Chamber, the
    second, the law itself, the regulations, and provisions for its enforcement.
Raccolta ufficiale delle leggi e dei decreti del Regno.
    The official collection of laws, decrees, and regulations issued since 1861.

Annuario Generale d'Italia.
    Issued from 1886 to date. Very useful for general information not otherwise
    available.

Annuario Statistico Italiano.
    A great mine of information on all the important phases of Italian life. Very
    reliable.

Il Nazionalismo Italiano. Atti del Congresso di Firenze. Florence: Casa Editrice
    Quattrini, 1911.
    Reports of the speeches and proceedings at the first Nationalist congress of
    1910. Important for the study of Nationalist ideology before the Libyan War.

Partito Socialista Italiano. *Rendiconto dell'VIII Congresso Nazionale: Bologna,*
    8–9–10–11 aprile 1904. Pubblicazione della Direzione del Partito. Rome: Mon-
    gini, 1905.
    The stenographic reports herein contained are not as accurately edited as
    those of the congresses that followed.
Atti della Direzione del Partito Socialista Italiano. *Resoconto stenografico del*
    IX Congresso Nazionale: Roma, 7–8–9–10 ottobre 1906. Rome: Mongini, 1907.
———. *Resoconto stenografico del X Congresso Nazionale: Firenze, 19–20–21–22*
    settembre 1908. Rome: Mongini, 1908.
Direzione del Partito Socialista Italiano. *Resoconto stenografico dello XI Con-*

*gresso Nazionale del Partito Socialista Italiano: Milano, 21–22–23–24–25 otto-
bre 1910.* Rome: Officina Poligrafica Italiana, 1911.

————. *Resoconto stenografico del XII Congresso Nazionale del Partito Socialista
Italiano: Modena, 15–16–17–18 ottobre 1911.* Milan: Società Anonima
"Avanti!", 1912.

————. *Resoconto stenografico del XIII Congresso Nazionale del Partito Socialista Italiano: Reggio Emilia, 7–8–9–10 luglio 1912.* Rome: Ediz. d. Direz.
del Partito Socialista Italiano, 1913.

————. *Resoconto stenografico del XIV Congresso Nazionale del Partito Socialista Italiano: Ancona, 26–27–28–29 aprile 1914.* Rome: Ediz. d. Direz. del
Partito Socialista Italiano, 1914.

SECONDARY WORKS

I. GENERAL: POLITICAL, SOCIAL, ECONOMIC, AND CULTURAL

Arias, Gino. *La questione meridionale.* 2 vols. Bologna: Zanichelli, 1921.
  One of the best works on the Southern question; exhaustive bibliography.
Avenati, C. A. *La rivoluzione italiana da Vittorio Alfieri a Benito Mussolini.*
Turin: Ghirardi, 1934.
Azimonti, Eugenio. *Il Mezzogiorno agrario qual'è. A cura di Giustino Fortunato.*
Bari: Laterza, 1919.

Bachi, Riccardo. *L'Italia economica nel 1911.* Turin: Soc. Tip. Ediz. Naz., 1912.
————. *L'Italia economica nel 1912.* Città di Castello: S. Lapi, 1913.
————. *L'Italia economica nel 1913.* Città di Castello: S. Lapi, 1914.
————. *L'Italia economica nel 1914.* Città di Castello: S. Lapi, 1915.
Barbagallo, Corrado. *L'Italia dal 1870 ad oggi.* Quaderni della Querra No. 87.
Milan: Treves, 1918.
  An excellent brief synthesis from the Unification to the First World War.
Billot, A. *Histoire des années troublées, 1881–1899.* 2 vols. Paris, 1905.
Bobbio, Aurelia. *Le riviste fiorentine del principio del secolo, 1903–1916.* Flor-
ence: Sansoni, 1936.
  A thoughtful work on the Florentine reviews, especially *Il Regno, La Voce,
Leonardo,* and *Il Marzocco.* The author traces the development of ideas of
the Florentine movement critically.
Borgese, G. A. *Goliath: The March of Fascism.* New York, 1938.
  The work of a tortured spirit for whom history is a living experience.
Brenna, Paolo G. *L'Emigrazione italiana nel periodo antebellico.* Florence:
Bemporad, 1918.

Cabrini, Angiolo. *La legislazione sociale, 1859–1913.* Rome: Bontempelli, 1913.
  A good study of social legislation in Italy from Cavour to Giolitti. The
author was a Reformist Socialist who was expelled from the party in 1912.
Cappa, Alberto. *Due rivoluzioni mancate: Dati sviluppi e scioglimento della
crisi politica italiana.* Foligno, 1923.
  The author is an independent thinker who views both the Risorgimento
and the post-war in Italy as two "revolutions that missed." The work is more
interesting as the revelation of a state of mind in post-war and early Fascist
Italy than as an analysis of events.
Carano-Donvito, Giovanni. *L'Economia meridionale prima e dopo il Risorgimento.* Florence: Vallecchi, 1928.

Castellano, G., *Introduzione allo studio di B. Croce*. Bari: Laterza, 1920.
An excellent introduction to the mind and works of one of the greatest thinkers of modern times.

Cavaciocchi, Alberto. "La Massoneria italiana dal 1870 ai nostri giorni." *Gerarchia*, III (Dec., 1924), 744–56.
This article has been used too indiscriminately without reference to the author's Fascist bias.

Cavalli, Armando. "Correnti messianiche dopo il '70." *Nuova Antologia*, CCLXXIV (Nov. 16, 1930), 209–15.

Cesare, Raffaele de. *La fine di un Regno*. Città di Castello: Lapi, 1900.

——. *Mezzo secolo di storia italiana sino alla pace di Losanna*. 3rd ed. Città di Castello: Lapi, 1913.
The Conservative origins and attitudes of the author must be kept in mind in using his work.

Cilibrizzi, Saverio. *Storia parlamentare politica e diplomatica d'Italia da Novara a Vittorio Veneto*. 5 vols. Milan, 1923–40.
This is the basic work for the history of Italy after the Risorgimento; it is very factual and complete, and it does not limit itself to political history. Good documentation.

Colajanni, Napoleone. *Il progresso economico*. Rome: Bontempelli, 1913.
The work of a real scholar; reliable and important for a true understanding of the period.

Coletti, Francesco. *Economia rurale e politica rurale in Italia: Raccolta di studi*. Piacenza: Fed. Ital. dei Consorzi agrari, 1926.
A collection of writings on rural conditions.

Comandini, Alfredo. *L'Italia nei cento anni del secolo XIX*. 5 vols. Milan, 1939.
The basic work for a day-to-day account; indispensable for chronology of nineteenth century in Italy.

Corbino, Epicarmo. *Annali dell'economia italiana, 1861–1914*. 5 vols. Perugia, 1931–38.
The fundamental work on economic history.

Croce, Benedetto. *Storia del Regno di Napoli*. Bari: Laterza, 1925.
The great work on the Kingdom of Naples; important for an understanding of the South.

——. *A History of Italy, 1871–1915*. Trans. by Cecilia M. Ady. Oxford, 1929.
One of the pioneering works in the field. Croce's treatment of living history has been called a *laudatio temporis acti*.

——. *Storia d'Europa nel secolo decimonono*. 3rd ed. rev. Bari: Laterza, 1932.

——. *Cultura e vita morale: Intermezzi polemici*. 2nd ed. Bari, Laterza, 1926.

——. *Etica e Politica*. Bari: Laterza, 1931.
Contains some of Croce's best thought on liberalism.

——. *La letteratura della nuova Italia*. 5 vols. Bari: Laterza, 1929.
To be consulted for the relation of cultural life to other phases of Italian life.

Curcio, Carlo. *L'eredità del Risorgimento*. Florence, 1931.
A rather careful work whose conclusions must, however, be weighed thoughtfully.

——. *Il pensiero politico di Bertrando Spaventa*. Naples: Morano, 1924.
The examination of the political thought of one of the original thinkers of the Risorgimento period.

Dresler, Adolf. *Geschichte der italienischen Presse*. Munich and Berlin, 1933–34.
An indispensable reference work on the Italian press.
Destrée, Jules. *Figures italiènnes d'aujourd'hui*. Brussels and Paris, 1918.
Biographical sketches of Giolitti, Sonnino, Battisti, D'Annunzio, Salvemini, Barzilai, Luzzatti, Bissolati, Ferrero, and Corradini.

Enciclopedia Italiana. Treccani.
The "greatest encyclopedia in the world"; a real monument of scholarship and learning. To be consulted on all points of Italian (and world) history. Exhaustive bibliographies at the end of articles.

Ferrari, Aldo. *Principi e forme della lotta politica nella terza Italia, 1871–1925*. Milan: Rassegna Internaz., 1925.
A good short synthesis; relates all phases of the history of the period with the basic social and economic developments.
Fischer, P. D. *Italien und die Italiens am Schlusse des neunzehnten jahrhunderts*. Berlin: Springer, 1899.
Foerster, Robert F. *The Italian Emigration of Our Times*. Harvard Economic Studies, Vol. XX. Cambridge, Mass., 1919.
The definitive work on Italian emigration.
Fortunato, Giustino. *Il Mezzogiorno e lo Stato italiano: Discorsi politici, 1880–1910*. 2nd ed. 2 vols. Florence: Vallecchi, 1926.
The great work of one of the authentic liberals; fundamental for an understanding of the Southern question.
Franchetti, Leopoldo. "Un mezzo secolo di unità nell'Italia meridionale." *Nuova Antologia*, XLVI (May 1, 1911), 83–97.

Garlanda, Federico. *La Terza Italia*. Rome, 1902.
———. *The New Italy: A discussion of its present political and social conditions*. Trans. by M. E. Wood. New York and London, 1914.
A translation of the preceding work; constructive criticism of Liberal Italy by a serious-minded contemporary.
Genin, Federico. *Sessant'anni di governo costituzionale*. Turin: V. Bona, 1909.
The work of an anti-Giolittian deputy.
Giretti, Edoardo. *I trivellatori della nazione italiana*. Rome: Libreria Politica Moderna, 1913.
An anti-protectionist booklet; revealing.
Giovannetti, E. *Il tramonto del liberalismo*. Bari, 1917.
Giuliano, Balbino. *L'esperienza politica dell'Italia*. Florence: Vallecchi, 1924.
Giusso, Lorenzo. *Le dittature democratiche dell'Italia*. Milan, 1927.
An attempt to rationalize Italian governments from 1870 to 1922 into "democratic dictatorships."
Gobetti, Piero. *La rivoluzione liberale: Saggio sulla lotta politica in Italia*. Bologna: L. Cappelli, 1924.
A profound essay by one of Italy's great political thinkers. A deep probing of causes, developments, and personalities. More important for post-war period.
———. *Risorgimento senza eroi*. Turin: Ediz. del Baretti, 1926.
A justly famous study of obscure, but significant Risorgimento influences; it gives an interpretation of *Giolittismo* as mere administrative ability.
Gori, Agostino. *Il popolo italiano, nella storia della libertà e della grandezza della patria, dal 1800 ai nostri giorni*. 3 vols. in 4. Milan: Vallardi, 1928–29.

Hentze, Margot. *Pre-Fascist Italy: The Rise and Fall of the Parliamentary Regime.* London, 1939.
A good attempt. The author's treatment, however, seems to be dominated by certain preconceptions that obscure rather than clarify the basic issues of the study.

King, Bolton, and Thomas Okey. *Italy Today.* 2nd ed. London, 1904.
An old work by two well-known English students and lovers of Italy. Still good for reference.

Labriola, Arturo. *Storia di dieci anni, 1899–1909.* Milan: Il Viandante, 1910.
An informative, illuminating study by the contemporary Syndicalist; it makes a penetrating diagnosis of evils, although it is perhaps too much preoccupied with a class interpretation of events.

Lémonon, Ernest. *L'Italie économique et sociale, 1861–1912.* Paris: Alcan, 1913.

Licitra, Carmelo. *Dal liberalismo al fascismo.* Rome, 1925.
A philosophical attempt to explain the change.

Lodi, Luigi. *Venticinque anni di vita parlamentare: Da Pelloux a Mussolini.* Florence: Bemporad, 1923.
A detailed study of Italian ministries from 1898 to 1922; good work of reference for the period.

Mattei, Rodolfo De. "La critica antiparlamentaristica in Italia dopo l'unificazione," *Educazione Fascista.* VI (April 1928), No. 4, 193–201.
———. *Il problema della democrazia dopo l'unità.* Rome: Istituto nazionale fascista di cultura, 1934.
This and the preceding work are both essential for an understanding of the so-called antiparliamentary criticism in Italy; they are well documented and thorough; but the conclusions are drawn with too much emphasis on purely ideological premises.

McClellan, George B. *Modern Italy: A Short History.* Princeton, 1933.
The author states that his study is drawn only from secondary sources.

Messeri, E. *Cinquant'anni di vita economica e finanziaria italiana.* Rome: Loescher, 1912.

Michels, Robert. *Italien von Heute: Politische und Wirtschaftliche Kulturgeschichte; 1860–1930.* Zurich, 1930.

Miranda, Luigi. "Un teorico del liberalismo: Mario Missiroli." *Nuova Antologia,* CCXIII (July 1, 1921), 74–82.

Missiroli, Mario. *La Monarchia Socialista: Estrema Destra.* Bari: Laterza, 1914.
A famous work by one of Italy's great journalists. Missiroli is the exponent of a theocratic conception of history that dominates his profound study. Very critical of Giolitti, who is seen as one of the artificers of the Socialist monarchy in Italy.

Monti, Antonio. *1861–1936: Dal Regno all'Impero; nel LXXV annuale del Regno d'Italia.* Milan: Vallardi, 1936.

Morpurgo, Emanuele. *La democrazia e la scuola.* Turin: Bocca, 1905.
The thesis is that Italian democracy must be governed by the people—by an educated and cultured people.

Nitti, Francesco S. *L'Italia all'alba del secolo XX.* Turin, 1901.
———. *La ricchezza dell'Italia.* Turin, 1905.
A study of the distribution of wealth and poverty in Italy.

Okey, Thomas. "United Italy," Vol. XII, *Cambridge Modern History* (1910).
Orano, Paolo. *I Moderni.* 5 vols. Milan, 1914.
———. *Lode al mio tempo: 1895–1925.* Bologna: Apollo, 1926.
Oriani, Alfredo. *La lotta politica in Italia.* 3 vols. Florence: La Voce, 1921.
    The work of an independent thinker little known in his lifetime. Salvatorelli says of Oriani that "as a writer his aspirations were greater than his powers of realization."
———. *Rivolta ideale.* Bologna: L. Cappelli, 1930.

Papafava, Francesco. *Dieci anni di vita italiana: 1899–1909; Cronache.* 2 vols. Bari: Laterza, 1913.
    A fundamental work, representing the thought of an authentic liberal. To be contrasted with Labriola's work cited above.
Papafava, Novello. *Fissazioni liberali.* Turin: Gobetti, 1924.
    More important for post-war period; a good presentation of Liberal fixations during the crisis brought on by fascism.
Pingaud, Albert, *L'Italie dépuis 1870.* Paris, 1915.
    The emphasis is on foreign relations.
Pino-Branca, Alfredo. *Cinquant'anni di economia sociale in Italia.* Bari: Laterza, 1922.
    A basic work on social and economic history.
Plebano, Achille. *Storia della finanza italiana dalla costituzione del regno alla fine del secolo decimonono.* 3 vols. Turin: Roux and Viarengo, 1899–1902.
Porri, V. *L'evoluzione economica italiana nell'ultimo cinquantennio: I Cavalieri del Lavoro.* Rome: Tip. della Camera dei Deputati, 1926.
Preziosi, Giovanni. *La Germania alla conquista dell'Italia.* Florence: La Voce, 1915.
    A study of German capital in Italy before the First World War.
Prezzolini, Giuseppe. *Amici.* Florence: Vallecchi, 1922.
    Biographical sketches of famous friends of the author, including Croce, Einaudi, Papini, Jahier, Soffici, Panzini, and Salvemini.
———. *La coltura italiana.* Florence: La Voce, 1923.

Quintavalle, Ferruccio. *Storia dell'unità italiana: 1814–1924.* Milan: Hoepli, 1926.
    A basic manual; reliable, factual, with helpful chronological prefaces to chapters.

Rasco. *Il primo gabinetto del nuovo regno.* Rome, 1901.
    On the Zanardelli-Giolitti Cabinet of 1901.
Reale Accademia Nazionale dei Lincei, Roma. *Cinquanta anni di storia italiana.* Pubblicazione fatta sotto gli auspici del Governo. . . . 3 vols. Milan: Hoepli, 1911.
    The great work published on the occasion of the celebration of fifty years of Italian unity in 1911. Indispensable for social, economic, and financial history.
Riccio, Peter M. *On the Threshold of Fascism.* New York, 1929.
    An attempt to present the group of the Florentine reviews as the precursors of fascism.
Rosi, Michele. *L'Italia odierna: due secoli di lotte, di studi e di lavoro per l'indipendenza la grandezza della patria.* 2 vols. Rome, 1922–27.

182   ITALY IN THE GIOLITTIAN ERA

Rosi, Michele. *Storia contemporanea d'italia*. Rome, 1934.

Ruggiero, Guido De. *Il pensiero politico meridionale nei secoli XVIII e XIX*. Bari: Laterza, 1922.

——. *Storia del liberalismo europeo*. Bari: Laterza, 1925.

——. *The History of European Liberalism*. Trans. by R. G. Collingwood. London, 1927.

The definitive history of liberalism by a great scholar and profound thinker.

Salvatorelli, Luigi. *A Concise History of Italy*. Trans. by Bernard Miall. New York, 1939.

Salvemini, Gaetano. *Appunti di storia del risorgimento italiano: 1815–1918*. Trento: Tridentum, 1920.

——. "L'Italia politica nel secolo XIX," in *L'Europa nel secolo XIX*. Vol. I. Storia Politica. Padua: Antonio Milani, 1925.

Santoro, Michele, *L'Italia nei suoi rapporti economici dal 1860 al 1910*. Rome: Tip. popolare, 1911.

Saporito, Vincenzo. *Trenta anni di vita parlamentare: delusioni e speranze per la patria*. Rome: Fratelli Palombi, 1926.

The parliamentary memoirs of a man of the Sonninian Center. Bitterly anti-Giolittian.

Sforza, Carlo. *Makers of Modern Europe*. Indianapolis, 1930.

Contains sketches of Giolitti, Bissolati, and Pius X, as the Italian makers.

——. *The Real Italians: A Study in European Psychology*. New York, 1942.

In regard to Giolitti advances the now notorious story of the "tailor" (Giolitti) and the "hunchback" (Italy).

Silone, Ignazio. *Der Fascismus: seine Entstehung und seine Entwicklung*. Zurich: Europa-Verlag, 1934.

The work of a famous novelist; stresses the background and development of Italian fascism.

Sordello, pseud. *Giuseppe Mazzini e la lotta politica: 1831–1920*. Rome: Libr. Politica Moderna, 1922.

A polemical, Republican pamphlet.

Sturzo, Luigi. *Italy and Fascism*. Trans. by B. B. Carter. London, 1926.

A basic work on its subject; contains an analysis of political developments since the Risorgimento.

Tagliacozzo, Enzo. *Voci di realismo politico dopo il 1870*. Bari: Laterza, 1937.

An excellent booklet on the group that began to agitate the Southern question.

Tittoni, Tommaso. *Nuovi scritti di politica interna ed estera*. Preface by Guido Mazzoni. Milan: Treves, 1930.

Valenti, Ghino. *L'Italia agricola dal 1861 al 1911*. Rome, 1912.

Vallardi, Antonio, ed. *Mezzo secolo di vita italiana: 1861–1911*. Milan: Vallardi, 1911.

Contains articles by various experts on phases of Italian history.

Valsecchi, Franco. *Das Moderne Italien: politische Geistergeschichte seit 1900*. Hamburg, 1935.

Vigo, Pietro. *Annali d'Italia: Storia degli ultimi trenta anni del secolo XIX*. 7 vols. Milan: Treves, 1908–1915.

Villari, Luigi. *Italy*. New York, 1929.

Vinciguerra, Mario. *Un quarto di secolo: 1900–1925*. Turin: Gobetti, 1925.
   A creative little book, with main stress on cultural and intellectual developments.
Viti de Marco, Antonio de. *Un trentennio di lotte politiche: 1894–1922*. Rome: Collezione meridionale edit., 1930.
———. *Per un programma d'azione democratica*. Florence: Aldino, 1914.
   A reprint of an article in Salvemini's review, *L'Unità*. Vol. II, Nos. 30 and 41.
Volpe, Gioacchino. *L'Italia in cammino: L'ultimo cinquantennio*. 3rd ed. rev. Milan: Treves, 1931.
   Like Croce's history it is a creative pioneering work on the period from the Unification to the First World War in Italy.

Wallace, William K. *Greater Italy*. New York, 1918.

Zingali, Gaetano. *Liberalismo e Fascismo nel Mezzogiorno d'Italia*. 2 vols. Milan: Treves, 1933.
   The first volume is important for period before fascism.

II. PARLIAMENTARY HISTORY, POLITICAL PARTIES, AND POLITICAL THOUGHT

Arangio-Ruiz, G. *Storia constituzionale del regno d'Italia: 1848–1898*. Florence, 1899.
Arbid, Edoardo. *Cinquant'anni di storia parlamentare del regno d'Italia*. 4 vols. Rome: Tip. della Camera dei Deputati, 1898–1907.
   Treats of parliamentary history only; down to the end of the nineteenth century.
Arcoleo, Giorgio. *Il Governo di Gabinetto nei governi parlamentari*. Naples: Jovene, 1881.
   Advocates the formation of extra-parliamentary cabinets.

Barzilai, Salvatore. *Luci ed ombre del passato*. Milan, 1937.
   The memoirs of a great parliamentary speaker.
———. *Vita parlamentare: discorsi e profili politici*. Preface by Ferdinando Martini. Rome: Tip. edit. nazionale, 1912.
Boffi, Ferruccio. *Il pensiero politico di Antonio Salandra*. Città di Castello: Lapi, 1914.
Bonghi, Ruggiero. "Una questione grossa: La decadenza del regime parlamentare." *Nuova Antologia*. XLV (June 1, 1884), 482–97.
———. "L'ufficio del Principe in uno Stato libero." *Nuova Antologia* (January 25, 1893).
Bonfadini, Romualdo. "I partiti politici in Europa e particolarmente in Italia." *Nuova Antologia*, XLIX (February 15, 1894), 620–39.

Caetani, Leone. *La riforma elettorale: il sistema proporzionale e l'evoluzione del parlamentarismo*. Rome: Casa edit. ital., 1909.
Chiesa, Eugenio. *La corruzione politica: Discorsi alla Camera dei Deputati*. Preface by N. Colajanni. Rome, 1913.
Ciccotti, Ettore. *Montecitorio: Noterelle di uno che c'è stato*. Rome: Mongini, 1908.

Cimone, pseud. (Emilio Faelli). *I 508 di Montecitorio.* Rome-Turin: Roux and Viarengo, 1907.
Colajanni, Napoleone. *I partiti politici in Italia.* Rome: Libr. politica moderna, 1912.
    A rare booklet.
Cotugno, Raffaele. *Montecitorio: La degenerazione del Parlamento.* Lucera: Ed. Frattarolo, 1923.
    More important for post-war period. Has some clever witticisms on the best-known Italian parliamentarians.

D'Orazio, Ettore. *Fisiologia del parlamentarismo in Italia.* Turin: S.T.E.N., 1911.
    A rare and unusual book; studies the Italian parliamentary regime psychologically.

Ferrari, Aldo. "Destra e Sinistra, 1871–1881. *Rassegna storica del Risorgimento,* Vol. XIII, 1925.
Ferrari, Celso. *I partiti politici.* Turin: Bocca, 1909.
Fortunato, Giustino. *Pagine e ricordi parlamentari.* 2 vols. Florence: Vallecchi, 1926–27.
    The parliamentary memoirs of the great student of the South.
Fovel, N. Massimo. *Il partito radicale nell'ora presente.* Rome: Bontempelli, 1914.
Fradeletto, Antonio. *Dogmi e illusioni della democrazia.* Milan, 1913.

Giusti, Ugo. *Le correnti politiche italiane attraverso due riforme elettorali dal 1909 al 1921.* Florence: Venturi, 1922.
Groppali, Alessandro. "La crise des partis en Italie," *Revue Internationale de Sociologie,* XIII (March, 1905), No. 3, 215 ff.

Jacini, Stefano. *I conservatori e l'evoluzione naturale dei partiti politici in Italia.* Milan: Bigole, 1879.
———. *Un conservatore rurale della Nuova Italia.* 2 vols. Bari: Laterza, 1926.
    The biography of the famous author of the Agrarian Inquiry by his grandson.

La Pegna, Alberto. *Per l'idea democratica.* Milan: Rassegna Internazionale, 1925.
    The collected speeches of an ex-member of the Radical party; contains biographical sketches of some important Radical leaders.
"La prima prova del suffragio allargato." *Nuova Antologia,* CLXVIII (November 16, 1913), 334–38.
Lémonon, Ernest. *De Cavour à Mussolini: Histoire des partis politiques italiens.* Preface by M. Louis Madelin. Paris: A. Pedone, 1939.
Lowell, A. Lawrence. *Governments and Parties in Continental Europe.* 2 vols. Boston and New York, 1896.
    Lowell's is still the classic study on the Italian parliamentary regime (chaps. iii–iv); a penetrating treatment on local government.
Luzzatti, Luigi. *Grandi italiani, grandi sacrifici per la patria.* Bologna: Zanichelli, 1924.

Malatesta, Alberto. *Il Parlamento italiano da Cavour a Mussolini.* Milan: Agnelli, 1933.
    The author, an ex-Socialist, is not to be confused with the famous Anarchist, Errico Malatesta.

Manes, Carlo. "I partiti politici nell'ora presente." *L'Eloquenza,* III (December 20, 1913), Nos. 9–10.

Maranini, Giuseppe. *Le origini dello Statuto albertino.* Florence: Vallecchi, 1926. To be consulted on the debated question of the origins of the Italian Constitution.

Meis, Angelo Camillo de. *Il Sovrano.* Bari: Laterza, 1927. A brilliant essay written in 1868 by an independent Southern thinker.

Michels, Robert. *Zur Soziologie des Parteiwesens in der modernen Demokratie: Untersuchungen über die oligarchischen Tendenzen des Gruppenlebens.* Leipzig, 1911.

———. *Political Parties: A Sociological Study of the Oligarchical Tendencies of Modern Democracy.* Trans. by Eden and Cedar Paul. New York, 1915. A translation of the preceding book.

Minghetti, Marco. *I partiti politici e la ingerenza loro nella giustizia e nell'amministrazione.* 2nd ed. Bologna: Zanichelli, 1881. The author was a member of the Right who studied some of the evils of the Italian parliamentary system after his own and his party's fall in 1876.

Mosca, Gaetano. *Teorica dei governi e governo parlamentare: Studi storici e sociali.* 2nd ed. Milan: Soc. Anon. Istituto Editoriale Scientifico, 1925. See text of present work, chap. ii, for an analysis of Mosca's famous book.

———. *Il principio aristocratico ed il democratico nel passato e nell'avvenire.* Turin: Paravia, 1903.

———. *The Ruling Class (Elementi di Scienza Politica).* Trans. by H. D. Kahn; ed. and revised with an introduction by Arthur Livingston. New York and London, 1939.

Nitti, Francesco S. *Il partito radicale e la nuova democrazia industriale: Prime linee di un programma del partito radicale.* Turin: Soc. Tip.-Edit. Naz., 1907.

Nota, Alfredo. *Sessant'anni di eloquenza parlamentare in Italia: 1848–1908.* 2 vols. Modena: Formiggini, 1911–12.

Ogg, Frederic A. *European Governments and Politics.* 2nd ed. New York, 1939.

Palma, Luigi. *Questioni costituzionali: volume complemento del corso di diritto costituzionale.* Florence: G. Pellas, 1885.

Papafava, Francesco. "Socialismo e liberalismo." *Giornale degli Economisti* (Series 2), XIX, 248–64.

Pareto, Vilfredo. "The Parliamentary Regime in Italy." *Political Science Quarterly,* III (December 1893), No. 4, 677–721.

Paulucci di Calboli, Barone G., and Antonio Casulli. *Il pensiero di Giorgio Arcoleo.* Milan: Alpes, 1927.

Perticone, Giacomo. *Gruppi e partiti politici nella vita pubblica italiana, dalla proclamazione dell'unità alla guerra mondiale.* Modena: Guanda, 1938.

Piccolo, Francesco, ed. *I liberali italiani dopo il 1860.* Florence: Sansoni, 1934.

Rabizzani, Giovanni, and Ferruccio Rubbiani, ed. *Sonnino.* Milan: Risorgimento, 1920.

Raccioppi, Francesco. *Commento allo Statuto del regno.* Preface by Luigi Luzzatti. Turin: Unione tip.-edit. torinese, 1904.

Salandra, Antonio. *Politica e Legislazione: Saggi raccolti da G. Fortunato.* Bari: Laterza, 1915.

———. *La politica nazionale e il partito liberale.* Milan, 1912.

Salvatorelli, Luigi. *Il pensiero politico italiano dal 1700 al 1870.* Turin: Einaudi, 1935.

Sanctis, Francesco de. *Scritti politici.* Ed. by Giuseppe Ferrarelli. 4th ed. Naples, 1924.

Schiavi, Alessandro. "Programmi, voti ed eletti nei comizi politici del 1909." *Riforma Sociale,* XX (1909), 378–407, 519–66.

Siliprandi, Provido. *Capitoli teorico-pratici di politica sperimentale in considerazione dei mali d'Italia e della necessità di riformare lo Stato.* 3 vols. Mantua: Stab. Tip. della Gazzetta, 1898.

Sonnino, Sidney. *Discorsi parlamentari.* Published by the Chamber of Deputies. 3 vols. Rome: Tip. della Camera dei Deputati, 1925.

Spaventa, Silvio. *La politica della Destra: Scritti e discorsi raccolti da B. Croce.* Bari: Laterza, 1910.

———. *Discorsi parlamentari.* Rome, 1919.

Tortoreto, Angelo. *I Parlamentari italiani della XXIII Legislatura: cenni biografici dei deputati e senatori.* Rome: Roma, 1910.

Turiello, Pasquale. *Governo e governati in Italia.* 2nd ed. 2 vols. Bologna: Zanichelli, 1882.

Un Deputato (Sidney Donnino). "Torniamo allo Statuto." *Nuova Antologia,* LXVII (Jan. 1, 1897), 9–28.

Vajna, De Pava M. *Popolarismo e nasismo in Sicilia.* Florence, 1911.

Viana, Mario. "Giovanni Borelli poeta artista letterato agitatore politico." *La Vita Italiana,* Aug. 1933.

Viazzi, Pio. *Il partito repubblicano.* Genoa, 1913.

Viterbo, Michele. *Sidney Sonnino.* Milan: Imperia, 1923.

III. THE CHURCH, CATHOLICS IN POLITICS, CHRISTIAN DEMOCRACY

Bastgen, H. *Die romische Frage.* 3 vols. Freiburg: 1917–18.

Benedetti, Achille. "Intervista coll'altro presidente del Consiglio, il conte Gentiloni." *Giornale d'Italia,* Nov. 8, 1913.
The article that shook democratic-liberal Italy.

Bonomelli, Geremia. *La Chiesa.* Cremona, 1913.

Borgese, G. A. "Romolo Murri e il modernismo" in *La Vita e il Libro,* II, 328–37. Turin: Bocca, 1911.

Buonaiuti, Ernesto. *Le modernisme catholique.* Trans. from the Italian by René Monnot. Paris: Rieder, 1927.

Comandini, Ubaldo. *Politica ecclesiastica e politica scolastica.* Rome: Bontempelli, 1913.

Crispolti, Crispolto. *Pio X e un episodio del partito cattolico in Italia.* Rome: Bontempelli, 1913.

Crispolti, Filippo. *Pio IX, Leone XIII, Pio X, Benedetto XV.* Milan, 1932.

Curàtulo, Giacomo Emilio. *La Questione romana da Cavour a Mussolini.* Rome, 1928.

Gentile, Giovanni. *Il Modernismo e i rapporti tra religione e filosofia.* Bari: Laterza, 1909.

Halperin, S. William. *The Separation of Church and State in Italian Thought from Cavour to Mussolini.* Chicago, 1937.
  An illuminating little work; contains excellent bibliographical footnotes.

Jordan, Louis Henry. *Modernism in Italy.* Oxford, 1909.

"La sovranità della Chiesa rispetto alla sovranità dello Stato." *La Civiltà Cattolica,* III (July 6, 1911), 129–46.
"L'azione dei cattolici nei recenti comizi." *L'Osservatore Romano,* Nov. 6, 1913.
Luzzatti, Luigi. *Dio nella libertà: Studi sulle relazioni tra lo Stato e la Chiesa.* Bologna, 1926.
———. *God in Freedom: Studies in the Relations between Church and State.* Trans. by Alfonso A. Costa. New York, 1930.
  A translation of the preceding work.
Luzzi, Giovanni. *The Struggle for Christian Truth in Italy.* New York, 1913.

Mariano, Raffaele. *Papa, Clero e Chiesa in Italia.* Florence: Barbèra, 1903.
Meda, Filippo. *Il programma politico della democrazia cristiana.* Bergamo, 1906.
———. *Discorsi parlamentari: XXIII Legislatura.* Florence: Libr. edit. fiorentina, 1913.
Mondini, Luigi, and Ernesto Vercesi. *Da Cavour a Mussolini.* Milan, 1929.
Murri, Romolo. *Della religione, della Chiesa e dello Stato.* Milan: Treves, 1910.
———. *Battaglie d'oggi.* 4 vols. Rome: Soc. I. C. di Cultura, 1903–04.
———. *La politica clericale e la democrazia.* Ascoli Piceno: G. Cesari, 1908.
———. "La Lega Democratica e l'azione pubblica dei cattolici italiani." *Rassegna Contemporanea,* IV (Oct.–Dec., 1908), 90–105.

Pernot, M. *La politique de Pie X.* Paris, 1910.

Rosa, Enrico, S.J., *L'Enciclica 'Pascendi' e il modernismo.* Rome: Civiltà Cattolica, 1903.
  Important. Most definitely anti-Modernist.

Salvatorelli, Luigi. "Ernesto Buonaiuti, pellegrino di Roma." *Cultura,* XII (1933), 375–91.
Sassoli De Bianchi, Conte Dott. Filippo. *Religione e patria: Questioni del giorno.* Florence: San Giuseppe, 1913.
  Collection of writings and speeches. Anti-Masonic, Giobertian.
Sercia, Giacomo. "Il modernismo religioso contemporaneo." *Rassegna Contemporanea,* II (April–June, 1908), 330–40.
Suardi, Gianforte. "Quando e come i cattolici poterono partecipare alle elezioni politiche." *Nuova Antologia,* CCLVI (Nov. 1, 1927), 118–23.
Sturzo, Luigi. *Church and State.* Trans. by B. B. Carter. New York, 1939.
  A luminous work by the eminent Catholic thinker and historian.

Toniolo, G. *L'Unione popolare fra i cattolici d'Italia.* Florence: U.P.C. d'Italia, 1908.

Vaussard, Maurice. *L'intelligence catholique dans l'Italie du XXe siècle*. Paris: V. Lecoffre, 1921.
Studies of some of the more outstanding Catholic leaders in Italy.
Vercesi, Ernesto. *Il movimento cattolico in Italia: 1870–1922*. Florence: La Voce, 1923.
A basic book.
———. *Tre Papi: Leone XIII; Pio X; Benedetto XV*. Milan, 1929.

IV. SOCIALISM

Angiolini, Alfredo. *Cinquant'anni di socialismo in Italia*. Florence: Nerbini, 1900.
One of the earliest attempts at a complete history; very informative, and well illustrated.
Angiolini, Alfredo, and Eugenio Ciacchi. *Socialismo e socialisti in Italia: Storia completa del movimento socialista italiano dal 1850 al 1919*. Florence: Nerbini, 1920.

Bacchelli, Riccardo. *Il diavolo al Pontelungo*. 2nd ed. Milan: Ceschina, 1929.
An interesting historical novel based on the attempted Anarchist-Bakuninist Bologna insurrection of 1874.
Balabanoff, Angelica. *My Life as a Rebel*. 3rd ed. New York and London, 1938.
The author was a member of the Left-wing faction of the Socialist party. Her memoirs, however, must be used with care since they are completely undocumented and betray many unaccounted-for and violent biases.
Bettinotti, M. *Vent'anni di movimento operaio genovese*. Milan, 1932.
Bissolati, Leonida. *La politica estera dell'Italia: 1897–1920*. Milan: Treves, 1923.
A revealing book; especially illuminating on the personality of its author.
Bonomi, Ivanoe. "Il Congresso Socialista di Bologna." *Nuova Antologia*, CXL (May 1, 1904), 129–30.
———. *Le vie nuove del socialismo*. Palermo, 1907.
Important on the origins of Socialist reformism.
———. *Dieci anni di politica italiana*. Milan: Unitas, 1924.
———. *Dal socialismo al fascismo*. Rome: Formiggini, 1924.
———. *From Socialism to Fascism: A Study of Contemporary Italy*. Trans. by John Murray. London, 1924.
———. *Leonida Bissolati e il movimento socialista in Italia*. Milan: Martinelli, 1929.
A very sympathetic study of a fellow Reformist.

Caggese, Romolo. "Leonida Bissolati." *Rivista d'Italia*, New Series, III (May 15, 1920), 80–101.
Campolonghi, Luigi. *Camillo Prampolini e il suo tempo*. Paris: Respublica, 1932.
Ciccotti, Ettore. *Come divenni e come cessai di essere deputato di Vicaria*. Naples, 1909.
Ciccotti, Francesco. *L'Italia in rissa*. Milan: Rassegna Contemporanea, 1925.
More important for post-war period.
Colajanni, Napoleone. *L'Italia nel 1898: Tumulti e reazioni*. Milan: Soc. edit. lombarda, 1899.
Important on the events of 1898.

Colajanni, Napoleone. *Il socialismo.* 2nd ed. Palermo-Milan: Sandron, 1898.
Croce, Benedetto. *Materialismo storico ed economia marxistica.* 3rd ed. rev. Bari: Laterza, 1918.
––––––. "Come nacque e come morì il marxismo teorico in Italia (1895–1900): Da lettere e ricordi personali." *Critica,* XXXVI (1938), 35–52, 109–24.

Feroci, Guido. *Socialismo e massoneria.* Rome: Mongini, 1910.
   A rare pamphlet by one of the younger members of the Socialist party. Anti-Masonic.
Forges-Davanzati, Roberto. "Dopo i Congressi di Modena e Firenze." *Rassegna Contemporanea,* IV (Oct.–Dec., 1908), 168–74.
Fovel, N. Massimo. *I 'moti' di giugno e il dovere della democrazia.* Florence: Tip. Galileiana, 1914.
   A Radical's view of Red Week of 1914.
Frignani, G. *Appunti per la cronaca del fascismo romagnolo.* Bologna, 1933.

Granone, Liborio. *La crisi socialista.* Catania: Il Domani, 1914.
   The crisis of Italian socialism viewed by a Reformist, Bissolatian Socialist.

Labriola, Antonio. *Scritti vari di filosofia e politica.* Bari: Laterza, 1906.
   The writings of a philosopher and a Socialist thinker.
Labriola, Arturo. *Marx sull'economia.* Lugano: L'Avanguardia, 1908.
   The theoretical case for syndicalism by its greatest Italian exponent.
––––––. *La guerra di Tripoli e l'opinione socialista.* Naples, 1912.
––––––. *Il socialismo contemporaneo: Lineamenti storici.* Rocca San Giovanni: Casa edit. abruzzese, 1914.
Lanzillo, Agostino. *Giorgio Sorel.* Rome: Libr. edit. Romana, 1910.
   One of the best works on the theorist of syndicalism.
––––––. *La disfatta del socialismo.* 2nd ed. Florence: La Voce, 1918(?).
Lazzeri, Gerolamo. *Filippo Turati.* Milan: Risorgimento, 1921.
   A pamphlet.
Leone, Enrico. *Il sindacalismo.* Milan: Sandron, 1907.

Marazio, Annibale. *Il Partito Socialista Italiano e il Governo: 15 febbraio 1901– 4 marzo 1905.* Turin: Unione tip.-edit., 1906.
Mazzali, Guido. *L'Espiazione socialista: Appunti per una storia critica del socialismo italiano.* Preface by Adriano Tilgher. Milan: La Cultura, 1926.
   More important for post-war period.
Meda, Filippo. *Il Partito Socialista Italiano: dalla Prima alla Terza Internazionale.* Milan: Vita e Pensiero, 1921.
   A study of Socialist congresses without documentation.
––––––. *Il socialismo politico in Italia.* Milan: Unitas, 1924.
Megaro, Gaudens. *Mussolini in the Making.* Boston and New York, 1938.
   An excellent study of Mussolini's life and activities to 1914.
Michels, Robert. *Il proletariato e la borghesia nel movimento socialista italiano.* Turin: Bocca, 1908.
   An essential study of the social bases of the Italian Socialist movement.
––––––. *Storia del marxismo in Italia: Compendio critico con annessa bibliografica.* Rome: Mongini, 1909.
   Contains a complete Bibliography in the Appendix.

Michels, Robert. *Sozialismus und Fascismus: Sozialismus in Italien. Intellektuelle Strömungen.* Munich: Meyer and Jessen, 1925.
————. *Storia critica del movimento socialista italiano.* Florence: La Voce, 1926.
   The fundamental work on Italian socialism to 1911; contains chronology, charts of derivations, and Bibliography.
Mondolfo, Rodolfo. *Sulle orme di Marx.* 3rd ed. 2 vols. Bologna: L. Cappelli, 1923–24.
   More theoretical than historical. Basic.
Mosso, Angelo. *Vita moderna degli italiani: Saggi.* Milan: Treves, 1906.

Nenni, Pietro. *La lutte de classes en Italie.* Preface by Filippo Turati. Paris: Nouvelle Revue Socialiste, 1930.
   More important for post-war period.
Nomad, Max. *Rebels and Renegades.* New York, 1932.
   See the chapter on Errico Malatesta.

Orano, Paolo. *Andrea Costa.* Rome, 1910.

Pareto, Vilfredo. *Les systèmes socialistes.* 2 vols. Paris, 1902–03.
   Theoretical.
Pietri-Tonelli, Alfonso de. *Il socialismo democratico in Italia.* Parma, 1913.
Prezzolini, Giuseppe. *La teoria sindacalista.* Naples: Perrella, 1909.
   A profound study, interestingly written.

Ragghianti, Angelo. *Gli uomini rossi all'arrembaggio dello Stato.* Preface by Biagio Bruni. Bologna: Zanichelli, 1914.
   A description of the Socialist "state within the state" in the Romagna and Emilia.
Ranzi, Fabio. "L'Equivoco dell'antimilitarismo dopo il Congresso Socialista di Firenze." *Rassegna Contemporanea,* IV (Oct.–Dec., 1908), 125–38.
Rigola, Rinaldo. *L'evoluzione della Confederazione Generale del Lavoro.* Florence: Ediz. della Critica Sociale, 1921.
   Contains statistics.
————. *Rinaldo Rigola e il movimento operaio nel biellese: Saggio sulla storia del movimento operaio.* Bari: Laterza, 1930.
Rosselli, Carlo. *Socialisme libéral.* Pari: Valois, 1930.
   A fine study of socialism as the party of liberty and on the limitations of the Italian movement.
Rosselli, Nello. *Mazzini e Bakounine: Dodici anni di movimento operaio in Italia (1860–1872).* Turin: Bocca, 1927.
   Fundamental for the origins of the Italian working-class movement as well as for the famous Mazzini-Bakunin feud.
————. *Carlo Pisacane nel Risorgimento italiano.* Turin: Bocca, 1932.
   The definitive biography of a Socialist thinker, hero, and martyr of the Risorgimento.
Rota, Ettore. *Una pagina di storia contemporanea—Gaetano Salvemini.* Milan: Albrighi, Segati & Co., 1919.
   A profound essay on Salvemini.
Rubbiani, Ferruccio. *Il pensiero politico di Leonida Bissolati.* Florence: L. Battistelli, 1921.
   Contains good extracts from the writings and speeches of the Socialist leader Bissolati; good introductory notes.

Salucci, Arturo. *Il crepuscolo del socialismo.* 2nd ed. Milan: Corbaccio, 1925.

Salvemini, Gaetano, *Tendenze vecchie e necessità nuove del movimento operaio italiano. Saggi critici.* Bologna: L. Cappelli, 1922.

A fundamental book, too often ignored in the study of Italian socialism. It contains a collection of the author's writings and speeches, and an illuminating introduction.

Sorel, Georges. *Reflexions sur la violence.* Paris, 1908.

An influential book; first widely read in Italy.

Treves, Claudio. *Polemica socialista.* Bologna, 1921.

Contains reprints of some of the author's more important articles which first appeared on the *Critica Sociale.*

————. *Un socialista: Filippo Turati.* Paris: S.F.I.C., n.d.

A pamphlet.

Turati, Filippo. *Trent'anni di "Critica Sociale."* Bologna: L. Cappelli, 1921.

A collection of Turati's important articles which first appeared in the great Socialist review he founded and edited.

————. *Le vie maestre del socialismo.* Bologna: L. Cappelli, 1921.

Many of the author's speeches are gathered in this work.

Zibordi, Giovanni. *Saggio sulla storia del movimento operaio in Italia: Camillo Prampolini e i lavoratori reggiani.* Bari: Laterza, 1930.

A fine essay on the work of social uplift in one of the most backward of the northern regions. Contains also a short biographical sketch of the work of the so-called "evangelical" Socialist, Prampolini.

Zoccoli, Ettore. *L'Anarchia.* Torino: Bocca, 1907.

V. NATIONALISM, NATIONALIST CURRENTS, THE LIBYAN WAR

Anzilotti, Antonio. *La crisi spirituale della democrazia italiana: per una democrazia nazionalista.* Faenza: Tip. Novelli and Castellani, 1912.

Arcari, Paolo. *La coscienza nazionale in Italia: Voci del tempo raccolte e ordinate da Paola Arcari.* Milan: Libr. Edit. Milanese, 1911.

The result of an inquiry on the existence of a national consciousness in Italy.

Arcari, Paola Maria. *Le elaborazioni della dottrina politica nazionale fra l'unità e l'intervento; 1870–1914.* 3 vols. Florence: Casa Edit. Il Marzocco, 1939.

A basic work for the study of the new nationalism in Italy. Contains many extracts from documents.

Askew, William C. *Europe and Italy's Acquisition of Libya, 1911–1912.* Durham, N.C., 1942.

Dr. Askew's excellent diplomatic study was not available to the author before the present book was finished. References to this study were made in the footnotes as the present text was going to press.

Barzilai, Salvatore. *Dalla Triplice Alleanza al Conflitto europeo.* Rome, 1924.

Bevione, Giuseppe. *Come siamo andati a Tripoli.* Turin: Bocca, 1912.

Borgese, G. A. *Gabriele D'Annunzio.* Naples: R. Ricciardi, 1909.

One of the really great studies of D'Annunzio.

Borgese, G. A. "Nazionalismo" in *La Vita e il Libro*. 2 vols. Vol. II, 286–327. Turin: Bocca, 1911.

Busetto, Andrea. *Nazionalismo, guerra e democrazia; con un proemio sull'elogio della guerra ed un appendice*. Venice: L'Avanguardia Nazionalista, 1914.
Extreme Nationalist viewpoint; in praise of war.

Caroncini, Alberto. *Problemi di politica nazionale: Scritti scelti e presentati con una Prefazione da Arrigo Solmi*. Bari: Laterza, 1922.
The writings of a Nationalist Young Liberal.

Casoni, Giambattista. *La guerra italo-turca*. Florence: Bemporad, 1914.

Castellini, Gualtiero. *Tunisi e Tripoli*. Turin: Bocca, 1911.

Cian, Vittorio. *Luigi Federzoni*. Piacenza: Soc. Tip. Edit. Porta, 1924.

Coppola, Francesco. "Dal liberalismo al nazionalismo. In morte di Enrico Corradini." *Politica*, XXXVI (Feb.–April, 1932), 5, 24, 101–02.

Corradini, Enrico. *La Patria lontana*. Milan: Treves, 1911.
A novel by the leader of the Nationalists. Its characters are interesting as symbols of various aspects of Nationalist philosophy.

———. *Il volere d'Italia*. Naples: Perrella, 1911.

———. *L'ora di Tripoli*. Milan: Treves, 1912.

———. *La conquista di Tripoli; lettere della Guerra, di Enrico Corradini*. Milan: Treves, 1912.

———. *Sopra le vie del nuovo impero*. Milan: Treves, 1912.

———. *Il nazionalismo italiano*. Milan: Treves, 1914.
Contains some of the more important writings and speeches of its author.

———. *Discorsi politici, 1902–1923*. Florence: Vallecchi, 1923.
A collection of speeches.

———. *L'unità e la potenza delle nazioni*. Florence: Vallecchi, 1922.

———. *La rinascita nazionale: Scritti raccolti e ordinati da Goffredo Bellonci*. Florence: Le Monnier, 1929.

D'Andrea, Ugo. *Enrico Corradini e il nazionalismo*. Rome–Milan: Augustea, 1928.

Ercole, Francesco. "Il pensiero e l'opera di Enrico Corradini." *Educazione Fascista* (March 20, 1932), p. 193 ff.

Federzoni, Luigi ("Giulio De Frenzi"). *Per l'italianità del "Gardasee."* Preface by Scipio Sighele. Naples: R. Ricciardi, 1909.

———. *Presagi alla nazione*. Milan: Imperia, 1924.

———. *Paradossi di ieri*. Preface by R. Forges-Davanzati. Milan: Mondadori, 1926.

Ferrari, Celso. *Nazionalismo e internazionalismo. Saggio sulle leggi statiche e dinamiche della vita sociale*. Milan: Sandron, 1906.

Flora, Francesco. *D'Annunzio*. Naples: R. Ricciardi, 1926.
A penetrating study of the mind and work of the poet.

Lassere, Pierre. *Georges Sorel, theoricien de l'impérialisme: Ses idées; Son action*. Paris, 1928.

Maffi, Maffio. "Corradini e il 'Regno.'" *Politica*, XLI (August, 1937), 70–85, 121–22.

Malagodi, Olindo. *Imperialismo: la civiltà industriale e le sue conquiste.* Milan, 1901.

Mantegazza, Vico. *Tripoli e i diritti della civiltà.* Milan: Treves, 1912.

Maraviglia, Maurizio. *Momenti di vita italiana.* Rome: Casa edit. pinciana, 1929.
   The work of one of the founders of the Italian Nationalist party.

Merli, B. *La guerra italo-turca.* Rome: Ediz. Voghere, 1914.

Michels, Roberto. *L'Imperialismo italiano: Studi politico-demografici.* Milan: Società Editrice Libraria, 1914.
   One of the earliest and best studies on Italian imperialism. Basic.

Mondaini, Gennaro. *Manuale di storia e legislazione coloniale del Regno d'Italia.* Parte I. *Storia coloniale.* Rome: A. Sampaolesi, 1927.
   A good reference work on Italian colonial policy.

Musatti, Alberto. "La passione nazionale di Enrico Corradini." *Nuova Antologia,* LXVII (April 16, 1932), 455–68.

Nazionalisti e cattolici: Discorsi di F. Aquilanti, F. Meda, E. Martire, G. De Frenzi, F. Coppola, M. Maraviglia, A. Pagano, V. Leonardi. Rome: Associazione Nazionalista, 1913.

Nothomb, Pierre. "Enrico Corradini, theoricien du nationalisme." *Revue generale* (Brussels), LIX, (1926), 539–60.

Occhini, Pier Ludovico. *Enrico Corradini e la nuova coscienza nazionale.* Florence: Vallecchi, 1924.

Papini, Giovanni, and Giuseppe Prezzolini: *Vecchio e nuovo nazionalismo.* Milan: Studio edit. lombardo, 1914.

Pascoli, Giovanni. *La Grande Proletaria si è mossa.* Bologna: Zanichelli, 1911.
   The famous speech delivered at Barga on November 27, 1911.

Pavoni, C. *Enrico Corradini nel giornalismo e nella vita nazionale.* Rome: Casa edit. pianciana, 1930.

Piazza, Giuseppe. *La nostra terra promessa.* Rome, 1911.
   Libya seen as the promised land.

———. *Lettere dalla Tripolitania.* Rome: Lux, 1911.

Picardi, Vincenzo. *Il Congresso Nazionalista di Firenze.* Rome: Coöper. tip. Manuzio, 1911.

Rocco, Alfredo. *Che cosa è e che cosa vogliono i nazionalisti.* Padua, 1914.

Salvatorelli, Luigi. *Irrealtà nazionalista.* Milan: Corbaccio, 1925.
   More important for postwar period, although it is really the study of a state of mind, the Nationalist.

Sarfatti, Gualtiero. "Le qualità militari del popolo italiano." *Rassegna Contemporanea,* IV (Oct.–Dec., 1908), 138–57.

Sciortino, G. *Esperienze antidannunziane.* Palermo, 1928.

Sighele, Scipio. *Pagine nazionaliste.* Milan: Treves, 1910.

———. *Il nazionalismo e i partiti politici.* Milan, 1911.

———. *Ultime pagine nazionaliste.* Milan, 1912.

Silva, Pietro. *L'Italia fra le grandi potenze, 1881–1914.* Rome, 1931.

———. *Il Mediterraneo dall'unità di Roma all'Impero italiano.* Milan, 1937.

Solmi, Arrigo. "La guerra di Libia e il Dodecaneso nei documenti segreti della diplomazia russa." *Politica,* VI (1923).

Todischo, Antonio. *Le origini del nazionalismo imperialista in Italia*. Rome: G. Berlotti, n.d.

Torre, A. "La preparazione diplomatica dell'impresa libica." *Rassegna di politica internazionale*, IV, (1937).

Valli, Luigi. *Che cosa è e che cosa vuole il nazionalismo*. Florence: Quattrini, 1911.

VI. GIOLITTI AND *GIOLITTISMO*

A. B. "M. Giolitti," in "Questions Diplomatiques et Coloniales." *Revue de Politique Exterieure*, XVIII, No. 408, 214–21. Paris: 1914.

Alazard, Jean. *L'Italie et le conflit éuropèen: 1914–1916*. Paris, 1916.
    The author devotes his first chapter to *Giolittismo*, following the common policy of attributing practically all the evils of Italian political life, and foreign policy to Giolitti.

Bacchelli, Riccardo. "Il Ministro Sabaudo." *La Ronda*, III (Nov.–Dec., 1921), Nos. 11–12, 773–97.
    Giolitti as the faithful servant of the Savoy dynasty.

Barbagallo, Corrado. "Gli uomini dell'Italia odierna: Giolitti." *Rivista d'Italia* (Milan), XXIII (1920), Fasc. 8, 478–88.

Brizzolesi, Vittorio. *Giolitti, dalla conflagrazione europea alle dimissioni del V Gabinetto Giolitti*. Novara: Istitutio Geografico De Agostini, 1921.
    Important for the war and postwar period.

Burzio, Filippo. "Giolitti." *La Ronda*, III (Aug.–Sept., 1921), Nos. 8–9, 517–40.

———. *Politica demiurgica*. Bari: Laterza, 1923.
    Reprints the preceding article; a penetrating essay not only on Giolitti, but on other phases of Italian political life.

Castorina, C. *Sicilia e Giolitti*. Catania, 1909.

Chiusano, Vittorio. *Giovanni Giolitti*. Turin: Carlo Pasta, 1913.

Claar, Maximilian. "Giovanni Giolitti (1842–1928) und die liberale Parlaments-diktatur in Italien." *Zeitschrift für Politik*, XVIII (1928), 231–39.
    An excellent article; it delves below appearances both in the case of the parliamentary dictatorship and in that of Giolitti's stand on Italy's entrance into the First World War.

Dillon, E. J. "Giolitti's New Italy: Vitality of the Nation." *Contemporary Review* (London), CIV (Dec. 1913), 866–77.

Ex-Deputato. *Vita di Giovanni Giolitti*. Ferrara: Ghelfi, 1929.

Fovel, N. Massimo. "Il 'Giolittismo.'" *Rassegna Contemporanea*, IV (Oct.–Dec., 1908), 106–24.

Giolitti, Giovanni. *Memorie della mia vita, con uno studio di Olindo Malagodi*. 2 vols. Milan: Treves, 1922.

———. *Memoirs of My Life*. Trans. by Edward Storer. 2 vols. London and Sydney, 1923.

"La grande requisitoria antigiolittiana." *Rivista Popolare* (Dec. 15, 1913).

Noak, Friedrich. "Crispi und Giolitti." *Deutsche Revue* (Stuttgart), XLVI (1921), Bd. 3, 257–65; Bd. 4, 45–53, 182–88.

Palamenghi-Crispi, Tommaso. *Giovanni Giolitti; saggio storico-biografico, con documenti dell'archivio Crispi.* Rome: L'Universelle imprimerie polyglotte, 1913.
   Polemical, anti-Giolittian.
Pareto, Vilfredo. "Due uomini di stato." *La Ronda,* III (July, 1921), No. 7, 437–48.
Prezzolini, Giuseppe. "Pace giolittiana." *La Voce,* IV (Oct. 24, 1912), No. 43, 915.
   The author's conclusion was that after the Libyan War Giolitti could not any longer be regarded as the "Minister of the Underworld."

Quirielle, Pierre de. "De Giolitti à Giolitti: La politique italiènne." *Revue Hebdomadaire* (Paris), XXIX (1920), Tome 7, 149–69.
———. "M. Giolitti et ses memoires." *Revue de Paris* (Paris), XXX (1923), Tome 1, 838–64.
———. "Giovanni Giolitti." *Correspondant* (Paris, 1928), Tome 312 (New Series Tome 276), 340–57.
   The author's writing on Giolitti is always distinguished.

Russo, Domenico, "M. Giolitti." *Correspondant* (Paris, 1920), Année 92, Tome 280 (New Series Tome 244).

Salvatorelli, Luigi, ed. *Giolitti.* Milan: Casa Editrice R. Caddeo & Co., 1920.
   Giolitti's parliamentary and electoral speeches arranged topically. A fundamental work for an understanding of Giolitti.
———. "Giovanni Giolitti und seine auswärtige Politik." *Europäische Gespräche,* VII (1929), 117–37.
Salvemini, Gaetano. *Il Ministro della mala vita, con scritti di Ugo Ojetti e Luigi Lucatelli.* 2nd ed. Rome: La Voce, 1919.
   A famous work—and epithet.
———. *Le memorie di un candidato.* Florence: Libreria della Voce, 1912.
———. *La elezione di Molfetta: Memoria per la Giunta delle Elezioni.* Florence: L'Unità, 1914.
———. *I documenti pansiniani per la elezione di Molfetta: Note e osservazioni di Gaetano Salvemini.* Florence: L'Unità, 1914.
———. *La elezione di Bitonto: Memoria per la Giunta delle Elezioni.* N.p., 1914.
   The last four titles deal with the "Giolittian" elections of 1913, in Apulia.
———. "Il metodo giolittiano." *L'Unità,* IX (Oct. 7, 1920), No. 41, 167.
Spectator, pseud., "Giovanni Giolitti." *Nuova Antologia,* CCLX (August 16, 1928), Series vii, 365–79.

VII. PERIODICALS

Magazines

La Civiltà Cattolica (Rome).
   Catholic organ, directed and edited by members of the Society of Jesus.
La Critica: Rivista di letteratura, storia e filosofia (Bari, 1903 to date). Bi-monthly.
   Croce's famous review; began a cultural revolution in Italy. Fundamental for any study of modern Italian history.

Critica Sociale: Rivista quindicinale del socialismo (Milan, 1891–1922). Fortnightly.
Founded and edited by Filippo Turati; a fundamental source for the study of Italian socialism.

L'Eloquenza: Antologia critica cronaca (Rome, 1911 to date). Bi-monthly.
Characterized by its title. Reported the great speeches in the country and in Parliament. Contains much material not otherwise available.

France-Italie (Paris, 1913–14). Monthly.
This review had a short life. Its purpose was to promote Franco-Italian cultural relations.

Giornale degli Economisti.
Essential for economic studies.

Hermes (Florence, 1904–1906).
Edited by G. A. Borgese. One of the Florentine reviews, in beautiful format.

Nuova Antologia (Rome).
A fundamental source and a mine of information. Its contributors have been the leaders of Italian life. Influential. Reliable.
Nuova Rivista Storica (Rome).
An Italian historical review; to be consulted for purely historical subjects.

Politica (Rome, 1918).
A Fascist organ; to be used with care.

Rassegna Contemporanea (Rome).
Contains informative articles on contemporary events.
Il Regno: Rivista politica, letteraria, artistica. (Florence, November 29, 1903–December 26, 1906).
Edited by Enrico Corradini. Nationalist.
La Riforma Sociale: Rassegna di scienze sociali e politiche (Turin, 1894–   ).
Edited by F. S. Nitti and L. Roux. Important especially for social studies.
Rivista d'Italia (Milan).
Carried periodically studies on significant contemporary personalities.
Rivista Popolare di politica, lettere e scienze sociali (Rome, 1895–1923).
Semi-monthly. Edited by Napoleone Colajanni.
Rivista Storica Italiana (Rome-Turin).
La Ronda; letteraria mensile (Rome, 1919–1923).
Chiefly a literary review, exponent of a Leopardian, neo-classical revival, but many other subjects treated by famous contributors.

L'Unità: problemi della vita italiana (Florence, 1911–20).
Gaetano Salvemini's great review; posed and attempted to suggest solutions for some of the great problems of Italian life.

La Voce (Florence, 1908–1916). Weekly.
The most famous and the most influential of the Florentine reviews. Founded and edited by Giuseppe Prezzolini. It was intended as an organ of moral,

spiritual, artistic, social, and political reëducation of the Italian people. Its contributors—among whom were Papini, Salvemini, Amendola, Croce, Gentile, Slataper—brought a strong new voice to Italian cultural life.

Newspapers

Avanti! (Rome, 1896–1911; Milan, 1911–   ).
    The great Socialist daily, became one of the best and most influential in the world. It counted among its successive editors Leonida Bissolati, Enrico Ferri, Giovanni Bacci, and Benito Mussolini.
L'Avvenire d'Italia (Bologna).
    Catholic. Edited by Cesare Algranati.

Il Corriere della Sera (Milan).
    A daily that became an Italian institution. From the beginning of the century its editor for many years was Luigi Albertini. Nationalist and Liberal, it reflected Lombard, and particularly Milanese, industrial developments. Anti-Giolittian, pro-Libyan.

La Gazzetta del Popolo (Turin).
    Conservative. Has been edited by B. Cerri since 1902.
Il Giornale d'Italia (Rome).
    Founded by Sidney Sonnino in 1901. Conservative. Sometimes regarded as an official organ of the Government. Expansionist in colonial matters; mildly imperialistic; anticlerical, therefore Liberal.
Il Giornale del Mattino (Bologna).
    A Democratic party organ.

L'Idea Nazionale (Rome).
    An organ of the Nationalist party; founded as a weekly on the anniversary of Adowa, March 1, 1911, by Luigi Federzoni, Enrico Corradini, Maurizio Maraviglia, Francesco Coppola, and Roberto Forges-Davanzati. It was turned into a daily in September, 1914. It fought bitterly Roman social democracy, freemasonry, official socialism.

Il Mattino (Naples).
    The great organ for the South; its editor was Edoardo Scarfoglio. Giolittian in internal affairs, expansionist in colonial affairs. It had able writers and correspondents, among whom were Ettore Marroni and Lorenzo Zammarano (Paris), Carlo Scarfoglio (London), Jean Carrère (Rome). G. A. Borgese also contributed to this newspaper.
Il Momento (Turin).
    Catholic. In good relations with the Roman Curia, and well disposed toward Giolitti.

La Nazione (Florence).
    Giolittian.

L'Osservatore Romano (Rome).
    Organ of the Vatican.

Il Resto del Carlino (Bologna).
    An enlightened, critical, Liberal daily, anticlerical, Giolittian.

Il Secolo (Milan).

A Democratic party organ. Dominated by the Radicals. Right-wing Liberal-Conservative. Anti-Libyan.

La Stampa (Turin).

Distinguished, loyal North Italian paper. Giolittian. It was always interested in colonial and military matters.

La Tribuna (Rome).

Liberal, anti-Socialist, Giolittian. Has been edited by Olindo Malagodi since 1910.

INDEX